"Divorce does not have to carry a life s question that divorce has traumatic impact on everyone involved, the scars it leaves do not have to be permanent."

> From the Introduction by Robert Coles, M.D.,
> best-selling author of *The Spiritual Life of Children*

ADULT CHILDREN OF DIVORCE

". . . offers concrete steps for concerned parents who want to minimize the damage done before, during and after the split. At stake for adult children of divorced parents: the ability to break the divorce cycle and safeguard a marriage."   *USA Today*

"*Adult Children of Divorce* gives all of us who come from divorced families important insights into ourselves along with hope for creating healthier, happier relationships in our own lives."

> Dr. Barbara De Angelis

"A rare combination of engaging writing, solid scholarship, clinical wisdom, and theoretical consistency, this book offers hope to those who have experienced the despair that accompanies the divorcing process."

> Donald Shouldberg, Jh.M., Ph.D.,
> Director, Marriage and Family Services,
> the Menninger Foundation

"This book is a vitally important contribution to contemporary America. . . . *Adult Children of Divorce* represents a beacon of light in a world of fragmented families. The authors are to be congratulated for creating this book, which offers adult children of divorce a second chance for a fulfilling life."

> Norman L. Paul, M.D.,
> coauthor of *A Marital Puzzle*

"Given the enormous incidence of single parent families (single by virtue of divorce) and the number of kids thereby affected, this book strikes me as a timely one and one that will make a contribution to the many souls who are struggling to make sense of a fundamentally senseless experience."

> Roy W. Menninger, M.D.,
> President, the Menninger Foundation

ADULT CHILDREN OF DIVORCE

Breaking the Cycle
and Finding Fulfillment
in Love, Marriage, and Family

———/———

Edward W. Beal, M.D.,
and Gloria Hochman

Delta

A Delta Book
Published by
Dell Publishing
a division of
Bantam Doubleday Dell Publishing Group, Inc.
666 Fifth Avenue
New York, New York 10103

ISBN: 0-385-30593-1

Reprinted by arrangement with Delacorte Press

Manufactured in the United States of America

Published simultaneously in Canada

March 1992

10 9 8 7 6 5 4 3 2 1

RRH

This book is dedicated to:

Our **grandparents**

Herman Beal and Ann Vejraska
Chris Beck and Carrie Ward

Samuel and Ethel Ochman
Adolph and Elsie Honickman

Our **parents**

Edward Beal and Wanita Beck
Sarah and Abe Honickman

Our **spouses**

Kathleen Redpath
Stanley Hochman

Our **children**

Alan, Amy, and Maryalice Beal
Anndee Elyn Hochman

And to **their children**

Acknowledgments

This book would never have happened without the inspiration and determination of Bob Miller, editorial director of Delacorte Press, who conceived the idea. He knew how much to push and how little to interfere, and his meticulous and perceptive editorial comments helped shape our writing. It would not have happened, either, without the encouragement of Anne Boas, my former student; Lisa DiMona, my agent, whose faith in the book was unwavering; and Ann Redpath, my sister-in-law and president of Redpath Press, who helped convince me that writing this book was an appropriate extension of my career.

Writing a book with a coauthor is like a marriage. Gloria and I spent a long time getting to know each other and talking about what each of us could bring to this project. Finally, in a leap of faith, we began. It has been a wonderful learning experience. I want to thank Gloria for her prodigious work, for her persistence in helping me clarify the complexity of divorce, and for being herself and letting me be myself.

Obviously this book could not have come about without the thousands of hours patients and others have spent discussing their lives with me, agreeing to be interviewed, and sharing their most private thoughts. These individuals and their families must remain anonymous. However, they and their stories are the backbone of the book. It is through them that you will see yourselves, and it is they to whom I express my sincere thanks and appreciation so others may benefit.

My interest in the family was stimulated by my training in adult and child psychiatry in the late 1960s and early 1970s at the Menninger Foundation. In those days there was little clinical interest in the family as a unit, but Arthur Mandelbaum understood and encouraged me.

My special appreciation to Dr. Murray Bowen, whom I met in 1971 as part of the Group for the Advancement of Psychiatry's Committee on the Family. There my interest in the family and divorce flourished. Dr. Bowen's ability to remain himself while generating endless ideas and provocative questions has been of inestimable value to me—a generous and treasured gift.

My long association with the faculty, staff, and clinical associates of the Georgetown Family Center has been rewarding professionally and personally. Each has stimulated my thinking and contributed to my productivity. Collectively they were of enormous help in sponsoring the six Georgetown Symposia on Divorce. My awareness of the social, legal, economic, and demographic dimensions of the family and their relevance to divorce grew out of planning and coordinating these symposia. Countless lawyers, judges, and masters of the court in the greater Washington, D.C., area have educated me about the legal aspects of the problem. Kathryn Wallman, executive director of the

Council of Professional Associations on Federal Statistics, helped me understand the importance of the U.S. Decennial Census—the denominator for all other population-based sampling, both private and public. I thank Paul Glick, formerly of the Population Division of the U.S. Census Bureau, and E. Mavis Hetherington, who were guest speakers at my first symposium. Both seemed far ahead of their peers in the study of divorce.

More recently, Barbara Foley Wilson, demographer of the Division of Vital Statistics of the National Center for Health Statistics, provided the latest data on marriage and divorce rates and exposed me to literature on courtship and cohabitation.

My thanks to Kathryn A. London, Family Growth Survey Branch of the Division of Vital Statistics of the National Center for Health Statistics, for her guidance and for her excellent paper, "Are Daughters of Divorced Parents More Likely to Divorce as Adults?" To Bernie Brown, who helped design the questionnaires that appear in the book. To Amy Beal, Tracy Johnson, Sheila Kilcullen, and Sara Skilling for transcribing interviews and typing rough drafts. To Ann Redpath and Lynn Chertkov for reviewing the manuscript and offering suggestions.

To my wife, Kathleen, who claims I never read Strunk's *Elements of Style* but admits to still liking mine—my friend for thirty-three years, my wife for twenty-five, throughout my best teacher of love and commitment, of intimacy and friendship.

To our children, Alan, Amy, and Maryalice, who taught me the true meaning of sunshine and to appreciate "The Grateful Dead."

To my mother and father, Wanita and Edward Beal, who gave me the gift of life and common sense.

To my sisters, Mary Beth and Jane, who, quite frankly, put up with me.

To Reverend John P. McNamee and Sister Anne B. Doyle, who have nurtured my soul for twenty-five years.

Edward Beal

My wish for each of you who reads this book—which turns out to be more about family bonds than family breakup—is that you learn as much as I have about what you do, why you do it, and how you can do it differently if you choose.

Working with Ted Beal has taught me a sterling lesson in the way relationships work and how differences can be resolved. I thank him for his knowledge, his convictions, his tolerance, his patience, his confidence in me, his respect, and finally for his friendship.

I, too, want to thank Bob Miller, editor extraordinaire, for his devotion to this book, for his belief that it was important, and for being there when we needed him; Lisa DiMona, our agent, and the staff of the Raphael Sagalyn Agency for its guidance and faith.

I want to thank Drs. Salvador Minuchin, Bernice L. Rosman, Lester Baker, John Sargent, Michael Silver, Ronald Liebman, and the staff of the Philadelphia Child Guidance Clinic, who helped me understand the games families play and how to change the rules.

This book is about families, and I want to thank mine—a special, noisy, warm, and loving group of aunts, uncles, cousins, nephews, nieces, and in-laws who make life rich and rewarding. I want to thank my family of friends, and especially Cathy Kiel for her dedicated research efforts. I want to thank my mother, Sarah, whose gentle voice and reassuring smile I miss every day; my father, Abe, who has taught me that life is not measured by years, but by spirit; my sister, Charlotte, for the memories we share; my daughter, Anndee, for her friendship and her love, and my husband, Stan, who is my soul mate, my partner, my confidant, and my lover on our wondrous journey through life.

Gloria Hochman

Contents

Contents

ADULT CHILDREN OF DIVORCE

Introduction

This book is an important part of what I think it fair to call a cultural reconsideration of sorts—the serious concerns, and even misgivings, that any number of Americans, including our psychiatrists, psychologists, and social workers, are having about the prevalence of divorce in our society. Until recently, all too many of us who work with troubled families tended to regard divorce as a part of contemporary life—what couples do (no less than half of those married) when they don't get along well for a sustained period of time. I well remember sitting in psychiatric conferences ten or fifteen years ago and hearing divorce discussed casually, even with some considerable approval: better that way than the wrangling and discord of a marriage. I remember thinking to myself, often enough, that no real effort had been made to address the matter of divorce as a problem in itself, a serious one at that—a step with lasting consequences for the man and woman who take such action, not to mention their children. All the time the emphasis was elsewhere—divorce as a "resolution of conflict," as I once heard it put: two people squabble or worse; they are not suited for each other; they are under "stress"; and so, quite naturally, or so it seemed, they take action to end their marriage. Since about half of the marriages begun in America during the 1970s and 1980s have ended in divorce, that word "naturally" has not seemed (for many) to be inappropriate.

But those who work with divorced men and women, and with their children, have begun to know otherwise. The studies of Judith Wallerstein and her associates have been published in a variety of professional and lay publications in recent years—important and telling information about the serious psychological consequences for children of divorce. Now this book, the work of a psychiatrist—who has spent years with divorcing couples, with divorced men and women, and with their children—and an award-winning medical journalist, adds additional and highly significant weight to a position many doctors and psychologists or social workers are beginning to take—divorce as something to think about long and hard, as something to try strenuously to avoid, as something that ought prompt the deepest kind of psychological and moral introspection at its prospect.

In essence, Dr. Beal and Ms. Hochman are telling us that those who contemplate divorce not only require the usual kind of "counseling" assistance but a caveat of sorts: to break up a marriage is a move of enormous significance with psychological consequences that don't necessarily go away when a legal judgment has been rendered, and maybe not ever, since what has taken place has a life of its own in the minds of the divorced couple, and most certainly, in the minds of their children. Best, then, to regard divorce (some of us now think) not as simply a common occurrence, hence a readily available alternative to the pain of a troubled marriage, but rather as a potential tragedy all its own—

hence a decision to be confronted with great and earnest and persistent seriousness. In a sense, religious doctrine aside, divorce *is* a moral matter as well as a psychological one—because when one prepares to do something that has potentially lasting implications for the way one will live one's life, and for the way one's children will live their lives, then one is sorting out rights and wrongs as well as questions of psychology, of "mental health," or of one's "personal welfare."

I hope this book will reach a wide audience of men and women who have reason to question their marriages, or who have, still, disturbing memories of marriages that didn't work—those of their parents. Dr. Beal and Ms. Hochman write lucidly, thoughtfully, sensibly—with a wisdom obtained from years of clinical work, done with great care and attentiveness. They have paid heed, as it were—learned certain lessons that I believe many others very much need to learn: what divorce really means for us Americans at the end of the twentieth century. If more of us knew, through their book, what they know, my hunch is fewer of us would be in divorce courts—the preferred choice being the utterly serious self-appraisal they recommend, often a kind of soul-searching done best with the help of others, be they physicians and therapists or members of the clergy. This is a book, one hopes and prays, that will prompt many of us to think of looking inward, seeking to change our ways—in order to be healed rather than to break up a bond whose significance is substantial indeed.

—Robert Coles

Preface

Family faces are magic mirrors. Looking at people who belong to us, we see the past, present and future.

—*Gail Lumet Buckley*
The Hornes: An American Family

No matter your age, chances are you have been closely touched by divorce. You may be the adult child of divorced parents, or good friends with someone who is. You may be married to a man or woman whose parents were divorced, or you may be thinking of marrying someone from a divorced family.

Perhaps you're a mother or father whose marriage ruptured in the 1960s or 1970s when divorce rates skyrocketed, and you are wondering what effect it is still having on your adult children. Or you may be considering divorce yourself and are concerned about what it will do to your children as they grow up. You may be one of a growing group of men and women who are considering marriage while your parents are thinking seriously about ending theirs.

You may be a lawyer, a mental health professional, a judge, or a member of the clergy who works frequently with divorced couples and members of their families.

Through the late sixties and seventies I, along with other mental health professionals, tried to help men and women through the crisis of divorce. We wondered what would happen to the children whose worlds had shattered, and we struggled to help parents understand their children's suffering while dealing with their own.

Most of the thinking then was that it was critical to get the family—parents and children—through the first couple of years, through all of the adjustments and changes and anger and sadness. Once that initial period was over, some professionals were hopeful, if not confident, that the children would have worked it out, that they would have been able to put the divorce behind them and go on to live their lives productively.

But even then, as a psychiatrist with a special interest in the family, I never considered looking at divorce as a short-term crisis. I always thought that the reasons for a couple's divorce were rooted in earlier family relationships that had not been resolved. And I expected that their children would wear the badge of those divorces for a long time.

As the years passed, I found myself working more and more with the children of divorce, traveling the road with them as they matured into adulthood and faced the rocky challenges of forming their own significant relationships.

Along the way, a lot of research has been done on how they have managed, or haven't. On whether or not they have been able to repair their crumbled childhood dreams.

On whether they have learned from their parents' mistakes, or are destined to repeat them.

The best-known study of children of divorce is by Dr. Judith Wallerstein, whose work was conducted over the past ten to fifteen years with her colleagues at the Center for the Family in Transition in Corte Madera, California. Dr. Wallerstein looked at sixty families in a suburban county in the San Francisco Bay area, and her study warns that divorce not only has a predictable effect on children when it occurs but shadows them into adulthood, intruding on their ability to take charge of their lives.

Even ten years later, according to Dr. Wallerstein, "They tell us that growing up is harder for children of divorce, every step of the way . . . they are entering adult hetero-sexual relationships with the feeling that the deck is stacked against them."

Other researchers, including E. Mavis Hetherington, a psychology professor at the University of Virginia, psychologist Sharlene A. Wolchik at Arizona State University, and sociologist Frank F. Furstenberg, Jr., of the University of Pennsylvania, have probed the effects of divorce, remarriage, and stepparent families on children of different ages and sexes who are at different stages in their development.

Dr. Hetherington found, for instance, that children from divorced families encountered more "negative life changes" than children from nondivorced families, and that these changes were associated with behavior problems even six years after the divorce.

And adults of divorce themselves tell us that they feel as though they are victims. They often say they feel done in before they start. They say, "My family disintegrated. I expect it will happen to me." Or "How can I keep it from happening to me?"

Today I see many people in their twenties, thirties, and forties who are getting a divorce; many of them come from families where there has been a divorce in the past. Some of them have parents who have been divorced three or four times. In many cases I have seen two, three, even four generations where divorce, like the family silver, seems to have been bequeathed from one generation to another.

It is not the divorce, initially, that brings them to my office. It may be the issue of commitment. Thirty-three-year-old Ginny, for instance, has been living with Eric for three years. She says she loves him, but whenever he mentions marriage, she arranges for her company to transfer her to California for three months.

It may be mixed emotions about parenthood. Consider Ronnie, so intense about his role as a father ("I'm never going to let my son go through what I did") that he is beginning to feel resentful . . . and ashamed that he feels that way.

Or the widespread fear that what happened to their parents will happen to them too. Colleen, thirty-six, an attractive, talented editor who has been married for four years, is terrified that no matter how hard she tries not to, she will end up like her mother, divorced at forty, inching toward a lonely and cranky old age.

Whatever the problem, divorce, where it has been present, inevitably moves into the foreground. My patients often blame the divorce in their family for all that has gone wrong in their lives. They say they have been deprived and "disenfranchised"; they feel that the aura of their parents' divorce lingers and interferes with their ability to form loving relationships of their own. They say they never had the opportunity to see how a caring relationship between two people works. They have doubts, fears, resentment, anger . . . and struggle to understand how they can pry themselves loose from a past that seems intent on tormenting them.

This book addresses that struggle. And it shows that divorce does not have to carry a life sentence. While there is no question that divorce has a traumatic impact on everyone involved, the scars it leaves do not have to be permanent.

Most research has looked at how well or how poorly the adult children of divorced parents function. Do they have poor self-esteem? Do they have difficulty finding jobs and pursuing careers? Do they use drugs? Are they sexually promiscuous?

A less well explored but equally critical issue—the one that ultimately determines the quality of life—is how well the adult children of divorce can establish and maintain, over a period of time, intimate, *mature* adult relationships.

Going through divorce is itself a regressive process: Everyone in the family slides down the maturity scale for perhaps two or three years. Some husbands and wives recover remarkably well. Some do not. But there appears to be a lingering effect on their children's ability, as they grow into adulthood, to initiate, establish, and maintain secure, stable relationships.

They are often caught up in the past, and the past is impossibly mingled with their present, intruding on their ability to develop and nourish closeness.

A review of the literature, interviews with adults of divorce, and my work with several hundred families of divorce have convinced me that divorce, in the short run, produces powerful and predictable symptoms in children no matter their age. But in the long run, it is not the divorce that determines whether children will be able to achieve intimacy as adults. It is their family style that makes the difference.

This often comes as a surprise to my patients, and it probably will to you too. That's what makes this book different from others that have explored divorce.

The adults of divorce you will read about are those whose parents divorced at different ages and stages of their development. They represent a variety of custody arrangements;

some come from families where the divorce was friendly, others from families where the divorce was acrimonious.

Some had continued and nurturing contact with the parent who did not have custody. Some rarely saw the other parent. Some parents remarried and the child acquired a complex network of new relatives and friends. In other cases, the custodial parent remained single.

The adults of divorce with whom I have worked come from middle-class families. Most of them are high achievers academically and in the workplace. They often hold important jobs and juggle weighty responsibilities calling for clear thinking, good judgment, and decision-making skills. Many are respected community leaders.

They are the adults of divorce who look the best in studies that measure educational achievement and socio-economic status. Yet there is no correlation between the professional success and their personal lives. These men and women are often "emotionally handicapped," unable to find satisfaction in their struggle to find and maintain an intimate relationship. They may be able to address meetings of two hundred fifty people, but they can't have a one-to-one conversation with the person with whom they are trying to be the closest.

This book will help explain why. It will help you understand what happened to you when your parents divorced and how that probably affected you. It will enable you to find the kind of family you come from, get to know that family a little better, and understand how the way you related to each other makes a difference in what is happening to you now.

Our goal is that you will read it slowly and carefully, absorb its messages, begin to nod your head as you recognize yourself and your family . . . and then go on to make necessary and rewarding changes in your life.

In Part One—The Power of Divorce—you will learn about the effect of divorce both on you as an individual and on society in general. We'll be talking about the difference divorce makes in the lives of children as they move through childhood and become adults. You will see how differently children in the same family may respond to divorce, depending on their gender, their age at the time their parents split, their birth position, their temperament and resilience, and, most important of all, the role they play in their families.

We will be taking a close look at the legacy of divorce—the complex web of relationships, the violated trust, the loss of valued connections—that absorb the thoughts and affect the behavior of children of divorce as they grow into adulthood.

We'll be discussing how divorce changes relationships between mothers and daughters, mothers and sons, fathers and their children. And we'll talk about the way families are disorganized by divorce and why the way they reorganize afterward is so critical.

Part Two—Where You Are Now . . . and How You Got There—will help you understand yourself and your family. You will learn whether or not you (and your parents) are "behaviorally mature," what that means, and why it is so significant. You'll have a chance to look at your family through a new prism—to rate its overall maturity before, during, and after the divorce.

You'll learn the difference between thinking and feeling, and how they get in the way of each other to chip away at the quality of your intimate relationships.

You'll see what we mean by "borrowing," when it works, when it destroys. As you read, you will be able to identify the kind of family you come from and you'll see how the repetition of or rebellion against your family style is interfering with your relationships now. You'll journey through developmental milestones and see how, as an adult of divorce, you may experience those milestones differently from adults whose parents stayed together. You'll learn about what happens during courtship, a pivotal time when long-dormant anxieties often surface, and learn how knowledge about your own behavior patterns can ease the way.

Part Three—Breaking the Cycle—will help you gain more control of yourself and, therefore, of your life. It will allow you to see, through specific techniques and new perspectives, how you can free yourself from the past without abandoning your emotional connection to your parents and other relatives. It will help you safeguard your own marriage and recognize your responsibilities to your children.

There is a set of questions through which you can rate your own "behavioral maturity" level and another that will help you identify your family style and show you how to modify your role in it.

Parts Four, Five, and Six—Siblings of Divorce, Sons of Divorce, and Daughters of Divorce—weave all you have learned into case histories that will make lightbulbs go off in your mind. You will see how family patterns are played out in adults of divorce. You'll learn why some children survive their parents' divorce with strength, understanding, and peace while others are seriously damaged by it. You'll see more clearly why specific people such as Richard, who defied the odds, and Tammy, who said she "never saw a normal relationship," react to divorce so differently. The section dealing with siblings of divorce will show you, with startling clarity, how and why children in the same family respond in their own unique way.

Through the mirror of these fourteen case histories, you will understand better what happened to you when your parents were divorced—what made it better or worse for you and how you are still reacting.

As you read, you may become upset about some of the behavior patterns and family styles you recognize as your own. It is important to make a note of that . . . and keep reading. The information that distresses you is significant. You need to learn why.

When you have finished reading the book, perhaps several times, we hope you will have gained a better understanding of your own family, have redefined yourself, and feel ready to move on to more satisfying—and lasting—relationships.

PART ONE

———/———

The Power of Divorce

CHAPTER ONE

─────/─────

The Changing Family

Barry is forty and scared. He has been living with Jennifer for fourteen months, and they have been happy. A few "details" in their relationship still need to be worked out, such as how often they visit her mother and what part Barry's child from an earlier marriage should play in their lives. But Barry thinks that this time he is in love.

"I think I want to spend the rest of my life with Jennifer, but something is keeping me back. Every time she mentions marriage, I find some reason to postpone the date. A new account at the agency [Barry works for a Boston advertising firm]; a crisis with Mitchell [his son]; the need to save a little more money. I'm beginning to wonder if I don't really love Jennifer, or what."

Hillary was married three years ago when she was thirty-four, twelve years out of college. More surprised than anyone, she ended up with her college sweetheart after having not seen him until their tenth class reunion.

"After graduation, we both realized that we were young

and unfinished and that we needed to work on ourselves,"
Hillary said. "We moved to different parts of the country—I
went to Washington, he went to Michigan, and we began
dating other people. A couple of times I thought I was in
love, but it never seemed to work out. Then Allan and I saw
each other from across the room at the reunion, and I think
we both knew that we were meant to be together.

"So why am I so uneasy now? We've just had a baby, a
beautiful daughter, Cara. I've stopped working temporarily, and plan to go back when Cara is about three. But lately
I've been waking up every morning with this awful feeling
of trepidation. Like something is going to go wrong. My
heart is pounding and I find myself in a cold sweat. I feel
like this terrific thing I have now won't last. And I'll be
helpless to do anything about it."

"I keep choosing the wrong person," says Claudia. "I
know it, but that's who attracts me." Claudia is twenty-nine,
is considered beautiful and talented by her friends, and has
already sold several of her paintings through a prestigious
gallery on New York's West Fifty-seventh Street.

"Fred had a mean streak," she relates. "He could be
wonderful a lot of the time, but when he got angry, he was
deadly. He had a temper that was ferocious. I mean, he
would get physically violent. After the third time he hit me,
I knew I had to break off the relationship.

"But Tony was no better. He didn't have a temper and he
was never violent with me. He just mistreated me. He'd say
he would call and he wouldn't. He'd make a dinner date
with me and not show up. Or he'd call fifteen minutes late
and say he was in Chicago unexpectedly. Once he showed
up to take me to a black-tie wedding wearing jeans and
Reeboks. My friends wanted to know why I put up with it
for so long. Can you believe I stayed with Tony for nine
months? Then he left. He met someone else. I think I'm
destined to go through life destroying myself."

Barry, Hillary, and Claudia believe they know why their

intimate relationships are causing them so much grief. Like millions of men and women their age—twentysomething, thirtysomething, maybe fortysomething—they are the adult children of divorced parents.

They share an unprecedented place in the history of this country, the first generations to come of age at a time where "blended families" is an expression everyone understands and the corner drugstore carries greeting cards that proclaim, "Congratulations on your divorce. Welcome to the first day of the *best* of your life."

They are the legacy of the sixties and seventies, the "divorce decades" when more people than ever before—one for every three couples who married in 1962 and one for every two who married by 1977—untied the knot.

Skyrocketing Divorce

Broken families are not new in this country. But as far back as the 1880s and through the early 1960s, most—from 60 to 90 percent—shattered because of a parent's death. And as we shall see later, disruption of a family because of death is a far less destructive experience for children than divorce.

Today growing up divorced has become the norm for substantial numbers of children, and most broken homes are the result of divorce or separation. Since 1972, when 1,021,000 couples split, more than a million children have been involved in divorce every year. According to research by sociologist Frank F. Furstenberg, one child in every ten will see his or her parents divorce, experience the remarriage of the parent he lives with, and go through that parent's second divorce—all before he is sixteen.

In 1989, the last year for which statistics are available, there were 2,404,000 marriages and 1,163,000 divorces and annulments nationwide, or one divorce or annulment for every two marriages. This means that almost 50 percent of children will grow up living without both their biological mother and father. Nothing this revolutionary—the virtual destruction of the two-parent family in this way and at this rate—has happened in more than two thousand years.

Society's Role

The divorce rate, which was relatively low in the fifties, skyrocketed in the "me" era of the sixties and seventies for social, economic, and religious reasons. There was the feminist movement, which gave many women the courage to confront and end loveless marriages. As women entered the work world, they gained a new capacity to be economically independent and felt freer to turn their backs on marriages they did not find fulfilling.

Medical science contributed by developing the birth control pill, which effectively separated marriage from sex. The moral climate became more flexible, and there were looser religious and civil restraints about the sanctity of marriage.

Even the church began to recognize that its ban on divorce and remarriage wasn't as influential anymore. Generations of Catholics, drilled to accept the premise that divorce and Catholicism don't mix, weren't buying it. And the general thinking of the Protestant church shifted to consider the new idea that a person's marital history may not, indeed, be the ideal way to judge the state of his soul.

A no-fault divorce psychology, the belief that people should not be held responsible for falling out of love, paved the way for no-fault divorce law, which permitted marriages to end because of temperamental incompatability.

The extended family, an elaborate relationship system that helps control conflict, became all but extinct for many of us. And without these family connections people dealt with less personal history, had a flimsier backdrop against which to define themselves, and had fewer people to react to what they did. It made divorce easier.

Freedom of choice! The legitimacy of self-interest! Increasing individuality for everyone! These were the hallmarks of the sixties. Nudged by a tantalizing palette of new age therapies, where "self-actualization" was the password, divorce became almost honorable—a sign of healthy growth—apart from each other. Along with multiple orgasms, full-time jobs, and maybe an affair or two, divorce seemed the appropriate and logical next step along the trail to self-fulfillment.

Unfortunately, the rush to embrace this new-found freedom was not accompanied by recognition of the role earlier constraints had played in maintaining society's stability and security.

Even the no-fault divorce law, fought for by women who thought it would equalize their rights and make divorce "civilized," has backfired, leaving many women impoverished after divorce, especially if they are older and have no marketable skills.

Lenore Weitzman, a sociology professor at Harvard University, says that "no fault" has become synonymous with "no responsibility." The results are a "systematic impoverishment of women and children."

And society has not yet caught up with the accommodations, such as on-the-job day-care centers and flexible work hours, that go hand in hand with freedom of choice.

New Views About Commitment

I see no reason why the trend toward divorce will not continue to escalate. Statistics show that children from a divorced marriage are themselves more likely to end up divorced, even if they have promised themselves they will never let it happen.

The whole issue of commitment is different today from what it once was. A lot of people get married with the attitude that if they're happy and the relationship is going well, then they're committed. But if they're not happy and things aren't going so well, then they are not committed. In our no-deposit, no-return society, the commitment they talk about is not necessarily to each other. If the marriage doesn't work, if it does not meet certain standards of perfection, it is easy just to exchange partners.

I see more people who are skittish about making a strong investment in marriage; when they do, they see it often as another stage of life, but not necessarily one that will last forever. There is a difference in perception about what marriage should be. More people use romantic love as the measure of happiness with their partner. When, inevitably, that fades or waxes and wanes through a marriage, divorce often becomes the acceptable way out.

Then, too, people are living longer, which makes them more vulnerable to divorce. Against today's stresses and pressures, many marriages may not be able to survive thirty or forty years. Some of us may not be biologically suited to stay together that long, and a marriage can withstand just so much stress.

The Divorce Spillover

The spillover from divorce touches the lives of us all, even those who come from intact families. The sense of transiency in relationships is contagious, and young people are nervous about making commitments because they have lost faith in their staying power.

Morris, a forty-year-old doctor, insists he will never marry even though his parents, Doris and Kenneth, have been wed for forty-two years and have what their only son acknowledges as a wonderful and loving marriage.

"We're living in different times, and I see too much," Morris says. "My patients—almost none stay together. They live together for a while. Then they break up. Then they live with someone else. Sometimes they even get married. But it seems to me it is with an insouciant attitude— you know, if it lasts, fine. If it doesn't, well, there's always divorce. That's not for me. I work four nights a week and every Saturday. I like what I do. I have a boat. I have friends. That's all I want."

"The idea of divorce impacts on intact families," confirms Norma Rolnick, a therapist who answers phone calls for a hotline sponsored by the National Organization for Women in Montgomery County, Pennsylvania. "Children get nervous if their parents have an argument, fearing that their lives will be shaken up the way so many of their friends' have been."

Patterns of divorce and marriage have become an intrinsic feature of modern family life rather than a temporary departure from tradition.

The Future

It is estimated that nearly half of all marriages will end in divorce and that close to 50 percent of children born in the 1980s will go through their parents' divorce before they are eighteen. Of these about 57 percent will live in a stepparent family. And since more than 50 percent of remarriages usually end within ten years, some children, especially those who are young when their parents divorce, will live in more than one stepparent family.

Almost no one disputes that a home headed by a mother and father who are compatible provides the best environment for a child's healthy development. A two-parent family, especially one where the parenting is constant and continuous, gives children the greatest emotional security. But it is unlikely that we can go backward to the family of the past (which was far from ideal, even though it might have been intact). It was a lifestyle that, for most people, is no longer economically feasible or personally satisfying.

Life has become more complicated. The balance between freedom of choice and a sense of responsibility is a fragile one and is a balance we're still struggling with. Freedom of choice has not come without its price. For parents who choose to divorce, the price may be worth it. For the children, though, it seldom is. As Frank Pittman, author of *Private Lies: Infidelity and the Betrayal of Intimacy,* has said, "Brutal marriages may be bad for children, but I'm not sure boring marriages are."

The Sting of Divorce

No matter how many years earlier the divorce occurred, my patients remember vividly the moment they learned about their parents' split. Judith Wallerstein, too, found in her research that even ten years later children "remembered all the exquisite, fresh detail as if it had happened a month ago."

And this is the way they often partition their lives. It becomes a marker for them: life before the divorce and life after the divorce.

Joel, now thirty-five, was eleven when his mother and father gathered him and his fourteen-year-old sister, Lori, in front of the fireplace in the living room of their suburban Philadelphia home.

"I can see it now," Joel told me. "Dad was wearing a blue sweater and gray pants. Mom was nervous and sat on the edge of the sofa as though she wasn't sure she could stay. Dad stammered a lot and finally mumbled, 'Mom and I don't love each other anymore. I'll be leaving next weekend to live in an apartment in town. I'll be seeing you as much as ever. . . .'"

Joel says he didn't wait to hear anymore. He jumped up from his chair and left the room, screaming, "I hate you." He slammed the front door and ran out into the night. "I think I've been running ever since," Joel told me. "I replay that moment over and over in my mind. And I see my life in two distinct parts—before the night my parents told me of their divorce and after. It's as though I'm two different people, and I can hardly remember the first one anymore."

It is not, however, that moment that is the critical one or the one that ultimately shapes the future of a child of divorce. Divorce is not a single event but a happening that is a long time in the making. It begins, sometimes openly, but often insidiously and subtly, long before the decision to end the marriage is reached. It continues, as I will explain, long after the divorce has been finalized. Sometimes it never ends.

The Child of Divorce Grown Up

Must you, a child of divorce, become an adult with problems? Are your problems likely to be different from those of adults who came from families who stayed together? Will you be better off, perhaps, than children who come from unhappy marriages but whose parents don't divorce? Will you be able to live a fulfilling, productive life? Or will your parents' divorce become a nagging filter through which you will always see yourself and your future?

This book will show the undeniable, dramatic, and profound effect that divorce has on children. It will show that its ghost may, indeed, live with them forever.

Coming from a family that has divorced *does* make you different from men and women who grew up in a family that stayed together. It *does* make you different from families where a parent has died. It has a significant effect on your future thinking and behavior. We'll talk about that later.

But, contrary to current thinking, you will learn that the divorce itself is not the crucial factor. It is the kind of family you come from, the way its members relate to each other, the patterns of behavior you grow up with and, unwittingly, imitate or rebel against, that are more likely to influence who you become. This would be true whether or not divorce occurs. For adults of divorce, it is the unique mix of your family's style and the divorce of your parents—how it was played out and your role in it—that spin together to determine your future.

Perhaps a Florida high school student said it best in a letter about her parents' divorce that was published in the *St. Petersburg Times.* She wrote:

> "When I grow up, I want to be something terrific. I want to be a photographer and take pictures of people, of their faces.
>
> "I want to know if it's possible to *SEE* love dying.
>
> "I missed it the first time around."

CHAPTER TWO

———/———

Cast Out of Eden

Children of divorce see themselves as being different from children whose families have stayed together. Whatever problems they encounter as they move through life, they tend to attribute them to their parents' divorce.

They view themselves through the prism of divorce that because it is so jolting, so shattering, becomes the organizing event of their lives. They identify their families as having been "unsuccessful" and see themselves and their subsequent relationships as more problem-filled, more anxious, and more at risk of failure. They mourn their lost childhood and what they perceive as the richness and protection of a family that stays together.

What the Surveys Show

An analysis of thirty-two studies, most of them conducted during the past fifteen years, reveals that adults of divorced parents have more problems and lower levels of well-being than adults whose parents stayed married. They are depressed more frequently, feel less satisfied with life, get less education, and have less prestigious jobs. Even their physical health is poorer. One study included 2,460 men and women from both divorced and intact families who were living in their own households. It confirmed that the impact of divorce endures throughout a person's lifetime and that the disruption during childhood remains a nagging concern.

Adults of divorce more often reported feeling less happy than those whose parents had stayed together. The former identified childhood and adolescence as the most unhappy time of their lives. Only adults who were themselves divorced said they were unhappier now. They admitted symptoms of poor physical health and more psychological anxiety and said that "bad things" frequently happen to them.

Those who were married reported equal happiness whether they came from families who had divorced or stayed together. But adults of divorce were more likely to admit that they had marital problems.

Married women who are adults of divorce felt their careers and their role as parents were more important than their role as spouses. Married men of divorce, on the other hand, valued their role as husbands more than they did their careers. But they were less interested in parenting than their wives who come from divorced families. Nonetheless, when they became fathers, they were no less adequate than men whose families had stayed together.

A study at Indiana University, reported in 1989, showed that college students with divorced parents are more sexually active than their classmates. The men preferred recreational sex to committed relationships, and most had had more than four sex partners before they entered college. The study's author, Robert Billingham, suggests that boys who have grown up without a father at home may model themselves after the stereotypical male behavior they see on television and in movies.

Women were more sexually aggressive than either men or women from intact families and often moved in and out of a series of brief relationships. This may happen because single mothers often become involved in short-term romantic flings after divorce, and daughters frequently copy their mothers' behavior.

Nonetheless these women, even more than women whose parents had stayed together, were determined that divorce wouldn't happen to *them*.

The Indiana University study supports what we know about cohabiting couples who are not married, a number that has risen from 450,000 in 1960 to two million in 1985. Adult children of divorce are a stunning 54 percent more likely to cohabit than their counterparts from parents who have stayed together.

In contrast to expectations, however, cohabitation has not ushered in an era of greater marital stability. One study reports that 38 percent of those who live together before marriage split within ten years (compared to 28 percent who did not cohabit first), and another indicates that women who cohabit have a marital breakup rate that is nearly 80 percent higher than those who do not.

I do not find this surprising. I have seen two distinct kinds of cohabitation. For some people, living together before marriage for a short time, usually a year or less, has evolved into a natural part of the courtship process, a step on the way to a wedding.

For others, it represents a lack of commitment and stability. Adult children of divorce who, as we will explain later, were the focus of their parents' problems and who are still reacting to their breakup, are more likely to move into a series of live-in relationships, often stormy and less committed. For them cohabitation, like divorce, represents an anxiety and discomfort about marriage. Cohabitation does not help them know each other better and it does not lead to stronger, more solid marriages. Their relationships are more risky.

A Problem That Lingers

Even men and women who believe they have "readjusted" feel as though they have a family problem that doesn't go away. It is something like families in which there is diabetes or cancer. It doesn't mean you'll get it, but you're aware of it and, at certain times, you think about it more.

With divorce, there are constant reminders, particularly at critical junctures such as graduations, holidays, or any kind of celebration. It is then that you can't avoid the fact you have half as many family members—or twice as many.

Even though children of divorce have a lot of company, it doesn't seem to matter. They still think of themselves as different. They think about relationships differently than children who come from intact families, and they often look at marriage ambiguously. On the one hand, they see marriage, rather than their own inner resources, as a way to restore and ensure stability in their lives. On the other hand, they are worried that their marriages will disintegrate just as their parents' did.

Even when they agree, as many do later. that the divorce made sense, they recognize that the model they saw as they grew up had serious problems. They wonder whether they will imitate that model. And there is a surprising number of adults who still don't understand why their parents were divorced. So they grope in the dark about how they can avoid making the same mistakes.

The adult children I see, the ones who are still experiencing pain and disappointment and frustration, confide to me their belief that it was their parents' divorce that set the stage for their problems.

Children of divorced parents are convinced that they have been cast out of the Garden of Eden. If only their parents had stayed together, they would feel more secure. They would be more stable. They would be capable of having more fulfilling relationships. They would achieve greater happiness.

My experience tells me that while the divorce certainly had a powerful effect, the belief that the divorce itself is causing all of their problems is a fantasy, a myth children of divorce have built up around themselves. If they look over their shoulder, they will find young people as insecure, unhappy, and frightened as they are. They will find others who, like themselves, are stumbling through relationships, are choosing the wrong partners, and are squeamish about commitment. And these are often people whose parents have stayed together for twenty-five, thirty-five, forty or more years.

The reason is simple:

Problems with relationships in the present occur because of unresolved relationships in the past, unsettled issues with a person's family of origin—mother, father, grandparents, sisters, brothers.

The main reason people have trouble with current relationships is that they haven't worked out their previous ones. This is true whether or not those past relationships include divorce.

It is in this arena that young men and women must struggle to understand their past, make peace with the important people in their lives, and be free to initiate and maintain their own intimate relationships with confidence. As you read on, you'll be able to see that and apply it to yourself and your family.

Divorce Matters

This doesn't mean that divorce doesn't matter. There is no question that divorce has a profound effect on children and adds incredible complexity to their lives.

Before they reach the age of eighteen, they have spent two or three years, perhaps one-sixth of their lives, in a major crisis that demands large chunks of time and energy devoted to restoring themselves. They were emotionally less available to develop peer relationships, to be fully involved in school, in sports, in routine play. And unless there was a strong supportive person in their lives, they usually felt distressingly isolated.

They were stripped of the innocence that is the domain of childhood. Their world came crashing down on them, and overnight the rules changed.

They found themselves often center stage in a drama they did not create and over which they had no mastery. And they learned, out of turn, out of time, that the behavior, even of the people who are supposed to love them the most, is subject to change.

Whatever their age when the divorce occurred, it undermined their sense of security, interrupted their routines, loosened the underpinnings that held their lives together. It introduced them to skepticism about the degree to which anyone can count on anything or anyone.

If, after all, your parents can turn your world upside down so drastically, whom then can you trust?

From the very beginning, from the day parents separate, the child's world crumbles. It is the behavior of the parents that determines whether the fallout will be temporary . . . or lasting.

Changing Relationships

When parents separate, the children's relationship with them changes, almost overnight. For one thing, parents at that point often are so overwhelmed by their own troubles that they become less sensitive to those of their children and less available to them. If there is another romance on the scene, that person often becomes the focus of attention with the children fading into the background. In other cases the relationship between parent and child becomes too intense and erupts in serious problems.

Different from Death

Divorce brings with it a disruption in the lives of all family members that is matched by no other event, not even death. When death occurs, the surviving parent and children are usually older. It doesn't happen because of conflict and it doesn't create the intergenerational complexities often bred by divorce.

Divorce, on the other hand, is voluntary, at least on the part of one parent. So in addition to sadness and depression, anger, resentment, and hostility of children are high. Some children refuse to see the parent who they feel is responsible for breaking up the marriage.

Years after the divorce many adult children are still not able to tolerate their parents' romantic and sexual involvement with another person, especially when they believe that the relationship broke up their family. As a result relationships between the adult child and that parent, usually the father, are less than satisfying.

The death of a mother or father stimulates an outpouring of sympathy and support; friends and family rally around the children because they understand their pain and want to offer solace. This is not the case with divorce. Friends and family do not perceive it as the death of a family. But for children, that's exactly what it is.

Recently twenty-one-year-old Howard, one of my daughter's schoolmates, lost his mother to cancer. His friends visited him at home, made cards, wrote letters and called him long-distance, in Minnesota, to express their condolences. They made a special effort to spend time with him when he returned to school to help him work through the crisis, and were understanding about his frequent lapses into silence or moodiness.

When I asked my daughter how the same friends reacted when Liz's parents were divorced—when her father moved out to live with another woman—she just shrugged her shoulders. "We didn't do anything," she responded.

Friends and family often feel uncomfortable about their roles when a divorce takes place. How do they treat the children? Do they talk about it (especially if the children seem reticent)? If they ignore it, will it go away? Friends tend to act as though nothing unusual has happened. One set of grandparents often vanishes from a child's life. And while in today's society divorce is not unusual, its impact on children is powerful and it makes their lives dramatically different.

CHAPTER THREE

―――――/―――――

The Difference Divorce Makes

There is no question that divorce makes a difference in the way a child grows up. He or she will live in a single-parent home for a substantial period of time, probably go through the remarriage of one or both parents, become involved in a staggeringly complex web of relationships, and—for 37 percent—go through another marriage ending in divorce.

What all of this means, however—whether it strengthens or cripples the child as he goes through life—has a lot to do with the nature of the divorce.

Each divorce is unique, and it is what has happened *before* the divorce, *how the divorce itself is played out* and, most important, what happens *after the divorce* that influences what ultimately becomes of the children.

There is no pat formula that can forecast the outcome for a particular child. Research on the effects of divorce are illuminating but often contradictory, depending on the age of the children being studied, where they are in the divorce process, and the quality of their relationships with their parents.

The most important factors—the ones that determine how a divorce will affect a specific child—are: *the unique characteristics of the child; the relationship that develops between the child and his parents—but mainly with the custodial parent, and, most important, the way the family reorganizes itself after the parents have separated.*

All families have their own styles of managing relationships and dealing with differences among their members. In some cases differences are handled by *open conflict,* perhaps even verbal or physical abuse. In others one spouse *becomes subordinate* and never expresses his or her opinion directly. Sometimes he or she may avoid sticky issues entirely by *distancing* himself or herself, physically or emotionally, from his spouse or pretending the problems don't exist. And frequently differences between husband and wife become diffused by *focusing on another member of the family,* often a child.

It is a child's distinguishing characteristics—such as his sex and age at the time of divorce as well as his own resilience—that have a lot to do with his *acute* responses to his parents' divorce. But it is these ingrained patterns of family behavior (and the degree to which those patterns occur around the time of the divorce and afterward) that shed more light on the *intensity* of the child's immediate response and, more important, on the long-term consequences.

Mental health workers who see children at the time of divorce are concerned with relieving their acute symptoms of distress and putting them back on their appropriate developmental track. They often don't look at the family's style of relating to one another. But it is this style that has the most influence on the child's capacity to develop intimate relationships when he or she grows up, the ultimate measure of a meaningful life.

It often comes as a shock that the child who seems to

have "adjusted" so well in the period after divorce and even during his or her growing-up years will struggle with relationship problems in adulthood. One has little to do with the other.

Keep this in mind as you read the diverse stories we will tell of adult children of divorced parents.

Children and Their Uniqueness

Age

I believe that the *intensity* of the children's response, no matter their age or developmental stage at the time of divorce, depends largely on how much they are the focus of their parents' anxiety. Distraught parents, by their words, actions, and body language, convey an implicit message to their children: we are frantic; therefore you have something to be frantic about too. Most children comply.

Parents who are calm and reasonable give their children the reassurance that eases them through these turbulent times. These children, even at the peak of divorce upheaval, will probably show fewer and milder symptoms.

Nonetheless, we cannot minimize the power of divorce, and I have seen duplicated in my patients the symptoms Judith Wallerstein and Joan B. Kelly describe in their study of divorcing families in Marin County, California. Their study, which describes graphically the acute effects of divorce on boys and girls of various ages, shows that their symptoms match their stage of development and reflect how they are able to appraise and cope with the crisis in which they find themselves.

The youngest preschool children, those aged two and a half to three and a half, regress. They are fretful, bewildered, and aggressive, and they need attention. In their play they construct unsafe toy worlds inhabited by hungry animals. They become possessive with their toys and anxious when separated from their mothers.

Older preschoolers (three and a half to almost five) are whiny, tearful, and aggressive. They are confused by the absence of a parent and typically told Dr. Wallerstein and her colleagues, "I don't have a daddy anymore" or "I'll need a new daddy now."

Some felt responsible for driving their fathers away. One girl insisted that her father had left because she was noisy at play; another savagely beat the "naughty baby doll." These children were not old enough to understand cause and effect; they saw the world as revolving around them, the study said, so their response was consistent with their stage of development. The self-esteem of younger children was so closely tied to their parents that parents' reactions became their gauge. They looked to them to know whether to be anxious. The more anxiety their parents showed, the more was felt by their children.

The five- and six-year-olds were restless, whined, and often threw temper tantrums; but their self-confidence was not as damaged, nor was their development as slowed, as the younger children's.

School-age children behaved differently. The immediate and most pervasive response among seven- and eight-year-olds was sadness. Unlike the preschoolers, who often denied what was happening to them, these children were exquisitely aware of their suffering and had considerable difficulty obtaining relief.

One little boy in the study talked about feeling as though he needed to cry all the time. Another's world seemed filled with symbols of death, damage, and loss. She talked about her dog's heart attack, then pointed to the therapist's doll and said, "Poor little thing, she doesn't have any eyes."

Children of this age, Dr. Wallerstein said, know what is happening to them, but they are too old to use fantasy to make it palatable as younger children can. So they are extremely sad and frightened about their futures. Crying and sobbing were common, especially among the boys. They worried that there was no safe place for them, and they were terrified of not being wanted anywhere. They missed their fathers desperately, and their longing was in some ways reminiscent of grief for a dead parent. They sometimes wondered if they would be the next to go.

Nine- and ten-year-olds understood the reality of the divorce clearly and struggled to give some order to the chaos in their lives. Often they hugged their feelings to themselves, not talking about them, trying not to think about them. They were ashamed by the divorce and embarrassed by their parents' behavior. Their schoolwork suffered; this was as true for excellent students as it was for poor ones. Relationships with their friends deteriorated, and they often became behavior disasters—destructive, hostile, bullying, rebellious, reclusive.

Surprisingly, Drs. Wallerstein and Kelly found that adolescents were often hit the hardest. Divorce interrupted their development at a critical point and seriously burdened their capacity to do what teenagers must do—separate from their parents and grow into adulthood. Teenagers were forced by the divorce to judge their parents, and they often became angry as the mother or father of their childhood fantasies vanished.

I have seen that children of any age with any kind of problem will have more problems as a result of the divorce. But it almost never occurs to most parents to do what might seem perfectly obvious under more normal circumstances —ask their children, at the time they learn about the divorce and frequently thereafter, what their concerns are. Do they worry about where they will live? Whether they will need to change schools? What they will tell their friends?

But anxiety incapacitates people—parents as well as children—and the most level-headed adults can become irrational and suffer from startlingly impaired thinking while they are going through a divorce. And so this is often the time when they are least aware of their children's needs.

Couples who postpone divorce until their children are grown and no longer living at home are probably not sparing them pain. A recent study of forty-eight college students who were living away from home when their parents separated said they were shocked and stunned, even though they knew their parents' relationships were tempestuous. Some blamed the parent who left home and tried to help the one who was spurned. Some avoided pleasurable activities; others became self-indulgent. And many felt disillusioned about marriage and resolved not to marry or have children.

Bonnie: Afraid to Have Children   Bonnie, who is thirty-seven, said it took her a long time to think seriously about marriage, and now that she is married, she can't bring herself to have children. She keeps thinking something will go wrong that she won't be able to foresee or control.

Bonnie was a senior in college when her parents separated and says she was shocked to learn about their breakup. While she was growing up in a suburb of Houston, she was her father's "cutie pie."

"I felt so supported and so loved, and I thought my parents had a wonderful marriage. They fought sometimes, and had their differences, but so did most of my friends' parents. When I went away to school, at seventeen, I thought everything was okay between them. I had no reason to believe differently.

"But one day when I came home for spring break, my mom broke down and told me she was filing for divorce. She said she and my dad had been having problems for a long time. Some of them were sexual, and that was hard for me to hear. It's hard to think about your parents that way. Some were just having basically different values. I told her to see a marriage counselor. She said they had already tried

—and failed. As far as she was concerned, the marriage was over.

"I remember feeling really angry at her. I thought she was being irrational and not giving my father a chance. My dad and I had always been so close. I couldn't imagine them not being together. I couldn't imagine not coming home to my house. I couldn't bear my mom moving to Arizona to be near her mother.

"I went back to school wishing it would all go away. But of course it didn't. I think my dad went through some kind of a mid-life crisis. He started dating a lot of women, moving them into our house. Once he even moved a woman's daughter into my bedroom. When I came home from school, I found all her things in my drawers and closets. I got so angry, I packed them up and dumped them on the lawn in trash bags.

"Since then, our relationship—my dad's and mine—has gone down the drain. I moved to Detroit. He seemed happy to see me go and leave him with his new life. He remarried and discarded me totally. He almost didn't come to my wedding. His brother and sister-in-law had to plead with him to be there.

"I can't figure it out. He sold our old house in Houston and moved away, but I don't know where. He hasn't tried to get in touch with me. And it looks as though I'll probably never see him again. It is like I was never his daughter. In three years I'll be forty and I still have nightmares about it."

Children to whom the divorce comes as a surprise are often devastated, no matter their age.

Peggy, who is thirty-eight, recently learned that her parents will be divorced, after thirty-nine years of marriage. "It's making me crazy," she told me. "I feel so depressed, like I'm about to have a nervous breakdown, and I can't think about anything else.

"It makes me feel as though my entire childhood was a fable, a lie. I wonder where I was when all this was happening. I thought we had a wonderful, close family. We did things together, went places. I never heard any shouting or screaming, and my parents always seemed to respect each other. I know life changes and people change, but you count on your family to be there until death does it part. I've never heard a marriage ceremony that said anything about divorce."

Males and Females

The initial impact of divorce is much more potent for boys than for girls; boys take longer to adjust and show many more behavior problems.

It has nothing to do with their intellectual level. I think it happens partly because boys and girls tend to express their feelings differently. And partly because boys are just more vulnerable to many kinds of stress than girls. More boys than girls have learning disabilities or phobias; more boys are slower to be toilet trained and mature more slowly. How often have you heard someone say, "You can't compare a girl of thirteen with a boy of thirteen. She is a young woman; he is still a baby."

Even in infancy the chances that highly premature girls will survive are greater than for boys. The reasons are uncertain, but the evidence is clear.

So it is not surprising that with the onset of a trauma as serious as divorce, boys, more than girls, tend to become antisocial, to misbehave, disrupt classrooms, and show aggression, even to exhibit violence such as biting, kicking, and hitting other children. They are likely, under stress, to become unable to control their impulses and show signs of hyperactivity. Some become noisy and raucous; others withdraw from their friends and spend a lot of time alone in their room.

Richard, now thirty-five, told me that after his parents' separation he just "went through the motions. I went to school. I didn't pay much attention to what was going on. It didn't seem very important anymore and I was having a lot of trouble concentrating. So my grades went from *B*'s to *D*'s.

"After school I would go to my room and play loud rock music. I'm not sure, even today, whether I did it to smother my pain or whether I was just looking for attention. It didn't matter. No one did anything about it. It's hard to remember, but I think I stopped feeling anything."

I have seen, time and again, that during the divorce period women often become more emotionally reactive and are more likely to do what they do naturally—they overfunction for their sons in the same way they did for their husbands.

The sons look to their mothers for cues. It is almost as though they don't know how they think or feel unless Mom tells them. And parents usually expect and demand less from boys in terms of being aware of and expressing their feelings.

They grow up, therefore, without having learned what to do with their emotions. The result is that as adults they are deficient in dealing with personal relationships that thrive or totter on the ability to recognize and respond to feelings. Many adult males wouldn't know a feeling if it hit them over the head.

Girls, on the other hand, often keep their feelings to themselves. Their grades may not drop, and outwardly they may seem to be handling the divorce well. They may seek attention and affection from adults more than boys do, but their behavior is not usually destructive and antisocial. (In the cases where it is, however, one researcher found that those girls tend to be less socially competent as time passes.)

Friends and family are often surprised at how "well-adjusted" the girls seem to be, and wonder what they are doing with their feelings. We know now that they often bury them and that their feelings of sadness, deep loss, and abandonment gnaw at them and show up in their behavior by the time they reach adolescence. Frequently they date and have sexual intercourse earlier, for instance, than girls who come from families where the father is absent because he has died. At that time they are more likely to become hostile toward their mothers; they sometimes run away or become sexually promiscuous and experiment with drugs and alcohol. Girls who show these characteristics are often those whose parents divorced when they were very young.

Girls also may have more trouble with heterosexual relationships as they approach adolescence and may not have the ability to interact appropriately with males. In some cases, especially where they have had unsatisfying contact or no contact with their fathers, they are inept in pursuing romantic relationships in a healthy way. They have no experience in relating to a loving father, and they missed the chance to acquire the social skills and confidence they need to relate well to boys and men. In many cases their memories of men may be laced with anxiety or even hostility and a sense of rejection.

Robin's Story: A Model Daughter . . . For a While "I remember feeling out of focus, fuzzy, as though nothing was quite real," says Robin, whose parents were divorced when she was ten. "I was always a reasonable, I guess you might say a somewhat controlled little girl, so I didn't do anything outrageous. I did cry a lot, but I did it privately. For everyone else, I put on a cheerful face. I saw my role as comforting my mother, who also concealed her real feelings, but who was plainly distressed.

"I kept thinking that this couldn't possibly be permanent. My parents were two rational people and always seemed to settle their differences without too much fuss. I kept wishing them back together and for a long time I believed it would happen. If only I acted the same, if I pretended nothing was wrong, if I continued to get good grades . . .

"By the time I was fifteen, I realized that though neither my mom nor dad had remarried, they were not going to get together. We were never again going to be the happy little family of my childhood. That's when I got angry. Something snapped inside me and it was as though the divorce happened at that point. There was no payoff, I realized, for being good."

That was when Robin's behavior became troublesome. It started with skipping a few classes, missing some tests. Her grades toppled, and she seemed to care about nothing but whom she would be dating next weekend.

"I went out with anybody," Robin says. "And I began to have sex when I was sixteen. Suddenly I didn't care much about anything else. My mother was beside herself, but nothing mattered to me then. My mom was Miss Goody Two Shoes and where had it gotten her? My dad still didn't love her. I decided I would be different."

At eighteen, right after high school graduation, Robin married Ned, a house painter, whom she had met when her mother was having their apartment redecorated. They knew each other five weeks before they eloped. The marriage lasted a year.

Six months later Robin met Marvin and moved in with him three weeks later. That relationship broke up the following Christmas.

"I know that my parents' divorce screwed up my life," Robin says. "I'm trying to work it through now. Maybe if I had reacted when it happened, I'd have been better off. By now I'd be on a more even course. As it is, I have a long way to go."

Siblings and Family Position
Children often say that they survived their parents' divorce only because they had a brother or sister to share their trauma, and that they became closer to their sibling as a result.

Myra, now thirty-two, says that she and her sister, a year younger, became inseparable after they heard about their parents' divorce. "We were seven and eight, and I remember being afraid to let Linda out of my sight. I thought if something happened to her, I wouldn't be able to go on living. I think she felt the same way.

"Through the years we have stayed close. Now we each have our own friends and our own lives, but we talk to each other every day and our relationship is important to us. We have a shared history and we still talk a lot about Mom and Dad—the time they were together . . . and apart."

Others, however, relate that conflict escalated between them and their siblings or that each of them, especially those of different sexes, offered little support to the others. Often one child aligned herself with the mother while another took the father's side; this pushes them further apart. The marital conflict turns into a conflict between brothers and sisters.

"My sisters and I never talked about the divorce," remembers Richard, whose parents divorced when he was twelve and his sisters were ten and fourteen. We each kept pretty much to ourselves, and all of us spent a lot of time alone. My sisters had more friends than I did so I guess they talked to them. But we never shared our feelings with each other. Now that I think about it, I'm not sure why. It would probably have helped all of us."

Where there are several children, often those of the same sex will stick together and comfort each other. But boys and girls, because their reactions are so different, rarely share their feelings or even spend much time together.

Temperament, Resilience, and Personality

We cannot discount each child's own brand of personality, temperament and resilience that have a lot to do with how he or she will behave after the divorce.

Some boys and girls—we call them the "invulnerable

children"—seem to be able to overcome intolerable situations and emerge stronger and healthier emotionally. Others, experiencing more minor stress, crumble and fall apart. What makes the difference?

I think it has a lot to do with a child's inner resources, those he has inherited through biology and those he has garnered through his environment. Children who have a history of having been difficult temperamentally, who have been described by their parents as irritable, impulsive, and aggressive, do not do well when faced with a situation as stressful as divorce. These children tend to have few friends, pull back from help that is offered, and usually have serious difficulty in school. Their self-esteem is poor and they are unhappy and lonely.

The absence of a father in their home exacerbates their problems. If they develop a good relationship with their dad, or if their mother remarries and they do well with their stepfather, they will often improve.

Nathan: A Stepfather Helps   Nathan was ten when his parents were divorced. His mother, Roslyn, had known for some years that her husband was unfaithful but chose to look the other way. Roslyn's self-esteem, despite her being attractive and creative, was "in the cellar," and she couldn't face being single again. However, her husband, Sammy, gave her no choice. One Sunday he packed his bag and told her the marriage was over.

The next day he visited his son to tell him he would be living elsewhere but would continue to see him. Nathan had always had a quick temper and was aggressive in his play with other children. As a result, he had few friends.

Nathan's face registered nothing when his father gave him the news, but he jumped up from his chair and threw it across the room, shattering the glass door on a china closet. Then he locked himself in his bedroom, where he remained for two days without eating or speaking to anyone.

The third day he dressed for school and told his mother

that he wanted to hear no more about the divorce. He was not interested. He did not care. Furthermore, he said, he had always hated his father and was glad to see him gone.

Nathan's behavior worsened. At school he told no one about his parents' breakup but attached himself to a rowdy, aggressive crowd of boys, boys he knew his parents would not approve of. Soon his teachers were complaining about his disruptive behavior in class, and his grades, which had been average before the divorce, plummeted.

Meanwhile, his mother, her self-esteem lower than it had ever been, began to go out with several single female friends who urged her to change her hair color and wear more flattering dresses. Through them she met Roger, a pleasant, low-key manager of a children's clothing shop. Roger was ten years younger than Roslyn, but they found instant rapport, and within eight months Roger moved in.

Nathan would have nothing to do with him. But Roger, who had four younger brothers and three nephews, was patient. He never pretended to take the place of Nathan's father, whom Nathan now saw once a month, but gradually introduced him to new interests like fishing and stamp collecting. On Sunday mornings Roger and Nathan would go bike riding together and would stop for breakfast on the way home.

In less than a year Nathan was a different child. His school grades were up. His temper was more controlled. And he acquired new friends, including Jeff—also from a divorced family—with whom he could share his feelings.

CHAPTER FOUR

———/———

Relationships—
Children and the Parents
They Live With

Children learn from their parents in two ways: through identifying with them and through interacting with them. In families that stay together, children have a chance, as part of their daily living, to identify, interact with, and learn from the views and behavior of both parents. And they can observe interaction between their parents. Children learn that femininity means more than just "mother as woman" but has something to do with the way their mother relates to their father; they learn about masculinity from their father's reactions to her.

After divorce occurs, 90 percent of children live with their mothers. While there are indications that more fathers will have custody of their children in the future, most adults from divorced families were raised by their mothers. Does it matter? Does it cause adjustment problems? Do children grow up impaired because their main access was to one parent, usually their mother?

Most studies have looked at children who live with their

mother since it's the most common arrangement. And they show that it is the mother's stability, mental health, general competence, and ability to maintain order in the family that counts heavily in the way children adjust to the divorce initially. Even in the absence of a father, a highly functioning mother, while having her hands full, can pick up the slack. And her children will do reasonably well.

However, in the long run, the absent father and the mother who overcompensates for him may transmit to their children a way of life marked by a sharp imbalance in intimate relationships. These children never see two adults assuming appropriate shares of their responsibilities in their relationships with their children. Girls, especially, often grow up overfunctioning in the same way their mothers did, which leads them to marital partners who can't or won't hold up their part of a relationship.

Despite popular belief, some research over the past two decades suggests that living with Mom may not always be in the best interest of sons. Children seem to do better when living with parents of the same sex after the divorce.

Girls who live with their mothers and boys who live with their fathers are often better adjusted. They are more competent socially, more mature, and more cooperative, and they have higher self-esteem.

I have seen (and so have other researchers and clinicians) that in the two or three years after the divorce the quality of the relationship between the divorced mother (who has custody) and her children depends on whether the child is male or female. The conflict that occurred between husband and wife seems to filter down to the mother and son, and a more cooperative relationship seems to develop between mother and daughter.

Mothers and Sons

The relationship between a mother and the son or sons of whom she has custody is the most problem filled just after the divorce when the mother is most emotional and least rational. However, the problems sometimes linger. One study showed that mothers still had difficulty controlling their sons six years after the divorce, that they tended to nag them and complain about them. There was affection between them as well, but even after this length of time the relationship often was ambivalent and intense.

This happens for several reasons. For one thing, mothers often see their husbands' characteristics in their sons and unconsciously react in a negative way to them. It is not surprising since boys are often a lot like their fathers, who are their natural role models. Imagine what this does to a son! Some of the very qualities they may like most about themselves and perhaps about their fathers may be the things their mother doesn't like at all.

To complicate the situation further, once the father is out of the house, a mother often turns to her sons as their father's stand-ins and has the same expectations of them that she did of her husband. If the husband was remote and not outwardly affectionate, the mother may demand that the son be different—and become annoyed with him because he is not.

Society's expectations don't help either. One of my patients, a forty-two-year-old woman who was having a stormy relationship with her eighteen-year-old son, revealed that her son's scout leader had told him shortly after the divorce, "Now you're the man in the family." Boys don't want to replace their fathers; it confronts them with unbearable emotional conflict and precipitates behavior that is often hostile, antisocial, aggressive, or just plain contrary.

The behavior of boys often improves dramatically when

the mother remarries. I think that mothers see men differently (and more positively) at that point in their lives, and it
is reflected in the way they treat their sons.

Mothers and Daughters

On the other hand, the relationship between divorced
mothers and their young daughters often becomes
stronger, at least for a while. Girls generally are more similar to their mothers than to their fathers. Also, in our society, parents think about and treat girls differently from
boys. They think of girls as warm, supportive, and sensitive,
and more concerned about relationships.

Girls and mothers tend to develop close bonds and focus
on each other after the divorce. There is often a tacit agreement between them that men are disappointing; the divorce validates that that is the case. This triangle—mother
and daughter united against father—seems to work well for
a while, until either the mother remarries or the daughter
grows older, becomes interested in men, and develops relationships of her own. Then a daughter's bond with her
mother unravels.

Consider Lori. After her parents' divorce she and her
brother Joel continued to live with their mother. Lori, then
eleven, and her mother became closer than they had ever
been. Lori's father had left because he had met and
planned to marry another woman; Lori hated him for doing
that and for breaking up what she had perceived to be a
happy family. For four years, she would have nothing to do
with her father. She would not read his letters or answer his
telephone calls, and she dumped his birthday gifts in the
trash without even opening them.

When she was sixteen, she began dating a boy she had
met at a cousin's wedding. But she preferred to spend more
time with her female friends and saw him only about once a
month. He was the only boy she dated while she was in high

school. In college, however, Lori found herself suddenly attracted to men, wanting their attention, and wanting to have sex with them. She would write letters to her mother about the dance marathon she and Jack won, about the candlelight dinner Harry arranged for her birthday, about Burt, the young man in her chemistry class who just asked her to join him for a weekend in New York. All the while, Lori's relationship with her mother disintegrated. Her mother didn't share her daughter's enthusiasm about her newfound popularity.

"She kept telling me that college was for learning, not for playing around," Lori says. "And she warned me about men—how they were interested in you only for sex. She told me not to get too excited about any man because he is sure to let you down.

"It made me angry. I knew she was trying to protect me, but what did she want? Did she expect me to avoid men all my life? So I just stopped telling her, stopped writing to her about the important things in my life. Just stuff like, 'How are you and Joel [her brother]? I got a B in political science.' You know, the safe stuff. And our relationship kept stretching further and further apart."

A study by Dr. E. Mavis Hetherington found, interestingly, that this same kind of mother/daughter pattern does not occur when the father has died. I believe the difference comes because the closeness after death is not based on a negative view of the father or of men in general. In fact, the mother's memories of the deceased father tend to be positive ones, and this attitude is transmitted to the daughter, who is freer to pursue heterosexual relationships based on a healthier view of men. The disruption of the family by death is not seen by anyone as a case of winners or losers, as is often true in divorce, and the way the family organizes itself around the crisis is very different.

If the divorced mother remarries, it is a sign that she is looking at men differently; if the bond between mother and daughter was based on looking at men negatively, that bond is now weakened.

The greatest conflict then occurs between the daughter and the stepfather, because she has so thoroughly bought into her mother's earlier views of men. For her the new marriage is tantamount to a betrayal.

If, however, the mother does not remarry or makes a bad second marriage, the daughter faces new problems. As she grows up, begins dating, and cultivates relationships with men, she finds herself in a no-win situation. If she finds men pleasing and goes on to develop healthy relationships with them, she is betraying her mother and loosening the tie that binds them. If she does not, she betrays herself and is not able to move into fulfilling heterosexual relationships of her own.

Custodial Fathers and Their Children

When fathers have custody of their young children, it often indicates unusual family circumstances. It may be that the father was heavily invested in caretaking and entered the marriage in a role somewhat different from that of the traditional "breadwinner" father. Or it may be that the mother has been judged "unfit" by the court to raise her children or that she has agreed to relinquish custody to her husband because of a higher priority—a career, another relationship, or the feeling that she could not be an adequate mother at the time.

In any case, there is more evidence now that living with their fathers may be beneficial to boys and detrimental to girls. In fact, one study revealed that boys between the ages of six and eleven whose father had custody of them were more socially competent, were warmer in social relationships, had higher self-esteem, and were more mature, more independent, and less demanding than boys who grew up with their mothers or even in intact families.

Girls who live with their fathers, however, did not do as well when measured for the same characteristics, which supports the idea that there is something significant—and positive—about the continuous relationship of a child with the same sex parent. It has a lot to do with the intuitive nature of a parent's involvement with a child of the same sex. Unlike mothers who have custody of their sons, fathers seem to be able to set rules and enforce them in a way that does not create power struggles between them and their sons.

Older boys who have more to say about where they want to live frequently choose their fathers. Even boys who have lived with their mothers for a period of time sometimes move in with their fathers when they reach adolescence. In many cases, it is with the full sanction of the mother, who says she can no longer manage her son's behavior.

Tracey had legal custody of both Gregg, seven at the time of divorce, and Wanda, age nine. By the time Gregg was thirteen, Tracey declared he was "impossible." He was flunking in school, refused to do any chores at home, stayed out too late, and was involved with a rowdy group of friends whom she suspected of using drugs.

She asked her husband, with whom she had remained on friendly terms, to take him. Now five years later Gregg is being graduated from high school in the top 10 percent of his class. He holds an after-school job with a weekly newspaper and has developed a sense of responsibility that surprises even his mother. His father says it hasn't been easy. The key, he says, was clear rules and limits, but with enough flexibility and reason that conflict could usually be avoided.

When boys grow up with their mothers and have little or no contact with their fathers, they often spend their adult years searching for Daddy. Ronnie, for instance, is a forty-five-year-old nationally known psychiatrist. His files are filled with poignant thank-you notes from grateful patients whose lives he has helped salvage. But he admits that his own life has been defined by an agonizing and consuming search for the father he lost when his parents divorced thirty years ago.

Until the divorce, Ronnie remembers his father, a busy doctor in a baggy gray suit, as a man who loved him intensely. He has memories of his dad bouncing him on his knee, taking him to baseball games, packing the family in a car on a minute's notice to head for an amusement park or a picnic or the zoo. But when Ronnie was thirteen, his father became someone he didn't recognize. He gave up family medicine for psychiatry, exchanged his baggy suits for high fashion sports coats, and after twenty-five years of marriage left the family.

At first, Ronnie's father moved to another part of the city, and Ronnie would visit him on weekends. Two years later he remarried and moved a hundred and fifty miles away.

"I hated what my father was doing, but I loved my father," Ronnie says. "He was such a driving force in my life. I wanted Daddy to like me. I wanted him to be proud of me. I wanted to please him. And I tried my best to have a relationship with him.

"It was different with my mom. Mommies are nurturing and they are there whether you please them or not. But daddies are not like that. That makes Daddy a very powerful person."

Ronnie dedicated that next seventeen years to cultivating a relationship with a father who didn't seem to be interested. "My father didn't seem to care what I did or how I felt or who I was. I would get angry and there would be periods of time when we didn't even talk. But I always came back. I was always the one to reach out again. The best we ever got was 'cordial.' "

During that period Ronnie was gaining prominence as a psychiatrist. He wrote articles for leading journals, hoping his father would read them and respond. He did not. After several years, in desperation, he stuffed what he calls "his life's writings," dozens of journal clippings, into an envelope and mailed them to his father. He waited for a call that never came.

After Ronnie was married, he tried again, urging his father to take an interest in him. "You're not going to live forever," he told his dad. "Let's try to enjoy each other." His father listened, then said, "You're right. Things shouldn't be this way between us." But his father did nothing to make their relationship better.

Ronnie didn't give up. No matter how often his father rebuffed him, he went back for more, hoping that each time would be different. When his oldest son was born, he took him to visit his dad. At thirty-six, he still felt exquisitely deprived of a father, but he wanted his son to know his grandfather. The continuity of life was important to him. "I wanted my father to do with my son what he should have done with me, what *his father* should have done with him. Maybe he would learn from looking at his grandson."

Ronnie was disappointed. His relationship with his father never improved. And it wasn't until a month before his dad died that he said to Ronnie the one sentence he had waited for all his life, "I'm proud of you."

"No matter the reasons for a divorce, it always feels selfish to a child," Ronnie says today, five years after his father's death. "Even if the reasons are proper, legal, ethical, and understandable, from a child's perspective you want Daddy—and Mommy. And you want them together.

"I still find myself looking for Daddy all over the place. Even now that he's dead. I only wanted him to notice me, to notice what I was doing and be proud of me. I wanted him to say, 'This is my boy.'

"I look for Daddy in other people, though not so much anymore, and it sets me up for disappointment. I don't suppose I'll ever get over it."

CHAPTER FIVE

———/———

The Family After Divorce

The period after divorce is a critical one because children are so vulnerable at that time. The way their parents treat them and each other teaches them indelible lessons—positive or negative—about relationships. They are lessons they will absorb and carry out in their own lives as they grow up.

Parents who are able to put themselves in their children's shoes, who can be rational and objective enough to tend to their children's feelings, give them the best chance of emerging from divorce in sound emotional health. The stability, mental health, and reasonable behavior of both parents are major predictors of children's ability to develop satisfying intimate relationships as adults.

Some divorces are angry and punitive. Others are friendly and cooperative. Most are somewhere in between, and the relationship between parents often changes—for the better or the worse—over time. But one thing is certain:

Divorce does not end the relationship between spouses who are parents.

Most of the time, the way two people behave in their marriage is the same way they behave during their divorce and for the first two or three years afterward. That way—the family style of relating to each other—influences the handling of issues that can make a difference in the way a child of divorce grows up. They include, but are not limited to, the child's access to both parents, visitation rights, and connections with extended family members.

In an angry and punitive divorce, heated custody fights often erupt and the children become the pawns, bargaining chips in a battle that turns into a full-scale war.

The intelligence of the parents doesn't count. It doesn't matter how loving they are or how caring. Their anger at each other eclipses their reason and their sensitivity toward their children. Their minds become muddled; they will trade houses for children and make no distinction between daughters and dollars. Even they are often horrified, years later, over their behavior. My patients often tell me that they knew the way they acted, around the time of divorce, was inappropriate, and that it was damaging to their children. They say they couldn't help themselves. A well-known magazine editor confessed, "I've written about divorce. I knew all of the right things to do. I just couldn't do them."

"Mom wants me to hate Dad," says Theresa, who is nine. "Dad wants me to hate Mom. Each of them tells me bad things about the other. So I don't know how to act when I'm with either one of them. I just don't say anything, and I feel guilty all the time."

Ben, a thirty-seven-year-old magazine editor, married to the head of a social services agency, had one of the most agonizing custody situations I have seen.

"I was afraid I would lose my son," he said, "and I became paranoid about it. My wife, Marie, said she wanted him. I said I wanted him. She would tell him he couldn't call me. I threatened to file for custody. She threatened to commit suicide. And my son got pulled at, like Play-Doh, from each of us."

It is not unusual for normally rational people such as Ben and Marie to taunt their children with such comments as: "Your mother is nothing but a whore," or "Your father was never any good. Look what he is doing to our family."

Sometimes the slurs are more subtle, but just as destructive. "Your *father* called. He won't be able to see you Sunday," or "It's a good thing you got this twenty-five-dollar birthday check from Grandmom. Maybe we'll be able to eat this week," or "You didn't get the sneakers I sent your mother money for? She must have gotten her hair done instead."

As one Philadelphia lawyer says, "You can't kick the crap out of each other without kicking the crap out of your kids."

In an effort to reduce the acrimony between divorcing couples, those contemplating divorce in Cobb County, Georgia, first must take a course designed to show them how their behavior may be damaging their children. The message they are given is that the marriage is ending, but the family is not.

A hundred years ago children almost always remained with their father after divorce, but custody shifted to the mother at the beginning of the twentieth century. Unless she was pronounced grossly unfit (mentally ill or alcoholic) and clearly not equipped to care for them, it was felt that mothers were the natural nurturers and had a biological connection with their children that was different—and stronger—than the fathers'.

Now, more fathers are protesting. Some are demanding sole custody. In other cases, mothers are walking out on their families, leaving fathers saddled with child-care responsibilities they hadn't bargained for. Joint custody, too, is becoming a more acceptable option.

Frequently fathers, particularly those who did not initiate the divorce, see custody of the children as the only way to maintain contact with their families. They are saying to their wives, "You can leave, but there is no way you will take my children with you." In other cases, where a husband's psyche has been brutally injured—often where his wife has been unfaithful—he may threaten a battle, even a court procedure, to prove she is an unfit mother.

In fact, 10 to 15 percent of divorce cases are accompanied by custody fights that end up in the courts. The father does not want the mother to have the children; neither does he want to pay her child support. The children often become the focus of an agonizing and wrenching custody dispute that is fought in and/or out of the courtroom. They are sometimes even asked to testify to a parent's wrongdoings, especially if they have witnessed adultery.

Beverly, Wendy, and Theresa—Bitter Divorces

Beverly, who is now thirty, remembers vividly the day she went to court with pictures of her father and another woman having sex. She had found them, by accident, as she was searching through her father's suitcase for a present he told her he had bought her on a recent trip to California. She was fifteen at the time and had known that her parents' marriage was a highly conflicted one. But she had no idea that her father was having an affair. She hid the pictures for months but volunteered them to her mother when her parents separated and her father insisted he wanted custody of his daughter.

"I can't imagine how either of them was able to put me in that position—going to court and appearing before the judge in his long black robe," Beverly says. "I was terrified. But I hated my father then for what he did to us. And I told him I would go to court with those pictures. I guess when I think about it my mom really had no choice. But my father

. . . I think he was a really bad person to let me go through that."

Beverly never had a chance to make peace with her father. He died when she was twenty-two and her visits with him, until then, were infrequent and strained. She says she is still having a difficult time dealing with men and thinks that harmonious relationships with them are probably beyond her reach.

Even where the battlefield is not the courtroom, children often end up as the bloodied soldiers. The parent who wants custody often tries to bribe or sway the children with tantalizing promises:

"If you live with me, you'll have a new room you can decorate yourself."

"You'll have more freedom. In a year, when you're sixteen, I'll buy you a car."

"We'll take long vacations every summer, maybe even Paris or London."

"I'll get you your own telephone with your own number."

A parent who doesn't get what he or she wants has a lot of power to make her spouse's life miserable. Sadly, the children are the trump cards.

"My dad kept telling me terrible things about my mother," says thirty-year-old Yvonne. "And my mother told me equally terrible things about my dad. Mom wanted me to tell the lawyers that Dad had abused me sexually. She said that we would embarrass him into giving us more money.

"Dad wanted me to say that Mom had been running around with other men for five years and that she used cocaine.

"I couldn't tell you whether either of those things was true. Maybe Dad did touch me where he wasn't supposed to when I was little, but it was nothing I could remember real well. And Mom did have a boyfriend who came around once or twice. He even sent her a dozen roses for her birthday when I was eight.

"But here I was, thirteen, and I loved both my parents. I didn't want to see them split up, and I didn't want to be in the middle of it. I used to stay late at school, just so I wouldn't have to come home to their screaming.

"When Dad finally left the house, Mom wouldn't let me see him. She said he was no good and he would be a bad influence on me. She said, if I wanted to go live with him to go ahead, but she would have nothing to do with me.

"What choice did I have? I didn't see my father for almost a year until their divorce was final. Then he got visitation rights.

"But nothing got better. He wasn't allowed to come in the house when he picked me up. And he had to show up with a specified woman friend, someone my mother knew, or she wouldn't trust me to go with him.

"When I got home, she pumped me for information about what had happened. Who else came? Was the woman friend there all the time? Did he try to touch me? What does his house look like? Did he say anything about her? What did we do? What did we eat? Did he give me any money?

"He did the same thing. 'How's your mother's boyfriend? Where is she working? Is she home when you come home from school?'

"Each one was looking for something mean to say about the other one. I tolerated it until I was nineteen, until I couldn't take it anymore. Then I told both of them—'No more questions. If you want to know about each other, use the telephone and ask.' "

Loyalty conflicts and guilt about choosing between parents grow up with children. Even as adults, in their thirties and forties, they remember being in court, asked to decide which parent they wanted to live with. They say that they never could have told the truth. Some select the parent who they think needs them the most. Others will choose the parent their sibling did not.

Many of my patients still dread holidays because they have so much guilt about where they will go and how the parent they don't choose will feel about their decision. Roger, who is fifty, still flies from Atlanta to Toronto every Christmas so he can spend part of the day with each of his parents.

Candy and Tim—the Friendly Divorce

More families are working toward what they describe as a "friendly divorce," one in which the parents will be, at the least, civil to each other, pleasant, and still interested in the other's well-being. A divorce that will not maim the children and will give more than lip service to the often uttered phrase, "We don't love each other, but we both still love you." This kind of divorce challenges parents to actions that match their words.

Considering the inherently rancorous nature of divorce, an astonishing number of couples are able to stay friends. When they can simulate, as closely as possible, the cohesion of the predivorce family, odds are that the children will benefit. They may emerge even stronger and better adjusted than children from intact but dysfunctional and unhappy homes.

Betty and Philip, for instance, had been unhappy in their marriage almost from the beginning. They both said it was nothing major, just a gradual growing apart as each developed new interests and shifting values. They had married in their early twenties and quickly had two children, Candy, then six, and Timmy, four. They knew they didn't want to continue living together, but both felt responsible for the children and didn't want to separate abruptly. They decided that for six months Philip would move to the third floor of their large home in Virginia, and he and Betty would pursue independent lives, but that the family would continue as a unit. All of them would have dinner together at least three times a week, and once each weekend there would be an outing planned around the children. Their relationship became more like that of a brother and sister.

When Philip moved out, it was just a few blocks away so he could continue seeing the children. He and Betty discussed an amicable financial settlement, one that would not compromise the children's lifestyle, and while each of them had a lawyer, there was little controversy about finances and visitation and none about custody.

"Betty is a wonderful mother," Philip said. "There could be no better mother for our children. So why would I quibble about what that is worth in terms of dollars and cents?"

Philip's job called for extensive travel, but when he was at home he spent a lot of time with the children, and they felt free to call him and visit as often as they wanted. Frequently they spent weekends at his apartment. Even when each of them remarried, a time ripe for incendiary behavior, there were few problems. The two couples continued the friendship, and Philip's parents still think of Betty as their daughter-in-law. In fact, Philip and his second wife, his parents, and his entire family attended Betty's second wedding.

Candy, now eighteen, says that except for a short period of disorientation when her father moved out, a time when her mother needed more propping up than usual, the divorce has not had a major impact on her life. In fact, she says there have been many advantages.

"I could see as I got older that it was appropriate for them to be divorced," Candy told me. "My father and his wife are older yuppies, interested in careers, material things, and acquiring prestige and power. My mother and her husband are people who feel strongly about relationships and self-expression. They like art and music and beautiful flowers. My mother is willing to see the good in other people and it's infectious. She has a healthy image of herself.

"I think I'm much more like my mother, but it has helped me to see my stepmother's point of view too. She stressed that I should build a career and prepare myself for independence. She said my achievements in my career will give me power in my personal relationships. She is even paying for my schooling. I don't happen to agree with her, but it's okay. I respect her beliefs and it doesn't interfere with our relationship."

Her brother, Tim, on the other hand, feels less content. In contrast to the experience of many boys whose mothers remarry, he did not become close to his stepfather, whom he saw as a taskmaster, unlike his own father, whom he clearly preferred. Soon after his father remarried, he and his new wife had a son who, even as a young boy, showed extraordinary giftedness and talent. Tim felt left out and began to retreat from his father and his new family. He recognizes that he needs help to work out his anxieties and is determined to repair his relationship with his dad.

Both Candy and Tim say that they would have preferred that their parents could have been happy and stayed together. Of course, there are some unavoidable problems. But they emphasize that their parents did many of what they consider to be the "right things."

"They told us about the divorce together and made it clear that they weren't divorcing us," Candy says. "And neither parent said mean things about the other one. Even today, with Tim not feeling comfortable with Dad, Mom is encouraging him to get closer."

Visits with Your Other Parent

Visitation with the parent who does not have custody is an important key to a child's reaction to a divorce. Children need to know that they are not being abandoned, and that no matter what takes place between the parents, they will always have a mother and father who are physically and emotionally available to them.

Girls need a loving father with whom they can express their growing femininity and learn to feel comfortable about relating to the opposite sex. Boys need to have an ongoing and close relationship with the father with whom they identify, who validates their masculinity, and whose approval is a central part of their universe. Without it, they are often puzzled about the kind of behavior expected from them and blunder through their lives like Ronnie, always trying to find Daddy.

Where visits with the absent parent—usually the father—are frequent and satisfying, the child is apt to adjust better and more quickly. Where they are not, he or she is at greater risk for problems, immediately and into the future.

A Canadian study that followed the academic performance of children after their parents' separation revealed that school-age children who did not see both their mothers and fathers regularly experienced a significant drop in grades. This was true regardless of the child's age or sex.

The benefits of visitation, however, depend on how cooperative the parents are. Where parents use their children as go-betweens, to elicit information about the other parent after each visit, where there is a lot of conflict about the visits—how often they should be, how long, how arrangements are to be made, and so on—it may actually hamper a child's ability to cope.

Divorce counseling often focuses on keeping the parent who doesn't have custody in the picture, on letting him (or her) know how critical it is that he be there for his children, and urging him not to stay away because seeing his children may be too painful or may make him feel too guilty. A relationship that was terrific before the divorce is not money in the bank if it isn't nurtured and maintained. And by the same token, where a relationship has been less than perfect, parents have another shot, after the divorce, at making it better.

Mothers are encouraged to break through their despair, to see beyond their own pain that both parents are important for a child's optimum growth and development. And fathers whose children don't live with them are urged to maintain consistent contact.

Under the best circumstances—when parents agree on who will retain custody, and visitation rights are frequent and flexible—it is still not ideal for either the child or the parents. Dad's day may be Sunday, but the child longs for him on Thursday. Dad makes a decision that feels uncomfortable to the child, and Mom is not there to modify it. When there is an argument with a teacher, a rejection from a friend, a "no-good, horrible, very bad" day when nothing goes right, the parent who could help the most may not be around

Where Is He When I Need Him?

"When I had nightmares," remembers Connie, now twenty, "I wanted to run to my dad and have him hold me and comfort me. But Dad was in his apartment with his girlfriend. Even though he told me he was always there for me, what was I supposed to do? Call him and say, 'I hope I'm not disturbing you, but I'm having this awful nightmare?' It's just not the same."

Advice about decisions—from what a seventeen-year-old should wear to the prom to the major he should choose in college—exerts the kinds of influences and values that shape a child's life, that give it texture. That texture frays because both parents are not available to him in the context of a united family. Visits, too, even when they occur regularly, create their own mix of pleasure and disappointment. And for both father and children they are an inadequate substitute for what they are trying to replace.

Parents as Strangers

Children often feel like strangers in their father's new life. They see themselves as guests rather than residents in his apartment. They're not sure how to act with his new friend. Or how they really feel about her. And they complain that their fathers don't get a chance to know and understand them. Visits are often over before anything important is said or done.

"We used to giggle and call Dad the ice cream man," says Jill, who was seven when her parents separated. "He would pick my sister and me up every Sunday, and it was always the same. Even we could see that he felt funny with us, like he wasn't the same father anymore.

"He would pick us up in time to have breakfast at a diner near his new apartment. Then he'd say, 'Okay, girls, what will we do today?'

"One Sunday it would be the zoo. Another Sunday, a movie. Once we went to the circus. But always, it ended with ice cream. 'Okay,' he'd say, 'It's ice cream time.' We knew what that meant. It was going-home time.

"Once, about three months after the divorce, my sister Elaine, a year younger than I am, said, 'Can we see where you live?' I kicked her under the table because I knew my dad didn't want us there. I knew he had a girlfriend and figured she was probably in the apartment.

"Dad's face got real red and he looked at his watch. Then he said, 'Oh, yeah. Sure. Next week we'll go to my place.'

"Next week didn't come for eight more months. By the time Dad took us to his apartment, I don't think either of us cared anymore. We knew we weren't real important to him."

Sometimes Dad's new life seems appealing, like a never-ending party to which children are invited only sometimes. This may be especially true when there is a romantic interest who wants to make a good impression on the children.

And it can feel unbearably threatening to the parent who lingers at home.

Ingrid, who was fourteen when her parents separated, loved to go to her father's elegant apartment in the heart of Manhattan. It had a spectacular view of Central Park, and there was always so much to do in the city. By comparison her life back in Westchester seemed boring and lusterless.

"Dad had all of these interesting friends who always seemed to be hanging around. Sometimes a couple of them would stay overnight. I had my own room with all of my own things, so I felt like I belonged. And we were always off for a buggy ride in the park or a shopping spree in Greenwich Village or a craft show in Connecticut.

"Mary, Dad's girlfriend, was fun and let me do whatever I wanted. Every week she would have another present for me. Sometimes it was a pretty pin for my hair or a new sweater or a necklace. She bought me perfume and even took me to get my first manicure.

"It wasn't until I was almost nineteen and Dad had had several Marys in his life that I realized he and I didn't know each other at all. I was still dazzled by the life he led and I liked being part of that.

"But it was all superficial. We never talked about anything important. He asked me about school and he'd tell me about some big deal he'd made that week. But the stuff that really mattered—how I felt and what I was like inside— was going on only between Mom and me."

Buck: "Uncle Dad"

Visits can be equally disheartening for the absent father, whom novelist Bryan Wooley has labeled "Uncle Dad." The father who leaves often is determined that he will stay close to his children, that he will not allow time and space to destroy their relationship. Many, like Buck, had no idea how difficult—and devastating—it would be.

"So many of my friends were divorced and their kids

seemed to look okay," Buck told me. "They had friends, got on with school, had their ups and downs, just like other kids. Besides, I was a devoted father. And I was intelligent. I read the books and the literature on divorce. I knew the right things to do. I would give my kids 'quality time.'

"I might as well have used the books for firewood," Buck says, ten years later. "What I became was irrelevant in my children's lives. My wife, to my chagrin and surprise, re-married eighteen months after our divorce was final—to a kind and gentle man who is a terrific father to my kids.

"Sure, they are still my kids. He didn't adopt them and he never rips me to them. But he's the one that's there when they break a leg playing football. He's the one that watched my daughter get dressed for her first date. He's the one that plans family picnics and vacations with them. He is the one that has an influence over what they become, who will always be a part of them. Me, I'm an outsider.

"I remember when I was at home, I used to complain about how messy the kids kept the house. Roller skates in the living room, bicycles on the front porch, stacks of school books thrown on the dining room table.

"Now, my apartment is neat and tidy. Everything is in its place. Even the towels in the linen closet are folded in the same direction and are color coordinated. A stack of blue, a stack of red. But I'd give anything to have the mess back again. A few chewing gum wrappers stuffed in the sofa pillows, a carton from McDonald's tossed in the sink. I don't have the mess anymore, but I don't have my kids either."

Buck eventually moved to the Midwest because he couldn't tolerate being a part-time father. "Now my kids are older, eighteen, twenty-four, and twenty-six, all single. They call me and I call them. But we are still like strangers. Each of them comes out for a couple of weeks in the summer. I start getting nervous in April.

"How will it be? Will we be able to talk? Will it be awkward? What will we do? Will they like me? Will I like them?

"I have heard that it gets better. As kids get older and have their own lives, you can make up for lost time. You don't have to compete with a father who is living in the house with them. You can explain better and they can understand better.

"Maybe that will happen. But I'm fifty-six now and the time that's gone is gone. I'll never have the chance to make it up. And neither will they."

Buck is not alone. The pain of feeling like a stranger in your child's life becomes intolerable for many absent parents, and it seems to them that it will be easier for them and their children if they stay away. Often they feel as though their children must know that they are interested, that they would be there for them if the children only wanted them.

But children see it differently. Lacking the skill or ability to dissect or understand their parent's actions, his or her behavior becomes the barometer through which they measure how much he or she cares. When there is not enough contact on which to build a relationship, a child gets a strong message. The message is: "My dad (or mom) doesn't care enough." The child's battered self-esteem is baggage he may lug into adulthood.

The Absent Parent

The amount of child care received from the parent who does not live at home is shockingly low, much lower than most of us would imagine. While studies vary, many indicate that as many as 40 percent of absent fathers have no contact with their children. One study showed that almost half of all children living with either mother or father had not seen their other parent in the preceding twelve months. Of those who did have contact, only a minority saw him or her an average of once a week. Sadly, only a little more than a quarter of the children even talked to their parents on the telephone as often as once a week, slept at his or her house at least once a month, or had a place in the other parent's home in which they could keep some of their things.

Even with a parent who starts out with good intentions, other priorities can take over. There may be demands made by new, intimate relationships, more time spent at work to support two households, travel, and just the inconvenience and discomfort of having to plan time with the children. If visits don't end, they frequently stretch further apart. And fathers often don't know how much their children long for time with them. Sometimes the custodial parent, who can see firsthand the effect on the children, will try to encourage a relationship. Much of the time, though, it doesn't work.

Leonard: "I'm Twenty-two and It Still Hurts"

Leonard, now twenty-two, is still smarting from his father's rejection. "I don't remember the details because I was only five," he says. "But I know that one day I had a father, and the next day I didn't. My mom packed our bags and we moved from Des Moines back to Baltimore where my mom's family lived.

"My mom explained to me that she and Daddy were going to be divorced because they couldn't get along anymore. It wasn't until I was in my late teens that I learned my father had been abusive, that he had hit my mother and me too when I was very young.

"We never heard from him. Apparently he supported us although my mom got a job as a producer for a television station, something she had done before she was married. I know my mom encouraged him to get in touch with me because, once in a while, I would overhear her talking to him on the telephone late at night when she thought I was asleep.

"Once I heard her tell him, 'You have a wonderful son to

be proud of. It has been four years since you have seen or talked to him. What's wrong with you?'

"I didn't think there was anything wrong with my father. I thought something was wrong with me. I had friends whose parents were divorced and their fathers took them out on weekends and they bought them things and did things with them. I felt really bad.

"I went through a hard time when I was growing up. When I went to camp, other kids whose parents were divorced had visits from both of them. I didn't. It began to bother me more and more, and it affected my ability to concentrate. It was hard to pay attention at school, and the only things I wanted to do were sports—physical things, where I could get out some energy and some anger. Maybe some sadness too.

"When I was seventeen and ready for high school graduation, my mom asked me if I wanted to invite my father. At first I said, 'no.' But it was out of spite. I kept brooding about it and all the time I knew I wanted my father to be there. So finally I told my mom and she sent him an invitation on which I wrote a little personal note.

"Every day I waited to hear. Maybe he would call. Maybe I would get a letter. Finally, Mom suggested that I call him on the phone. I was afraid and I asked her to do it.

"My dad is a professor at the University of Iowa, and he said there was a big conference that weekend, and he didn't think he could be there. But he must have thought it over because a week later he called and said he would come.

"I tried to act like I wasn't nervous about it. But I was more scared about seeing my father than I was about making a mistake in my graduation speech.

"But actually, it worked out okay. My mom's family treated him politely even though I know they all hated him. And my mom was terrific. She did everything to help the day go smoothly. Dad and I talked very little to each other, but he did say he was proud of me and hugged me once or twice.

"I was sure, after that, that we would be seeing each other from time to time. But it never happened. I called him a few times, once to ask him to buy me a jacket I wanted. I knew Mom could get me the jacket, but I needed something to let me contact my dad. I told him the kind of jacket I wanted, and he said, 'Okay, I'll send it this week.'

"That Saturday, I got a check in an envelope. No jacket, no note. Nothing. Just a check.

"I haven't stopped trying. But my self-esteem . . . well, I don't have much. When I meet a girl I like and she doesn't like me, it doesn't surprise me. If I'm left out of a party I expected to be invited to, I don't even care. My mom and her family are close and I feel terrific about them. But I still want a relationship with my father. I don't think I'll ever feel at peace until I get it."

Joint Custody: Does It Help or Hurt?

Does joint custody make life easier for a child of divorce? To the extent that it reflects cooperation between the parents, where the parents are both dedicated to making decisions about the child that reflect their joint interest in his or her welfare, I think it does.

Usually joint custody works best when parents live in the same city, the same neighborhood, and the child is able to attend school easily and keep the same friends.

Some children feel this is the best of all possible divorce worlds, while others give it mixed reviews. Some complaints are strictly logistical. The blouse Amy wants to wear today is in her father's house. Her chemistry notes are at her mother's. The friend she is seeing tonight is in her dad's neighborhood, but she is scheduled to stay at Mom's. She'd rather be at Mom's tonight, but Mom's friend is staying there. And so on. But in some respects joint custody mirrors as closely as possible the predivorce family because both of the child's parents are accessible to him or her on a more regular basis. The toxic emotions created by physical distance and sporadic visits are less likely to fester and get in the way of harmonious relationships.

In cases where joint custody is imposed by the court or decided upon as a face-saving device for a parent, it doesn't work so well. Here it is not the parents who have decided together that joint custody is best for their children. And court orders, while they can regulate living arrangements, can do nothing to quench the fire of personal conflict. When two parents (or four, in the case of remarriages) disagree on what is best for a child, someone has to have veto power. If the divorce is not a "friendly" one, the child may remain the object of controversy, joint custody not-withstanding.

I worked with one family in which there was a major difference of opinion among parents and stepparents on education for a child. On August 30—a week before school was to begin—the sixteen-year-old boy didn't know where he would be going to school or in which city. In this case, his parents had been coming to me for counseling. But additional problems surfaced because the stepmother was miffed that her husband and his ex-wife were making a decision about school that excluded her. I am now setting up a meeting with all four parents who, at least, are willing to participate. There is a lot going on in this family, and in order to know the play, I need to see the whole cast of characters.

The practice of joint custody is more common, with thirty-three states permitting judges to award it where they feel it is in the best interest of the child. But whether or not it will lead to improved psychological health of children as they grow up remains to be seen.

Access to Other Relatives

The access to grandparents, aunts, uncles, cousins, and other relatives is critical to the child of divorce. Children, for instance, who have grandparents living with them, or nearby, often feel less disrupted and more comforted; while much in their world is changing, some of the important people are still in place for them. The more communication and conversation children have with significant relatives—often it is an aunt or a grandmother—the more likely they are to come through the divorce less damaged. This is true even when the relatives are in the picture mainly because they are providing emotional support or concrete help to one of the divorcing parents. Their presence and participation in the lives of the children provide significant residual benefits.

Steve: Grandmom Was There

Steve, thirty-six, says he did not find his parents' divorce especially traumatic and thinks his grandmother may have made the difference for him.

"My grandmother had been living with us for six years since my grandfather died. My mom worked as an administrative assistant to a furniture manufacturer, and Grandmom stayed at home, doing all of the cooking and shopping. When I got home from school, she was the one who was there.

"Dad was a sales representative for a cosmetics chain, and he was on the road a lot. So we didn't get to spend much time together even before the divorce.

"Afterward it seemed as though nothing changed that much for me. My brother and I still had our grandmom. She always had chocolate cupcakes and milk waiting for us when we got home from school. She was the one who asked about our homework and talked to us about what happened that day.

"It's not that we weren't close with my mother. We were, and we were always excited to see her at night after work. And weekends we did things with my mom. She was the one who made the decisions. Dad never seemed to count much even when he was around. He stayed on the sofa and watched television while we went out with Mom. So for us nothing was really much different.

"I don't see my dad that much now, but I guess we have an okay relationship. We don't argue much or anything. He never got married again, and neither did my mother."

In cases like this, where the mother has not surrendered her parenting responsibilities, this kind of arrangement can work well. But mothers who believe that *their* mothers are intruding, who feel that their independence is being challenged, may pass the conflict on to their children.

Even when relatives such as grandparents or aunts do not live with the family, their availability and continued support of the children can make a difference in their ability to cope with the changes in their lives.

Other Changes and What They Mean

Changes such as having to move to a different neighborhood and changing schools, new concerns about money, and leaving old friends make life even more difficult. Recognizing the need for stability in the life of a child whose parents are divorcing, a Maryland law allows the custodial parent to remain in the same house for three years following the divorce. This avoids too many abrupt changes for a child who is struggling for order in his life.

Jesse, who was nine when his parents divorced, says that he used to crawl into bed at night and hide under the quilt, hoping to shut out the nightmare he was living through. "It was bad enough that Dad moved out. Bad enough that I didn't have a family anymore. But then Mom told me we would have to sell the house and move nearer to my grand-mother.

"That scared me, I think, even more than the divorce. I would lose all my friends, and I would have to try out for soccer in a new school. Mom went back to work and Lenny [his best friend] and I hung out together every day after school. Now I wouldn't have a best friend anymore either."

Jesse got lucky. He became so despondent that his parents took him to a psychiatrist, who helped him articulate his feelings. His parents, even though they were going through an angry divorce, conceded on the house and decided to keep it until Jesse had graduated from high school.

"As I look back," says Jesse, now twenty-six, "I don't think I could have survived it if I had lost my house. I remember thinking about killing myself."

Instant Poverty

Large numbers of children find themselves in dramatically altered financial situations after divorce. Several studies show that a year after divorce, men's living standard rose up to 42 percent. Women's and that of the children they were rearing plummeted by an average of 37 to 73 percent, depending on the study.

A California research project reports that five years after divorce, a woman's income is 30 percent of what it was during the marriage. A man's income is 14 percent more. According to the Bureau of Census, in 1985 only one-half of mothers owed child support received the full amount; one-quarter received only a partial amount, and one-quarter received nothing. Economic decline is often more pronounced among middle-class mothers.

"My mother, sister, and I ended up living in poverty," says forty-two-year-old Shirley, a bright attorney with one of Washington's largest firms. "I was seventeen and my sister was thirteen when Dad left. All through the divorce proceedings, there was a lot of arguing and screaming and hollering about money—how much Mom would get, how much we would get for school and clothes and spending money.

"My father changed attorneys three times because no one would work with him for any length of time. He was so crazy and unreasonable.

"Somehow he managed to conceal most of his assets, so Mom got practically nothing. We stayed in our house, but there were times we couldn't use the air conditioning because we couldn't afford the electric bill and we had to watch the heat in the winter—walk around with heavy sweaters.

"Meanwhile Dad, while he wasn't living in luxury, bought a house and furnished it, had a new car, and was always well dressed. Whenever we saw him, that is. I still resent him for it."

The Need for Supports

Some children have pleasant dispositions and are described by those who know them as easy to get along with, fun to be with, curious, and competent. This kind of child usually faces stress well, namely because he or she has higher self-esteem to begin with and a larger group of supports to call on. Sometimes those supports are friends. Sometimes they are family members. They may even be teachers or neighbors. The important thing is that not only are the supports there, but the child is able to take advantage of them.

The support person makes a difference in the way a child of divorce grows up. It is he or she who fills the gap left by parents, who are, at least for a while, likely to be tense, unhappy, frustrated, and unavailable. Without such support, even the most resilient, well-adjusted child may not be able to make it through divorce successfully.

In our society, unfortunately, there are few supports for

children of divorce. And there are no rituals to mourn what often feels to a child like the death of his family.

"The Banana Splits"

The need for support is becoming more visible, and groups such as "The Banana Splits" at the Woods Road Elementary School in Ballston Spa, New York, are helping children cope with the pain of their parents' breakup. The Banana Splits began in 1981 as an informal rap session and became, eventually, a district-wide program for children from elementary through high school age. The Banana Splits are saying things we should be listening to:

"I felt like the whole world was collapsing around me. . . . It's great to cry here because you know no one's going to make fun of you."

"At first, my parents couldn't even stay in the same room. When Mom dropped me off for the weekend, she wouldn't even pull in Dad's driveway. She would just shove me out the door. It made me feel like a creep for still wanting to see him. But I did."

"Parents should watch out about work. I know it's important since they have to pay for us to eat and stuff, but sometimes I'd rather just see my mom than eat. I mean, I'd rather be hungry than lonesome."

Groups like the Banana Splits are invaluable for children in the throes of divorce. Like all self-help groups, they offer comfort by providing a nonthreatening environment in which to express feelings with others going through the same experience. They do not, however, substitute for the support of an adult who stands with a child through the crisis years. And in the long run the child who has a best friend, in or outside his family, one with whom he can work out his feelings, makes a better adjustment. However, even this kind of support may not be enough for children who live in an environment of excessive stress.

CHAPTER SIX

―――――/―――――

The Legacy of Divorce

Growing Up Faster.

Often preadolescent and adolescent children of divorce grow up faster than other children their age. They carry more responsibility. They are expected to be more independent. And they have more power in decision making. Girls, especially, overfunction as a way of supporting a parent who has lapsed into depression or lost his or her ability to cope effectively.

In traditional families, children have limited input into family decision making. They are not the ones who decide on budgeting the money, moving from one home to another, making their parents' job choices, or determining how much contact there will be with the extended family.

In sharp contrast children of divorce have a say in almost everything. Their responsibilities change. So do their rights and privileges. I have seen young teenagers overturn their mother's (or father's) decisions, take charge of household routines, determine vacation plans, and set rules for younger children in the home. I have also seen them interrupt their parents' conversations, address their mom as "Cynthia" instead of Mother, even tell a parent to "mind your own business," or suggest that "I wish you'd just shut up."

Sheryl and Her Mother

Sheryl was only five when her parents were separated. Now, twenty years later, they are not yet divorced because as Sheryl says, "They can't quite let go of each other."

Sheryl and her mother were more like friends than mother and daughter, and Sheryl was exposed to all of the culturally enriching experiences that her mother felt would give her a well-textured life—opera, theater, concerts, craft shows. She taught her to ride a horse, to ice-skate, play tennis, and swim. But it was clearly Sheryl who made decisions in the family. Sheryl decided the big things like whether or not they should move and where, as well as the little things such as which dress her mother should wear to the theater. Because her mother had so much trouble making decisions and Sheryl considered her to be "wishy-washy," she had little respect for her. She talked back to her, interrupted her sentences, and referred to her by her first name by the time she was eleven.

Still, she was dependent on her mother in ways that seemed to her friends to be inappropriate and inconsistent. She called her on the telephone twice a day no matter where she was—at camp, visiting friends for a weekend, and later at college. She planned most of her vacations with her mother and when she returned from college had dinner with her almost every night.

Sheryl's career search took her from her home in Boston to Chicago where she worked for a financial consulting firm. She and her mother were concerned about how well she would do with independent living, and both were hap-

pily surprised. Sheryl found and furnished an apartment on
her own, learned to become a gourmet cook, entertained,
found new friends in a strange city, and managed with
extreme competence. Her personal relationships, however,
"leave a lot to be desired. Growing up, I learned how to
take care of myself. But I never learned how to relate to a
man in a healthy, loving way. I never saw anyone do that."

There are pluses and minuses to growing up a little
faster. Most parents who stay together are not skilled at
giving their children chores appropriate to their age. For
instance, a three-year-old is able to keep track of his toys
and put them away neatly after playing with them. A seven-
year-old can make her own lunch. A ten-year-old can keep a
shopping list, do his laundry, and keep his room clean. But
parents don't often ask that they do it.

Children of divorce have no choice. If the parent with
whom they live, usually the mother, has to or wants to work,
the children must pick up some of the slack. It doesn't
usually hurt them and, in fact, many adults of divorce, in
retrospect, say that the arrangement worked amazingly well
and propelled them on the road to competence and independence as an adult.

They admit that there were drawbacks. They were more
acutely aware of financial crunches that threatened their
security. And they were forced to see their parents, especially the one they lived with, as a person with frailties and
doubts. Trouble often came when the parent's demands on
the child interfered with his own activities or exceeded his
capabilities. Then there was anger, resentment or outright
rebellion. And some children complain of childhoods that
were lost to them. Too much energy had to be directed
elsewhere.

"That whole scene wasn't comfortable for me," says
Daryl, now twenty-nine. "I was thirteen when my parents
were divorced and I wanted my mom to take care of me, not
the other way around. I felt this big burden of having to be

self-reliant because, being an only child, there was no one around to support me. It made me serious and sober much before my time, and I still resent that. I got out on my own early, just to get away from it."

When Children and Parents Switch Roles

Children of divorce often become confidants of their parents, a role that is not appropriate for them. Even though Sally, a forty-two-year-old divorcée, knows that she should not be burdening her fourteen-year-old son with unpaid bills and discussing with him her nightmares about the two of them ending up as street people, she says she can't help herself. "He's there, he's accessible, and more than anything else, he's in this with me. I need to know I'm not alone."

Along with the responsibilities also come rights that children learn to expect, and the parent, sometimes without question, grants. Lisa, a thirty-six-year-old mother who works as an accountant for a major firm in Richmond, Virginia, has been divorced for three years. Recently she confided that her nine-year-old son had made the decision not to sell their home, even though it was too big and too costly.

"I wanted to rent an apartment, closer to my mother, and be able to save some money for summer vacation or new clothes," she said. "But Scott doesn't want to do that. He says his friends are nearby and he spends so much time alone [his mother leaves for work an hour before he goes to school and returns at seven, four hours later than Scott] that he wants to be in a place that feels familiar."

Scott's premise makes sense. His mother understands. But it is not a decision he would make if he were not a child of divorce.

What happens to these boys and girls when they grow up? Are they more independent, more competent, more self-reliant? Or do they tiptoe through life longing for their lost childhood?

How does it affect the way they raise their own children? Do they repeat their growing-up experiences, believing it strengthens their sons and daughters? Or do they indulge them to make up for their own overburdened past?

I have seen it go many ways. Some children become so self-reliant, perhaps in a narcissistic way, that they go through life unable to accept nurturing from anyone. This doesn't do much for their intimate relationships.

On the other hand, some men and women expect their intimate partners to fill the hole in their soul left by a parent who depended on them too much. That doesn't work well either. It places too heavy a burden on the other person.

Some adults of divorce (usually women) choose partners who depend on them as much as one of their parents did. They gravitate toward the neglected and rejected persons whom they attract because they are so skilled at assuming responsibility for others.

The experience of some children of divorce prepares them well for their futures. Early in life, they learn more than most of us about the give-and-take of relationships. They understand that no one, not even their idealized parent, is perfect, and they become more sensitive to the needs and vulnerabilities of others. As parents they respond with warmth and spontaneity to their children's need for nurturing and security, sometimes to a fault. Other times, unconsciously, they may resent their children for having parents so much more nurturing than their own. And it is not unusual for parents, in an effort to give their children what they didn't have, to become so intense that they become emotionally exhausted.

When Jerome's son, Matthew, was born, he vowed that he would want for nothing. "He will never have to worry about money, clothes, or the love of his father. I will always be there for him, no matter what," said Jerome, a well-to-do stockbroker.

Jerome's father had walked out on his family when Jerome was sixteen. At first he visited every month. Then he moved to another city and the visits trickled down to once or twice a year. Jerome's efforts to reestablish contact with his father were not successful. His dad was "polite, cordial," but definitely not interested in spending time with his son. He needed freedom, he told Jerome. "Someday you'll understand."

When his own son, Matthew, was seven, he was in an automobile accident that left him partially paralyzed. Jerome combed the country for doctors, researched medical books, challenged the doctors. He redesigned his home with ramps and doorways with special access and spent every night and every weekend with his son. He literally gave up his own life. He donated his golf clubs to a boys' camp, sold his boat, refused to take vacations unless Matthew could be with him. He glared at his wife when she took an evening out with friends.

Two years later, spent and anxious, he realized he needed help. It didn't take long for him, through therapy, to recognize that he was playing out his childhood and would have to exorcise the ghost of his father if he wanted his marriage and his sanity to survive.

CHAPTER SEVEN

The Web of Relationships

Divorce adds a new dimension to the lives of children. It forces them to confront a web of complex relationships that children from intact families, no matter the way family members behave with one another, do not have to face. Their lives do not necessarily need to become more troubled, but they will certainly become more complicated.

There is a new way of relating to the parent with whom you live and the parent who visits (or doesn't). Sometimes brothers and sisters are separated, divided between parents. With more joint custody today, a child often has more than one home, each with its own set of rules and standards. At Mom's you go to bed at nine; at Dad's you send for Chinese takeout at midnight. Mom prohibits sugar-filled snacks; Dad keeps a supply of M & M's in the cupboard. With Mom, you can go to the restaurant in slacks; Dad insists on a dress.

Then there is the mother's "boyfriend" and the father's "girlfriend." Children, even as adults, still feel uncomfortable when referring to them. "What do I say when I talk about them?" asks twenty-year-old Terri. "My father's lover? His woman friend? His friend? His companion? His partner? His live-in? His sweetheart? We need a whole new language to keep up with our behavior."

When a parent marries, there is a stepmother, a stepfather, his or her children from previous marriages, parents, extended family, and friends. Thirty-seven to fifty percent of the time there is another divorce and frequently a subsequent remarriage. There may be half brothers and sisters. It gets complicated, and it takes a lot of energy to juggle these entangled relationships.

"When I get married," twenty-six-year-old Myrna told me, "I'm going to have to have two weddings—one for my father's side of the family and one for my mother's. I haven't figured out yet what I'll do with the people from my mother's second marriage. [Myrna's mother now has a third husband.] Should I invite them to the wedding for my father's side?"

My daughter's college friend says she is thoroughly confused—and disillusioned. In her freshman year her parents, both researchers at a Philadelphia college, divorced. In her sophomore year each of her parents remarried. In her junior year both divorced their second spouses. By the time she was ready to be graduated, her parents had remarried each other.

A University of Michigan psychologist, Neil Kalter, once sponsored a student-run newspaper called "The Daily Divorce." The name illustrated that the divorce—no matter when it took place—never goes away.

In fact, divorce presents to children a series of neverending changes which they must struggle to integrate into their already chaotic lives. The first of these may come when the mother or father with whom they live begins dating.

Sex and the Single Parent

"I was pretty unhappy when Dad moved out," says Billy, then sixteen. "I knew Mom and Dad had been having problems, but I never expected them to divorce. We have a big family—Mom and Dad both have lots of brothers and sisters, and nobody ever divorced. I couldn't imagine it would happen.

"My mom was the kind of person you couldn't talk to much. She had her own ideas and she didn't pay much attention to what my sister and I said. What she said was the way it had to be.

"I missed Dad a lot and went to his house every weekend. I used to live for those weekends. But after a while I wondered why Mom didn't seem to care. She worked, so my sister and I didn't see her much during the week. And on weekends she seemed pretty happy to send us to Rockville, where Dad lived.

"Well, one weekend I came home early Sunday afternoon, and I found the hall closet full of men's clothing— jackets and pants with fancy labels like Perry Ellis and Ralph Lauren. There was a suitcase in the guest room and a man's shirts and socks in the drawers.

"No one was home, thank God, because I felt so sick to my stomach and my hands and face got all clammy. I went into the bathroom and threw up. Then I went back to my father's house and told him I couldn't live with my mother anymore."

Billy's situation is not typical. Usually parents are less abrupt about introducing their romantic interests into their children's lives. Nonetheless, whenever it happens, the realization that their mothers or fathers are out dancing, dining, and having sex with someone who is not their other parent is shocking and unsettling.

Sometimes it occurs just as a child is reaching that same stage in his own life, and the normal transition of events suddenly topples out of sequence for him. Parents who went through adolescence a long time ago are doing it again. Often they and their children are having the same difficulties at the same time with the singles scene. It makes their sons and daughters feel uncomfortable. They are forced to see their parents as peers. And they don't like it.

Does Mom Love Him or Me?

Children's sense of security and stability unravels as they watch their parents participate in this new arena of dating and mating they thought was reserved for them. What will happen to their relationship with that parent? Will his or her new love interest overshadow or even replace concern for them?

Their fears are not without merit. Often that's the way it happens. At least for a while. Sex therapist Phyllis Diamond says that some parents, after the marriage dissolves, focus exclusively and intensely on their children. Others are caught in what she calls the "hummingbird syndrome," a maze of dates and parties and social events they whirl through to prove to themselves that they are still sexually attractive. That's a powerful need for them then, but it is often at odds with their children's needs at the time.

There are no precedents. No previous generation of children or parents has had to struggle so strenuously with these issues, to negotiate so delicately a foreign, unmapped territory. Parents ask themselves: When should I start dating? How will I let my children know? Is it okay for them to know I'm having sex with someone? How will it affect their own sexuality? Will they think I'm promiscuous, and will it make them more likely to have early sex?

The single parent is going to date. And she or he is going to engage in sex—probably with more than one person. The critical thing is that it be done discreetly, with a sense of appropriate timing and with special sensitivity to children. And with recognition that children will have different reactions depending on their age.

Young children who still hope that their parents will get together again often see the other man or woman as an interloper, the person who will prevent their parents from ever reuniting. Jeremy, who was six when his parents divorced, asked his mother, "Why can't you go out with Daddy instead of these other men?"

The noncustodial parent has more freedom, so the need to introduce a child to his or her dates may not come up for a long time. But when it does, a child is often miffed and upset. When visits are only on Sunday, the hours are precious. A romantic interest usurping the time children want for themselves tells them that they are low priority. The damage to their ego can affect their self-image throughout their lives.

"I knew Dad had left us because of Margie," says twenty-nine-year-old Claudia, who thinks she is destined to go through life destroying herself. "But I never thought he would have the nerve to bring her around at a time when he was supposed to be seeing me.

"In the beginning, he didn't. I was about seven, and I think he knew how I would feel about it. But one day he picked me up at my mom's apartment, and I saw a woman sitting in the car when we got downstairs. I figured it was my aunt, my father's sister, but when we got closer, he said, 'Claudia, I want you to meet my friend Margie.'

"I hated her. She had broken up our family. It was all I could do to keep from bursting out crying. How could he have done this to me? Bring her here on my time? He had six other days in the week he could spend with her. I felt like I was just nuisance value. He *had* to see me because I was his kid, but I wasn't important enough for prime time.

"I wanted to jump out of the car and go back to Mom. But I also wanted to see my father. I missed him a lot. So I stayed. We went to a restaurant, but I couldn't eat. I felt sick to my stomach. Margie tried her best to be nice, but I wasn't hearing any of it. I just wanted my father to myself.

"Dad is back with Margie now after a half-dozen girl-friends in between. She was always in the background and, of course, I got used to the fact that he was involved with her. They never talk about why my dad isn't divorced or about them getting married and I don't ask any questions. But I remember that first time like it was yesterday. Dad put a gash in my self-worth that I've never recovered from. I have trouble believing I'm an okay person that someone could really care about."

For the person with custody, usually the mother, the issue is even stickier. It is difficult to conceal, for too long, her dating and sexual behavior. Children are exposed to it sooner, on a more regular basis, and when it isn't done gradually and thoughtfully, a child may carry the scars for a long time.

The adult children of divorce whom I have seen convince me that timing is critical. At first their need for the parent they live with is so intense they can almost touch it. One parent has gone; new romantic interests in the life of the other fill them with fear that this parent will abandon them too.

When parents do begin to date, their choices in partners make a difference in how well the children adjust, immediately and into adulthood.

Esther, twenty-four, says that her mother didn't go out right away. "It was at least a year after they split that she had the first date I knew anything about. I was sixteen, and I had a good relationship with Mom. I was scared about her going out and I told her how I felt. I was afraid she was going to forget about me because that's what happened to a lot of my friends.

"But Mom told me that she was scared too. She loved me, but she was lonely for the companionship of a man.

This was just a date and she needed my support to help her get through it. So we sort of did it together.

"I helped her fix her hair and I let her use the new perfume I had gotten for my birthday. When she left, she looked really pretty, and I went out with a friend.

"It felt funny. I wanted to come home early so I could be there when Mom got home. I wanted to hear all about her date. It was as though if she shared it with me, it would be less threatening. But I felt like our roles were reversing. I should be the one on the date and Mom should be waiting for me. Not the other way around."

Esther's mother had many dates after that. And Esther says that she began to feel more secure because her mother didn't make her feel like an outsider.

"She let me in on her feelings. She told me why she liked Harry and didn't like Jimmy. She told me what was important to her—someone who was considerate and who was nice to both of us. And she said that I should look for the same things in my dates—men who were kind and thoughtful.

"As far as I know, Mom never had sex in our house. At least not while I was there. That was something we couldn't discuss for a long time. It's hard for a kid to think of her mother as a sexual person. It wasn't until Tom came along that we talked about it."

Tom was the man Esther's mother eventually married, three years after her divorce. Esther felt comfortable with him right from the beginning. "He treated me like I was a real person, and he didn't try to take the place of my father. He was easy to be with, and he and Mom included me in a lot of things they did, if I wanted to do them. I never felt like I was in the way.

"And Mom still made time for me alone. I didn't feel like Tom meant everything to her and I meant nothing. And he understood that I still had a father and he never bad-mouthed him. In fact, he would ask me about my dad after I had spent a weekend with him, how he was and did I have fun? It was always in a pleasant way, never like he was interrogating me."

Esther says she feels lucky. Most of her friends with divorced parents experienced more trauma than she did about their parents' buzzing social life. Jason, she told me, once found his mom in bed with a man he hated. And Katie's mother told her that she would have to get used to sharing her with other people. "You are not my only priority," she told Katie when she was eleven. "I have a life too."

It is healthy for children to see intimacy between their divorced parent and another man or woman. When they do not, they have no role model for themselves. But too often their parents' dating patterns continue to disillusion them about relationships, and they grow up jaded about how reliable such intimacy can be.

Peter, for instance, saw his mother weave in and out of seven relationships that she called serious within four years. "I liked some of the men she dated," Peter said.

"I was nine when my mother and father separated. They didn't divorce until I was fourteen. But my mother began to go out right away. Each one of the men was, in her words, 'fabulous, marvelous, terrific.'

"But they lasted only a short time. The first one I got close to was Domenic. He was a regular guy who liked me and talked to me about what was happening in my life. I hoped Mom would marry him. But she didn't. And just like that, Domenic was out of my life too.

"The same thing happened with Stuart. I was more edgy with him, not because I didn't like him. I just didn't want to get hurt again. Mom went out with him for almost a year, the longest anyone ever lasted. Just when Stuart and I were feeling pretty good about each other, when I began to rely on him a little, they broke up. I never saw Stuart again."

Peter is thirty-three now and says he will never marry. He doesn't think relationships can last. He is a good-looking young man, has an impressive job with an interior design firm, and has had many liaisons with women. But he ends them before they become too serious. "I give myself no more than four months with a woman. Wherever we are at that point, it doesn't matter. I find a reason to end it."

Some children build an alliance with their mother or father's current love interest, hoping that their togetherness will help cement the relationship. Melissa, who was thirty-five when I met her, told me that she and her dad's girlfriend, Simme, became good friends.

"I was only ten, and I think Simme was about twenty-eight," Melissa says. "I loved her. She was so nice and so pretty and she had a lot of patience. We played games together and she took an interest in me. She was a wonderful cook, too, and she baked brownies and sugar cookies for me. I wanted Dad to marry her.

"I got real upset when I saw that Dad was dating somebody else, an older woman named Joyce. I was afraid to ask him about her, so eventually I told Simme. I told her to do something about it, to stop Dad from seeing Joyce. And to promise me that if she and Daddy ever broke up, we would still be friends.

"They did break up and there were several women after Joyce. Dad finally married Elyse. By that time I was numb. I was sick of trying to adjust to each new woman, sick of trying to make them like me and worrying about what I said and what I did or what I wore. It was like I was living on a merry-go-round that didn't stop long enough for me to climb off a horse. I didn't care much one way or the other."

Melissa says the incident with Simme affected her intensely and she missed her for a long time. Simme tried to see her, but her dad wouldn't permit it.

"He told me that Simme was no longer a part of our lives. That whole experience taught me that I have no control over anything. That anyone can do anything to me no matter how I feel about it. Since then, I try to protect myself. I try to be sure that I'm always in charge. I make the decisions. I make the choices. It works pretty well. It keeps my psyche out of trouble."

When Parents Remarry

The web of relationships becomes more tangled for children when parents remarry. Sometimes they have no sooner settled down after the divorce when they are faced with becoming part of a new family, one that often comes complete with a parent and his or her children. This is more the rule than the exception, since the majority of divorced people remarry. According to the United States Census Bureau, approximately thirteen hundred new stepfamilies are formed every day, and the number of stepfamilies increases about one percent a year, making it a common form of family life in this country. But common does not mean untroubled.

The relationship with the new parent must be worked through. How much authority will he or she have? How much control will the child's own parent continue to exert? When there are differences of opinion between the stepfather and the real father, who wins? What do you call the new parent?

Cindy's parents were divorced when she was twenty. When her father remarried five years later, his new wife's twenty-one-year-old son moved in with them. Cindy was stunned and angry that her father called this grown man "son." Worse still is the fact that *he* called her father "Dad."

Relationships are not only more complex, they are instantly thrown out of developmental sequence. The normal biological pace—courtship first, then marriage, then children—is out of sync. Children are part of the courtship, there before the honeymoon.

They are expected to become instant friends with brothers and sisters they have not grown up with, a scenario that predictably produces jealousy, rivalry, and resentment. How much must they share? How friendly can they be? Is Mom paying more attention to them than to us?

The oldest child may suddenly find himself the youngest. A girl with three brothers may now have two sisters. An only child may be part of a large family surrounded by four siblings.

Then there is a new set of rituals and routines that must be embraced without the advantage of having grown up with them. Fifteen-year-old Perry, whose father married a religious Jewish woman, was told he could not go out on Friday nights because Sabbath dinner was always eaten at home, nor could he ride in anyone's car until Saturday night when the Sabbath was over. Perry, a quiet and compliant boy, had not grown up with this lifestyle, and he was mystified and upset about the abrupt change. His father insisted he do what his "new mother" wished.

Of course, there are all of the peripheral people who are part of the new package—aunts, cousins, grandparents, even friends. These are the "strangers" in their families that children from intact homes never need to think about. Sometimes, a couple wants to "start over" with a baby of its own. Children then have to deal with brothers and sisters who are what they never can be, the beloved child of this new union, the creation of these two doting parents. They often feel shut out, like aliens in a foreign land.

How to sort out and juggle this maze of relationships and the cauldron of feelings they brew? It is no wonder that this bewildering and frightening task becomes the focus of a child's attention as he struggles, every day, for ways to master the new and unasked-for complexity of his life. And that it continues to influence his style of relating to other people in a close and intimate way as he or she grows up.

Since more second than first marriages fail, especially when children are involved, many of my patients have navigated these waters more than once. In fact, the number of children who are experiencing three or more transitions of this kind during childhood are growing rapidly. At a time when technology and new work and living styles are making our lives more impersonal, people are searching for intimacy more voraciously than ever. Families are still where most of us derive our comfort, our identity, our solace, and our support. When we don't find it the first time around, we are eager to try again.

Today there are more than four million households where at least one parent has remarried and at least one child comes from an earlier marriage. We call them "blended" families, reconstituted families, stepfamilies, second-marriage families. *The Brady Bunch* made it look as though it were a sugar-coated utopia, one in which the best of all ingredients blend into a livelier, fun-filled, more richly textured life. In the real world it doesn't happen that way. At every turn children are pushing their way through uncharted territory, wracked with shifting issues of loyalty, jealousy, guilt, and just plain confusion. The "instant" family is not just another version of the nuclear family they knew. It is a constellation unto itself, rife with stress, limping along trying to figure out how it works.

Nonetheless, many children find strength and pleasure in what California psychologist Constance Ahrons calls the binuclear family, the name she gives to the two-household families created by divorce. Couples who agree that they cannot live together, but can continue to be friendly and cooperative with each other, respect each other's households, and manage their responsibilities as parents, even when they remarry, can teach their children valuable lessons about relationships that they can carry into their adult lives.

How Children React

A child's reaction to remarriage depends a great deal on the age and sex of the new family members. We know that very young children often do well in their new families, perhaps because the memory of their original family is so dim. I have seen such children grow up unmarred by having been part of a divorce and remarriage.

For older children the picture is often less sanguine. A study that looked at children five years after remarriage found that both boys and girls had more behavior problems than children whose parents had not divorced. But there was a difference between boys and girls.

Boys seemed to benefit from having a stepfather, especially where the stepfather and mother were emotionally close and agreed on how the boy should be raised. They often looked forward to having a male role model and welcomed the idea of a father in the home again. When the stepfather's style of child rearing was authoritative—the love with limits concept—but not authoritarian or pushy, boys seemed to adjust the best.

For girls, on the other hand, as we pointed out in Chapter Three, their mothers' remarriage often precipitated problems. Their close relationship with their mother felt threatened. In fact, the closer the mother was emotionally to her new husband, the more difficult it was for the daughter to adapt and the less likely it was that she could accept her stepfather.

"I remember hating Paul with every fiber of my being," says Sonya, who was fourteen when her parents divorced. "And I hated Mom, too, for agreeing to marry him. When she and Dad divorced, she told me it was just the two of us now. My dad vanished and I never saw him again until I was twenty.

"Not that Mom and I didn't have our problems. She didn't always like the way I dressed, and she wanted me to go to bed too early on weekends. But nothing really major. I had lots of friends, but Mom was always there for me, and she never let me know, in any way, that she would marry again.

"Even when she began to date Paul, I thought they were just friends and I didn't feel upset about it. But then he began hanging around more. He wasn't mean to me or anything, but I could tell I wasn't important to him. He couldn't have cared less whether I was around or not. He made no effort to talk to me. Just 'Hi, kid. How are you doin'?'

"When Mom told me she was marrying him, it was instant hate. I just couldn't deal with it. From that moment on, I never accepted Paul or the marriage, and Mom and I drifted apart."

Today Sonya, at twenty-seven, is still drifting. She moved away from home when she was eighteen and began experimenting with drugs. She tried sex with both men and women and is still uncertain about her sexual orientation.

"I used to think that lesbianism or bisexuality was a biological thing," she says. "But now that I'm through with drugs and can think clearly, I have to be realistic enough to recognize that I may be reacting to my past.

"Who knows? I have lots of friends whose parents were divorced and they don't change their sexual preferences. But still it wasn't something I even considered or had any desire for until I was in my midtwenties. I'm trying to find out what I'm all about."

A survey of families in central Pennsylvania indicates that it is common for the father and children to grow apart when he remarries and children live with the mother. It may be that the father now focuses on his new family, losing interest in his former one, or that he is overwhelmed by the demands of two households. Or, says the study, mothers may become "more vigilant gatekeepers after their former spouses established a new family."

When that happens, children often roam through life searching for the love of the father who turned his back on them. Especially for boys, rejection from their father is a major blow to the ego, and they cannot believe that there isn't something they can do to reestablish contact.

"No matter how clear he made it through his behavior, no matter how many of my overtures he turned away from, I kept thinking all of my life that underneath he really loved me, and that there was some way I could reach him," says Frank. "I'm forty-five. He's sixty-nine and I'm still trying."

Adult children of divorce and remarriage, then more remarriage, often feel unsettled, as though their lives are just too complicated, too layered for them to wade through. As they embark on their own search for relationships, they try to sort out their feelings, to figure out just what it is they want from life and how they can go about getting it.

Marlene: "It's Too Complicated"

"The whole issue of relationships is still so weird for me," says twenty-seven-year-old Marlene. "When I think about families, my head spins."

Marlene's mother remarried three years after her divorce, when Marlene was twelve. Her stepfather, whose young wife had died, brought a three-year-old boy and a six-year-old girl into the marriage. At first Marlene thought it might be "fun" to have a brother and sister. She soon learned she didn't like it at all.

"Mom had worked most of my life. She was an engineer, and after the divorce she just kept on working. That's what I was used to. I didn't know any other way. She always talked about how much she liked her job and would never give it up. Well, she gave it up to take care of Sarah and Joshua. For me it was instant jealousy. She never did that for me.

"It was like all her values changed. She was willing to be a stay-at-home mom, drive in the nursery school car pools and be there for the first-grade Halloween parade. She had never done any of those things for me.

"And she fell all over my stepfather. She cooked for him

every night, snuggled up close to him while they were watching television, and nibbled on his ear. It was sickening.

"I guess he tried to be nice to me. He had a lot of money, and he was generous with it. He bought me a new, very expensive bicycle and got me the golden retriever I had always wanted. But he had a mean streak too. When you didn't do what he wanted you to, when you crossed him, he was nasty and sarcastic. And he always made snide remarks about my father."

As a result Marlene became closer to her father, who was determined to try even harder to hold his ground with his daughter. He visited twice a week and Marlene slept at his house every Saturday night. He couldn't compete financially with his ex-wife's new husband, but he showered Marlene with trinkets and small gifts that he could afford. And he tried to develop a close and lasting relationship.

The competition between the two men ended quickly. Two years later, when she was twelve, Marlene's mother divorced again. The stepfather moved out with his two children.

"But by that time I had learned to love the kids," Marlene says. "I wasn't too upset that Dan [the stepfather] was leaving. I had never gotten too close to him. But I wanted him to leave the children with us. They were my brother and sister. The day they packed their clothes, I remember that I just stood in the doorway of Sarah's bedroom sobbing. She was crying too. She said, 'Marlene, will you help me find my socks and panties?'

"I also missed Dan's mother, my stepgrandmother. She was a fun person, a sort of Auntie Mame type. She would always come bouncing in with a new hat and wonderful stories about her latest trip or her newest friend. I never knew my stepgrandfather. They were divorced for years and he lived in Arizona. She—I called her Grandma Katie— promised me she would visit and bring Sarah and Joshua.

"She kept her promise, and I think I got closer to all of them after the divorce than I was before. I didn't see Dan at all, but Sarah, Joshua, and I always went places together. Grandma Katie took us."

But Marlene now had a new conflict. Sometimes the weekend trips with Grandma Katie overlapped her Saturday visit with Dad. Mom had returned to work and had only weekends free, so she wanted her time with Marlene too.

"It got to be a big mess, and I felt as though I were one of those jugglers you see who tosses seven rings in the air and tries not to let any of them drop. I wanted to keep all of these people in my life because they were all important to me. And I was afraid to make the wrong move, choose the wrong person to be with that day. I was obsessed with holding on. I couldn't take any more loss."

Marlene had not yet fine-tuned her juggling act when her mom married again. This time her stepfather was older and kinder. He had a fuzzy gray beard and was easygoing. "Laid back," Marlene called him. He had two older daughters, nineteen and twenty-one.

"The twenty-one-year-old one, Patricia, was at college, but Missy moved in with us. She was really nice, and pretty, and she liked the idea of having a younger sister. She took me a lot of places with her, and my mom was pleased that we got along so well.

"I had another grandmother too, this time with a grandfather. And you couldn't help but love them. They were sweet, just like the grandparents you used to read about in books. He told stories about his childhood. She baked chocolate chip cookies.

"But it complicated my life even more. Now I had three sisters and a brother, a stepfather, a real father, four grandmothers, my original ones, whom I still saw pretty often, Grandma Katie, and this new one, three grandfathers and a whole lot of aunts and uncles and cousins.

"Holidays were, and still are, so anxiety producing. I

never knew where I should go or even where I wanted to go. It got so complicated that I was only with my mom on one holiday, Christmas. But the truth is that I wanted her to be with me every holiday wherever I was. Through all of these changes, she was the person I continued to live with and I still counted on her the most.

"Now I long for simplicity. I do love all of these people, and if we all were part of the same family, it would be fantastic. But they are all pieces of other people's families that happened to become part of mine through this crazy modern day way of life.

"As an adult I feel a big empty space where a family should be. These other people I see as good friends, maybe a little better than just good. But in the crunch they are not mine. And my mother and my father aren't anything to them. So I really can't be anything to them. Do you see what I mean? I'm not really anything to anybody."

CHAPTER EIGHT

———— / ————

What Lies Ahead?

Does Divorce Breed Divorce?

Divorce seems to run in some families the way diabetes or heart disease does. It is not the divorce that is the legacy, however. It is the family patterns leading to the divorce that seep into future generations.

There is plenty of evidence that adult children of divorce are more likely themselves to become divorced. This is more true of women than of men. Two studies show that women whose parents were divorced before they were sixteen will be from 59 to 69 percent more likely themselves to divorce than women from intact families. Males from divorced families have a 32 percent greater chance of divorcing than those from families that have stayed together. In contrast, daughters whose fathers had died had only a 35 percent greater risk of a shattered marriage than did women from intact families.

Even more stunning, daughters whose parents divorced

and remarried faced twice the risk of divorce than those living with both parents. But *widows* who remarry, seemed somehow to protect their daughters against divorce.

These studies reveal that no matter when the divorce took place, early or late in the daughter's life, her chances of divorce skyrocketed. The daughters most vulnerable were those who had last lived with both parents between the ages of ten and thirteen and who were living with a stepparent when they were fourteen. The stress of divorce and a quick remarriage, especially during adolescence, may have a layered and powerful negative effect.

As the divorce rate soars, the divorce cycle is destined to spiral.

While I believe that the family patterns we will be discussing are the primary villains because they make people less able to solve their marital conflicts, there are other reasons that contribute to the perpetuation of divorce in families. The emotional chaos experienced by children of divorce may push them into behavior—such as early sex, pregnancy before marriage, or delinquency—all of which are linked to higher divorce rates. And to escape the pressure at home, they may marry early, often to someone who is not an ideal choice. There is a study, however, that shows significantly more divorce among adults of divorce even when early sex and pregnancy are ruled out. They not only are likely to have unsatisfactory marriages, but also are less reluctant to end them. For one thing, they have seen that divorce is an option, and while it is stressful, they have seen that it may be the best solution to a miserable marriage. Girls who have seen their mothers cope successfully with divorce and independence may feel strong enough to do the same thing.

Why does the legacy of divorce seem to be transmitted to daughters more than to sons?

While both boys and girls who live with their mothers see the divorce from their mother's perspective, boys are less likely to identify with the problems their mothers are experiencing—loneliness, a sense of betrayal, a wariness about trust. This lack of identification, often perceived by the mother as an absence of sensitivity, escalates the acute problems between her and her sons in the period immediately following the divorce. But it allows them to move into adulthood less marred than their sisters because they were not as absorbed with and affected by their mother's problems. With the passage of time boys are often able to view the divorce from the perspective of both parents and understand their mothers better.

Girls feel a different sense of connection with their mothers because they are of the same gender and can feel their pain more exquisitely. They often share with them the feelings that are not picked up as intensely by the boys. And it affects their sense of commitment about future relationships in a more profound and lasting way.

When Trust Is Violated

Just as adults of divorce focus on the Eden that might have been theirs had their families remained intact, they are also focused on, even obsessed with, the issue of commitment. They struggle, in one way or another, with concerns about commitment throughout their lives. Some determine outwardly that they will never marry. Others say they will never again get close enough to anyone to let themselves be hurt so deeply.

Marian, a thirty-two-year-old lawyer, says, "When my parents announced they were going to get divorced, I felt like Mike Tyson had punched me in the stomach. I got clammy and nauseated, and the only thing I could think of was that it was all a mistake, that I had to do something to stop it. I wasn't a kid. This was only a year ago, but I felt like I was five years old again."

Although Marian lived only two hours away from her

parents, she admitted that she saw them perhaps four times a year, mostly on holidays. Her life was busy, happy (except for a romantic relationship that had recently ended), and generally satisfying. She did not feel dependent on her parents until she received the stunning news of their breakup. "I was thirty-one years old and it shouldn't have done this to me. Right? But it was awful. I couldn't imagine anything worse, and it affected me so much I couldn't do my work.

"I couldn't eat. I lost fourteen pounds in three weeks, and I would wake up in the morning with that sick feeling like when you're a kid and you don't want to go to camp.

"I knew their marriage wasn't perfect. Whose is? But you always count on them being together. I don't feel like I'll ever be able to trust anyone again. It's like my entire life was a dream and I woke up on another planet."

The actress Audrey Hepburn, in her early sixties, still describes her parents' divorce as the most traumatic event in her life. "I remember my mother's reaction," she told a newspaper reporter. "You look into your mother's face and it's covered with tears, and you're terrified. You say to yourself, 'What's going to happen to me?' The ground has gone out from under you." Hepburn says that "something of that feeling" has stayed with her through her own relationships. When she fell in love and married, she was always afraid that she would be left again, that someone else would take her loved one away from her.

Other adult children of divorce seek commitment aggressively and promise themselves that their relationships and their marriages will be different. Even more important, they will never do to their children what their parents did to them. Surprisingly optimistic, these adult children of divorce are shifting back to a more traditional, conservative philosophy about marriage. They disdain the avant-garde marriage forms of their parents and want no part of "open marriage" and "creative divorce." They believe in fidelity and in building a nest together.

They want to wrap their arms around commitment, and they talk lovingly about growing old together.

In *Bride's* magazine, Art Carey writes, "Some of us have embraced marriage too impetuously, hoping to escape our pasts by creating the kind of 'perfect' relationship our parents never had.

"Others, frightened by the fragility of marriage, and skeptical of the possibility of a lasting marriage, approach it with a vengeance."

Trust and the Extramarital Affair

Trust becomes a major issue for children whose mother or father has had an affair outside of marriage. Even when the affair is kept secret, even when the child is young when it happens, children know something is going on. They can sense that a parent is less attentive and see that he or she spends unexplained periods of time away from home. They may hear hushed telephone conversations, and they are aware that emotional energy is not focused on the family.

Often they blame themselves. They feel rejected and wonder what is wrong with them. Robin did not learn about her mother's extramarital affairs until she was nineteen and her parents separated. "Instantly I realized what had been going on for the past twelve years. I was furious. But in a way I felt relieved. All the time I was thinking my mother just didn't like me."

Research shows that parental affairs can set the pattern for their children's behavior when they become adults. Dr. Annette Lawson, a sociologist with the Institute for Research on Women and Gender at Stanford University, says that having affairs "appears to become a patterned response learned in childhood." Where a father boasts about his philandering to a teenage son, there is the hint of a family tradition in the making. Girls, on the other hand, often respond to the affairs of their fathers by growing up angry at men and insecure about their relationships with them. Because mothers are still felt to be the nurturing center of the family, a mother's affair frequently destroys her children's confidence in marriage and the family unit.

Marilyn and Eli: Unable to Trust

I see many adults who unwittingly sabotage their intimate relationships. In their reaction to their parents' divorces they remind me of children whose parents have abandoned them and who have been shuffled from foster home to foster home. After a while all but the most resilient build up defenses to protect themselves from more unbearable hurt and rejection.

"I was twelve when my parents were divorced, and I remember feeling ashamed and humiliated," says Marilyn, now thirty-three. "It was my mother who was leaving. She had found a boyfriend nine years younger than she was. He was twenty-five, a friend of her youngest brother. I couldn't believe it. My mother! Don't forget, this was twenty-two years ago. Mothers didn't leave their families. Maybe fathers, but not mothers.

"Overnight I felt like a different person, someone with a family to be ashamed of. I didn't want to go to school and I didn't want to see my friends. I could hear them whispering about me, saying nasty little things about my mother and her rock star boyfriend.

"My dad seemed stunned. I don't know to this day if he knew about Steve [the boyfriend] and that it might lead to divorce. Whether he figured it was a passing thing with Mom that would blow over in time. We don't talk about it—it's still too painful for me. Besides, Dad has his own life now. And I'm supposed to have mine. But the divorce diminished me, I think, forever. Before the divorce, I was close to my mom and I believed that she cared about me more than anyone in the world.

"I was an only child, and we went shopping together. She used to buy me pretty dresses and I'd have fun experimenting with her makeup. She would create funny hairdos for me. And she took me lots of places—to the zoo and the circus and to amusement parks. Dad was working a lot and traveling a lot, so it was usually just Mom and me. I trusted her and I felt secure as a child. I thought nothing could ever change that.

"Today I don't trust anyone. My friends say I'm attractive and I don't seem to have any trouble meeting men or getting dates. I've just been elevated to a senior vice president of the bank where I work, and I feel pretty confident about my job and my ability. But not about people. I figure the only person I can count on is myself.

"I still see my mother. She lives about ninety miles away from me. She and Steve never got married. But she had a few boyfriends after that and finally married one of them two years ago. I try not to get too close. I couldn't handle the pain of another rejection.

"I've decided never to marry. Every time a man moves in closer, I tell him, 'If you are starting to get serious'—I still use that expression—'don't.' I'm not interested in anything permanent. I have a pretty full life—I do aerobics three times a week, I belong to a little theater group where I play the piano, and my job is time-consuming and demanding.

"But these are all things I feel I can control to a large extent. If someone disappoints me at work or at the theater group, I can deal with it. That's the way people are. But I won't subject myself to that in a personal relationship. I've already experienced the ultimate disappointment. No one will ever do that to me again."

When people like Marilyn talk about trust, they are really describing predictability. If, for instance, your father always came home intoxicated on Saturday nights, it was unpleasant, maybe even terrifying, but it was behavior that you could count on. On the other hand, when someone's behavior changes dramatically—all of a sudden or over a period of time—trust is snuffed out.

It's reasonable for children to assume their parents will be there for them; and so for young children lack of trust and fright about what will happen to them are overwhelming when divorce occurs. These very young children, however, may have the best chance of recovery if they are exposed fairly quickly to stable, predictable environments that displace their early trauma. They can often grow up without the absence of trust becoming a major obstacle for them.

Unfortunately, it isn't that way for children whose families are characterized by a lot of conflict and irresponsible behavior. They learn, all along the way, that people are not predictable and can't be counted on. They move on to adulthood jittery about commitment. The situation is the same for children who come from families where the problems between the parents have been secret, where the process leading to the divorce was hidden. Suddenly, without warning, comes the divorce announcement . . . and their world turns upside down. They wonder where they were when all of this was going on. The message they get is that they can depend on nothing, and it affects the way they approach their own relationships.

Marilyn's story is not unique. But the Marilyns in our society do not show up in studies of children of divorce. On the outside they are popular, efficient, and productive. No one, not even they, would say they were paralyzed by their parents' shattered marriage. They are too private, too polished, too skillful at adjusting. Their trauma lies deep inside where friends, even close ones, fear to tread.

Sometimes, along the way, something happens that nudges them toward the therapist's office. Marilyn was nudged by Eli, whom she had been dating for a year and who wouldn't accept her rebuffs. She believed she loved Eli but told him that love to her meant sex and friendship and good times shared, but not marriage. Marilyn admitted that Eli had never disappointed her, that he lavished her with attention, he was always considerate and on time, and she missed him when he needed to be out of town for a week on business.

But Eli wanted more. He wanted marriage. He wanted children. If Marilyn was not able to make a commitment, he felt he would have to end the relationship. But he asked her to engage in therapy with him first. They would give it six months. If she still felt the same way, he would go away quietly.

It is not surprising that the issue of commitment is still a thorny one for Marilyn, one she would rather avoid. Before the divorce she was close to her mother emotionally. Closer, perhaps, than many twelve-year-olds. They spent time together, building what Marilyn perceived to be a special mother-daughter rapport.

But Marilyn was stranded midstream. After the divorce her mother left her home and eventually moved to another city about 150 miles away. She called frequently and visited once a month, but the closeness that Marilyn treasured was gone. The mother she counted on had disappointed her in the most fundamental way: by leaving her, physically and emotionally.

Through adolescence and early adulthood Marilyn never had the opportunity to develop the appropriate emotional distance from her mother, the distance that would have allowed her to pursue her own relationships without the shadow of her mother trailing her.

Marilyn's relationship with her mother is stuck at the level of a twelve-year-old; their emotional lives are cemented together. Despite her outward appearance of independence and competence, her need to resolve the relationship with her mother is powerful, intruding on her ability to move on with her life.

She sees her mother in Eli, a man who is attentive, caring, loving . . . and patient. But she is always waiting for the other shoe to drop. And she doesn't want to be there when it does.

All children of divorce have a Marilyn living inside of them to some degree. Their sense of trust has been violated in the most basic, most wrenching way by the most important people in their lives. Those who are more mature (and we'll talk later about attaining that maturity) come through it more successfully. For others, fears of betrayal follow them all their lives.

CHAPTER NINE

———/———

Lost in Time

A relationship that endures through time has an almost transcendental quality about it: part of what keeps it going is that it keeps on going. There is something about that kind of continuity that allows adult children, even those from miserable marriages, to look at their own futures differently. It is the difference between saying, "My parents ended up in a divorce and I don't want to be divorced," or "My parents had a bad marriage and I'm going to have a good one."

In the first case, the focus is on preventing an unhappy ending without addressing how to do that. In the second, it is on the quality of the marriage.

What Marlene, the woman who feels she belongs to nobody, is really saying is that she has been robbed of her roots, her history, and her continuity. In her case there were so many people added to her family network that most of them, as time passed, had limited meaning.

For others family history is eroded in a different way.

Divorce often brings with it the loss of one whole side of the family. Usually it is the side of the noncustodial parent, which often vanishes forever. It weakens their intergenerational ties and leaves them bereft of a past. In a world where the sustenance of a family may give us our best chance for survival, they become emotional refugees.

Even where contact remains, it is often less active than before. Frequently it is the quality of the ties between the parent who has custody and the other parent's family that ultimately determines how rooted the child may be.

Children Who Stay Connected

Caryn and Saul

Consider Helen and her husband, Melvin. George, their thirty-year-old son, was divorced from his wife, Alissa, when their children, Caryn and Saul, were seven and five. Alissa had been unfaithful to George almost from the day they were married. Even after the children were born, she would go dancing with other men several nights a week and leave them with their father. George says, still, that he would not have divorced her until the children were grown. He's a traditional type who believes, as do his family members, that marriages should stay together "for the sake of the children." He says he was willing to sacrifice his own happiness, or at least to postpone it.

But Alissa gave him no choice. She announced one day that she had met someone else and asked George to leave. Bitter as it was, they managed to settle the custody issue without dragging the children through a court hearing. Alissa would have custody of the children all week, but George would take them on weekends and every Wednesday night.

Alissa's parents were as heartsick about the breakup as were George's, and both sets of grandparents resolved to each other that they would not allow it to interfere with their relationship or with the children. They each agreed that they would not judge the circumstances of the divorce and that they would remain friendly with each other and the other parent.

"It's important that we do that if we want to see the children and keep them as part of the family," Helen says. "So I call Alissa a couple of times a week and I bite my tongue. If she and my son have disagreements, and they frequently do, I stay out of it even when it tears me up inside. I figure some day the children will be older and be able to make their own decisions about their closeness to us. But until then I have to be nice to my former daughter-in-law. Or I'll lose the kids."

Helen's grandchildren are fortunate. They are surrounded by a strong family network, one that will not allow divorce to wrench it apart. Even George's remarriage to Dina several months ago was handled with sensitivity to the children's feelings. Dina was introduced to them gently, and she was careful not to overwhelm them or pretend to be their mother. She made them feel comfortable with her and soon brought them into *her* family circle, also a close one. George and Dina waited for almost a year after they met to marry so the children would have time to adjust gradually.

If the marriage of George and Dina lasts—and the sturdy family ties give it a better than average chance—the children may grow up feeling nourished, rather than impoverished as Marlene did, by a supportive network of caring relatives.

Ellen and Deedee

The chances are also good for Ellen and Deedee, now nine and twelve. They are the offspring of a "friendly" divorce, one in which the parents, grandparents, and relatives have made a vow to maintain as much of the predivorce environment for the children as possible.

It was their father, Al, who decided that he wanted more from life than what he was finding with his wife, Sandra, and his children. He wanted to exchange his job in the East as a radio program manager for a chance to write sitcoms in Hollywood. He felt he had married too young, at twenty-one, and his values about life and what he expected from it were changing. Sandra wasn't happy about the split but believed that it was better that they separate than stay together unhappily.

Al's parents were devastated. They loved Sandra "just like our daughter." When Al left for the West Coast, they took Sandra and the children into their home for six months until she could make plans for her future.

After she moved into her own apartment, they continued to see her and the children at least once a week. And they talked with their son frequently to keep him, as much as possible, as part of the family.

When Sandra remarried three years later, her wedding was held at the home of Al's brother. After the ceremony Al's father congratulated the new groom and said, "You're getting a wonderful wife, and only for one reason—because my son is a fool."

When Connections Break

A plant cut off from its roots is unable to flourish. A person without roots, unconnected to a past, grows up without perspective and has less autonomy. A rich family history, well stocked with people, the stories they tell, and the secrets they share, provides us with a sense of who we are and frees us to move on, to build our own lives, to add to our history and pass it on to our children and grandchildren. Connection with as many generations as possible gives us the best opportunity for emotional security and stability. Having more open relationships with our parents allows us to make stronger marriages and become better parents.

Children who have been adopted frequently feel, with poignant intensity, their lack of connectedness to their biological past, and many of them are nudged, at some point in their lives, to engage in an agonizing search for their biological parents.

As thirty-year-old Janet, who was adopted when she was a baby, says, "Every time the continuity of life faces me—when I was graduated from college, when I got married, when I had my first baby—I felt this strong need to know where I had come from. It's not that my parents are not wonderful. I love them immensely. But the fact is, I share my biology with somebody else.

"I feel incomplete. I need to see someone who looks like me, who maybe talks like me, who plays the piano like I do. It doesn't matter what they are like. I know I may be disappointed, even sorry once I meet them. But that isn't the point. I need something for my own peace and something to pass on to my daughter."

Adults from divorced families often talk in the same way about the sadness they feel. "From the day my parents divorced, I felt as though I had lost, not just a father, but a whole family," says Emily. "Dad was the one who moved out, and my sister and I had 'visitation' with him. God, I hate that word, visitation. It's so unnatural to have to *visit* with your father—we hardly ever saw the rest of his family.

"His parents did try to see us a few times, but they had to arrange it through our mother, and they weren't getting along too well. So I guess they just gave up. Dad never took us there because they weren't getting along too well with him either.

"Dad has a younger brother, Uncle Joe, who isn't married. He was fun and he used to come often when we were little and bring us presents and take us for walks in the park and tell us funny jokes. Suddenly he wasn't there either.

"Dad's sister, Brenda, has two children, boys, about our age. But they moved to California about two years after the divorce. Once in a while I get a note from my cousin Lewis, who is a journalist in Paris. But it feels as though I am hearing from a stranger. We don't know anything about each other.

"The funny thing is, I remember that at the time of my parents' divorce, my best friend, Eleanor, lost her father too. He died in an automobile accident. And I remember that all the kids at school felt so sorry for her, and we made cards to send home to her and her mother. Later Eleanor would tell me about her aunts and uncles and cousins all coming over and taking her places and trying to take her mind off the loss of her father.

"I remember feeling really angry. I had lost my father too. But no one was comforting me. I found myself wishing my father had died instead. At least I wouldn't have lost everyone else too."

Barbara, thirty-seven, who is getting divorced for the second time, says the sense of isolation seems to intensify as she grows older.

"I don't even have any family to react to what's happening in my life. No one to scold me. Or soothe me. Or help me settle down. Or even care. When my friend Lena was thinking about divorce, her brother was furious with her. He sat her down and they talked for days about why she was doing it, if maybe there was some other way. I don't even have anyone to be furious with me."

Barbara's parents were divorced when she was five. Her mother never remarried. Her father, who lived with another woman but didn't marry her, died when Barbara was ten. She had almost no extended family; her father's family never saw her or her mother after the divorce, which was hostile and angry. Her mother's only sister lives in Montana with her husband and two sons. Barbara hasn't done more than exchange birthday cards with them for years.

"I have a few good friends," Barbara says, "but it's not the same as family. Family means roots. It means someone has to care. I feel like I've been cheated of all of that."

By the time she was thirty, Audrey Hepburn had not seen her father for twenty-four years, and she found that she had an urgent need to find him again. She knew he was living in Dublin, found his address through the Red Cross, wrote to him, and eventually paid him a visit. For the next twenty years she took care of her father's every need, until he died when he was an old man, in his nineties. "It helped me to lay the ghost," she has said to writer Edward Klein. "I went on suffering as long as I didn't see him." Still, Hepburn admits that she goes through life feeling as though she could lose everything at any moment.

Many children of divorce move through life the same way Audrey Hepburn did, with the troubling phantom of their absent parent always shadowing them. Sometimes they manage to file away the memory for a long time: it's too painful to deal with consciously. But it often surfaces, as it does for adopted children, when the continuity of life is an issue.

Consider Walter, who had not seen his father in almost thirty years. His parents had an angry divorce when he was four, and he and his mother moved to another city. He hardly remembers life with both parents, and his mother did not marry again. He does remember a series of "horror stories" about his father.

"Mom kept telling me what a bad guy he was, that he had all these affairs with women, that he was never interested in me. I knew that we got support checks from him every week without fail and that he called from time to time to see how I was, but that made no impact on me. My mom filled my mind with so much awful detail about my father's moodiness and rudeness that I assumed I felt the same way she did. Anyone who asked me about my father heard those same stories. He was not someone anyone would want to know.

"But now I'm getting married and I really want my father there. I don't know why. But it's like if he's not there, his ghost will be. My mother can't see it. She got hysterical when she heard I wanted to invite him. She acts as though they just got divorced last week. The wounds are still so fresh for her. So I guess I'll have to manage without him."

The unreasonable and misplaced loyalty Walter's mother expects from him resembles the dynamics between some Holocaust survivors and their children. These parents, like some parents of divorce, make a heavy emotional investment in their children to make up for their own unbearable loss. But they expect something in return: unconditional loyalty and devotion.

If they get it, it is usually at their children's expense. It places children of divorce in the middle of a no-win situation. When they are young, they are especially reluctant to initiate or even respond enthusiastically to overtures from their absent parent no matter how much they might want to; they are too dependent on their relationship with the parent with whom they live. They have no opportunity to form their own opinions about their father or mother or to develop an autonomous relationship with him or her. They end up viewing the missing parent through the eyes of the parent who remained. As they grow up, they become adults like Walter, still playing out the script of their childhood. They need help in learning what that script was and how they can change it.

As we will see in Part Two, the adult children of divorce must identify the kind of family they came from, understand the past that has been eluding them, and use that knowledge to make constructive changes in the way they think and behave.

PART TWO

———— / ————

Where You Are Now . . .
and How You Got There

You have already learned a lot about the power of divorce—
how it affects children and the difference it makes in the way
they grow up. You have seen that:

- The relationship children have with each parent
  changes dramatically after divorce.
- Children of divorce spend a major part of their childhood in a family crisis.
- They feel as though they have been betrayed and their
  sense of trust has been violated; this is an issue for
  them all of their lives.
- They have to confront a complex web of relationships
  that children from families who stay together never
  have to face.
- They often feel disconnected from their family history;
  sometimes they lose an entire side of their families.
- They tend to blame all of their problems on their parents' divorce.

- The *acute* (short-term) symptoms of divorce are to be expected and will subside in time. They are a response to the disruption created by divorce.
- The *chronic* (long-term) symptoms may be dormant for a long time and become evident years later when children grow up and are trying to form intimate relationships. These symptoms have less to do with the divorce and more to do with the family style they learned growing up.
- A good relationship with both parents, including frequent visits and telephone calls with the noncustodial parent, helps prevent many of the chronic symptoms from festering and following adults of divorce through life.
- Strong supports—an aunt, a grandmother, a best friend—can be significant in determining how a child gets through a difficult time of his life when his parents are likely to be less available to him.

In this part of the book—"Where You Are Now . . . and How You Got There"—you will learn why your family history is so important as you are trying to develop and nurture your own intimate relationships. You will see why courtship is a particularly difficult time for adults of divorce, learn what it means to be "behaviorally mature," and figure out the style of relating to people that most characterizes your family. Two sets of questions will help you determine where you are and how you got there. Later you'll learn how to break that cycle.

CHAPTER TEN

Looking Backward

Most adult children of divorce worry about their futures. They are starting in the wrong place. It is the past they need to work out, especially the relationships with their parents who were, in turn, influenced by *their* parents. They need to move backward in time, to look at their parents and grand-parents and learn how events that took place—sometimes before they were born—are influencing their behavior and their relationships now.

Most research has focused extensively on the *acute* crisis of divorce and the responses of children immediately and for several years afterward. But I see no correlation between the *acute* symptoms of divorce and the *chronic* symptoms that have penetrated their psyches in much less obvious but more critical ways.

I find, in fact, that younger children—who feel the most devastated in the beginning because they don't have the skills to cope with their parents' separation—often become well-adjusted adults. This is especially true if the parent they lived with remarried and the marriage was continuous and stable. If this happened, they developed a sense of continuity that obscured the memories of the earlier failed marriage between their parents and provided them with a model of marriage that gave them strength and security. Judith Wallerstein's research also revealed that young children, who looked the most distraught when their parents' breakup occurred, seemed less consciously troubled ten years later.

The acute symptoms, those that result from the disruption of the family, are to be expected and subside in time, especially with appropriate therapy. Grades return to normal. Relationships with friends resume. Anger and disappointment subside. In time, children usually make peace even with the parent who hurt them the most.

It is the chronic, less tangible turmoil, the one that results from the family style that led to the divorce, that is the most ominous. It lives hidden in our minds all through our lives. It alters the way we develop and interferes with our ability, as we grow up, to form healthy relationships. The person who looks okay, who seems to be doing okay, is often a skillful and practiced actor.

CHAPTER ELEVEN

——————/——————

The Anxieties of Courtship

Concerns about commitment, fears of abandonment, apprehension about history repeating itself, plague even the most well-adjusted men and women who have lived through the divorce of their parents.

There are pivotal points in a person's life when long-dormant anxieties rise to the surface. They are times when the junctures in life loom large. Courtship. Marriage. Birth. Death. Anxiety and apprehension increase, too, when a person approaches a significant milestone—age fifty if your mother died at fifty; the birth of your fourth child if that's when your parents were divorced; vacation time if that's when your parents' conflicts escalated.

It isn't surprising that the courtship period, when people are trying to carve out an intimate relationship, should be especially difficult. It is during this time that people struggle to learn about each other, when they come face-to-face with raw emotion, when they are doing more feeling than thinking.

Two strangers with different upbringings and different roles within their original families are trying to forge a relationship that will be nurturing and satisfying to both of them. No wonder patterns from the past poke through—for better or for worse. Issues of trust, responsibility, and sensitivity must be confronted. There are decisions to be made and differences to be resolved. How those differences are negotiated—what we do with anger, disappointment, joy, expectations—determines the course the courtship will take.

That course is highly predictable. And it is usually repetitive. No matter the partner, people generally behave the same way and approach problems in the same familiar style.

Unfortunately they are usually blind to their own behavior patterns. They don't see that they follow a script written for them when they were growing up. They don't know that like Walter, the man who wanted his father at his wedding, they are still *reacting* to the past instead of *acting* in the present. They don't understand their parents or won't acknowledge the influence they continue to have on them. Without realizing it, they are courting a powerful hidden agenda—to work out the unfinished business of their childhood in a new relationship.

A study of twenty-five hundred middle-class college students called "The Impact of Parental Divorce on Courtship" tells us that divorce, regardless of when in a child's life it occurs, increases certain kinds of behavior during courtship—earlier and more premarital sex, more cohabitation, and earlier marriages.

Moreover, where there was significant conflict around the divorce or the relationship with the parent (either mother or father) deteriorated after the divorce, the adult children were more likely to weave in and out of short-term relationships and were quicker to threaten to end the relationship if it wasn't working. Their chances of being divorced themselves also increased.

Children who came from highly conflicted families where divorce did not occur had some, but not all, of the same problems during their own courtships. They too were struggling to find satisfying relationships and tended to drift from one partner to another. But they were less likely to engage in early sex and cohabitation.

This study supports what I see every day in my practice: continuing conflict—whether or not the parents divorce—has lasting effects on children and influences their courtship patterns years later. In Part Six you will be reading the cases of Ginger, whose family did not resolve its problems after the divorce, and Donna, whose family was able to cooperate; you will see the striking differences in the kind of adults both women have become.

When a divorce resolves family conflict, children learn how to move on with their own lives productively. When it doesn't, they remain stuck, see the divorce as having solved nothing, and learn nothing about how to settle differences.

Adults of divorce, however, must grapple with still another layer of intangibles that complicates their struggle for personal intimacy—concerns about the continuity of life and the rupture of even the most sacred bonds.

Courtship is a time when these issues surface as palpable and undeniable. It is a time when people think about family and commitment and the future. It is a time when they ponder not only the relationship they are in but the network of relationships that forms their lives.

As we pointed out in earlier chapters, these are issues that have a life of their own in the minds of adults of divorce. Even where they recognize, perhaps years later, that the divorce was in the best interests of both parents, it doesn't stop them from wishing that they had come from an intact family and from wanting something different for themselves.

Sometimes it is a question of ever being able to make a commitment to another person with confidence that it will endure.

Sometimes it is an unflappable promise to themselves that their lives will not be a rerun of their parents'. As thirty-two-year-old Richard, a boy whose parents were divorced when he was six, says, "A good marriage is the best revenge."

In any case nagging concerns about their past and their future elevate the emotional temperature of their courtships. It is no wonder that so many people seek help at this stage of their lives.

CHAPTER TWELVE

Pursuing Intimate Relationships

The way adult children of divorced parents pursue intimate relationships has a lot to do with the *way* their parents handled the crisis of divorce, which in turn has to do with the way their parents related to each other in the first place.

It takes a lot of insight into our past to understand how we were "hurt" and how we reacted to that hurt, to learn about our own relationship patterns and how to change them so that we become masters of our future rather than victims of our past.

The chronic symptoms of adults of divorce, the ones that wreak havoc on relationships, are highly predictable. They are dictated by our family style and the part we play in perpetuating it. Every family has its own style, its own way of behaving, of relating and reacting to each other. This is especially true when it comes to dealing with differences between husband and wife.

Differences, often strong ones, are not the exclusive province of the family of divorce. They exist in every family.

It is not *having* differences in viewpoint that causes problems; it is the *reaction we have* to those differences, how they are handled, what we do with them, that matters.

What we do tends to be what we have been doing all our lives, from the time we were children. It tends to be what we have learned in our families when we were growing up, patterns we learned from our mothers and fathers, who learned them from *their* mothers and fathers. It is not unusual, after all, that without realizing it, behaviors that feel familiar get repeated, generation after generation. Just as stomach problems run in some families, headaches in others.

The relationship problems that may lead to divorce run in families. It is not necessarily genetic; people do learn coping traits. No one enters marriage with the idea that it will end in divorce; most people want to make it work. But it is the way they relate—the way they have been relating all of their lives—that determines whether their marriages will flourish or fail.

While most divorce research has focused on the nuclear family, I have followed generations of families and find that certain ways of doing things or reacting to situations are passed on in an uncanny way from grandparents to children to grandchildren, even when some of those people have never known each other. It is these ingrained, predictable ways that families have of reacting to each other, both in the presence and absence of stress, that determine, in large part, what happens to children when divorce occurs. Those behaviors—the destructive ones and the healthy ones—are likely to have far-reaching effects, not only on the children of divorce as they grow up, but on *their* children and on generations to come.

Anxiety and Relationships

Anxiety rubs off on people. What you absorbed from your family *then* surfaces in your anxiety level *now*. Without your being aware of it, that anxiety and how you respond to it often sabotage the formation of the intimate relationships you want so much.

There are lots of ways we handle anxiety. Some of us turn to drugs or alcohol or sex. Some of us develop eating disorders, such as anorexia nervosa or bulimia. Some of us bury ourselves in our jobs. But for all of us our anxieties come out, in one form or another, in the way we manage our intimate relationships.

As we said earlier, when parents divorce, the emotional anxiety level in children soars, no matter their age. But it is not this initial, time-limited, high-voltage anxiety that is the most bruising. It is the way relationships are disrupted and reorganized after the divorce that causes the chronic anxiety that shadows us through life.

It is this chronic anxiety—the result of the way we have, over the years, reacted to our families' patterns of behaving with one another —that builds and interferes with our ability to mold and maintain intimate relationships that work for us. It leads us to poor choices in partners and unproductive behavior with the very men and women who could be promising mates. We end up frustrated, feeling as though we have failed again, and wonder what is wrong with us. It doesn't do much for our self-esteem and confidence.

Some of the behavior patterns are complex, convoluted, and difficult to unravel. They may require extensive and skillful therapy. Others are simple and can be identified easily with a little bit of help. That's the way it was for Iris, who repeated her parents' behavior without realizing it.

"I grew up in a family in which criticism was a way of life," says Iris, "I can't remember my mom ever telling my dad or me anything nice that didn't have a 'but' with it.

" 'Your sweater is pretty, but you look better in red.'

" 'The melon is wonderful, but maybe a little too sweet.'

" 'You're a wonderful ice skater, but when you make that far turn, you'd look more graceful if you bent your left leg. . . .'

"My dad was like that too, but in a different way. He'd put down my mom in front of other people. If she expressed an opinion about something, he always took the other side. You could count on it.

"As a kid, I used to cringe and I would feel embarrassed. But you get used to it, and I thought that's just the way families were. I had no idea I would grow up doing the same thing."

During her early twenties Iris went through four relationships, all of which disintegrated within a year.

"The last thing Larry, my last boyfriend, said to me the night he left was, 'Iris, you ought to play a tape machine when you have a conversation with someone. You don't give a guy a break. You make him feel as though he can't do anything right.'

"The specific thing that had happened that night was our talk about Larry's new job. He was an advertising account executive and had just been given responsibility for two new accounts. Both were corporate, different from the entertainment clients he was used to handling. He was thrilled and so was I. I told him so and made him a special dinner, with candlelight and wine, to celebrate.

"But then I began to tell him how he would have to dress differently now and which clothes he'd need to get rid of and maybe he ought to change barbers. I didn't even know what I was doing wrong. I was only trying to be helpful. Even when he got up and left the table, I didn't know.

"But Larry turned out to be my best friend. When he told me what I was doing and how I had been doing it for the entire four months we had been dating, I felt sick to my stomach. I knew exactly what was going on. I was acting exactly like my parents. I was doing the very thing I detested in them, the thing that I think contributed to the end of their marriage. The next day I asked a friend to recommend a therapist. I knew I needed help."

CHAPTER THIRTEEN

―――――/―――――

Are You "Behaviorally" Mature?

The men and women I see are puzzled and frustrated. Many of them are accomplished in the world of work, juggling heavy schedules, supervising big staffs, sometimes making million-dollar decisions. In the arena of intimate relationships, they are inept. Why?

It has to do with what I call a person's level of "behavioral" maturity. Behavioral maturity has nothing to do with physical characteristics, nor does it have any relationship to intelligence or education, talent, or skill. It is the ability to know the difference between thinking and feeling and to distinguish whether the way you behave is influenced by your thoughts or your emotions.

Less mature people have a tendency to think narrowly. They believe that their thoughts and observations are the only ones that are accurate and that their behavior is, therefore, justified. It is difficult for them to entertain differences among people, and they are quick to assign blame to someone else. They think of themselves as the center of the universe instead of part of a larger world.

Someone who is "behaviorally mature" can accept changing conditions and absorb and manage the tension produced by change. During a divorce, for instance, when tension is high, the maturity level of everyone in the family usually plummets. However, the behaviorally mature person recovers more quickly and regains the balance between thinking and feeling that allows him or her to go on with life in a productive way.

Less mature people do not distinguish between fact and opinion. They don't have enough sense of their own individuality to say, "It's okay if you have an opinion and I have a different opinion. Let's talk about it." All of their arguments are personal. And they try to pressure each other to change their minds or their behavior.

Consider a couple that is arguing about vacations. He wants to go sightseeing in New York and she wants to lie on the beach in Hawaii. For a less mature couple, the argument might go something like this:

She: You are really thoughtless. I work so hard all year and I need the kind of vacation where I can just lie around and do nothing.

He: You know I hate the sand and I don't swim well and sitting in the sun all day gives me a headache. But you never consider me. It's always what you want to do. Besides, Hawaii is expensive. I wanted to buy a stereo system last month and you said we couldn't afford it. But you're willing to spend it for a trip to Hawaii. You are really selfish.

She: Talk about selfish. You bought three suits last winter and I'm still wearing dresses that are four years old. But I didn't stop you. I didn't say anything. I told you how good you looked. You could have said to me, "Honey, why don't you buy yourself a new dress?"

He: Who stopped you? If you wanted a dress, you could have bought it.

What we have here is simply a basic difference between two people about vacation plans. But it has escalated into a heated argument in which one blames the other for things that have nothing to do with vacations. They are exchanging feelings, not information. And nothing gets solved.

This couple has been unable to separate thinking and feeling. It would have been more productive for the conversation to have gone this way:

He: Here we are arguing about vacations. It is obvious that you want to do one thing and I want to do another. Let's see if we can figure out something that would please us both.

She: I really don't like New York, especially in the winter when it is so cold, and I want to get some sunshine.

He: Maybe there's a way we could do both. Hawaii for a week in the winter and New York for a week in the spring.

She: I don't think we can afford to do both. I need some new clothes and I need to save some money for that. You bought three suits last year, but I didn't get anything.

He: You may be right. I hadn't thought about that. And another thing, I think we may need a new roof on the house. I noticed the other day that the shingles are beginning to go.

She: I wish you had mentioned that before. A new roof is expensive. Maybe we really can't afford Hawaii this year in any case.

He: What do you think about compromising? This year, New York. The new roof. A few new dresses for you. Next year, Hawaii.

She: Well, I can't say I'm not disappointed. But that seems to make sense. Maybe I can look for the dresses in New York while you're going to the museums I don't enjoy.

This kind of maturity—the kind that enables us to distinguish thinking from feeling—gives us the capacity, when we get into an emotionally charged situation, to be aware of how we are responding and to reflect on it. Once we begin focusing on what the other person does or does not do, we get into the area of blame. When that happens, an argument, usually one that can't be settled, inevitably results.

It is this ability to distinguish between thinking and feeling within ourselves and between ourselves and others, and learning to use that ability to direct our lives and solve our problems, that is the central feature of mature growth and development. It gives us the freedom to move back and forth between intimate emotional closeness with another person and pursuit of our individual dreams. And to find pleasure in each. It gives us the objectivity to participate in highly emotional situations because we can exercise logical reasoning when we need to. It allows us to calm anxiety and deal with fairly severe stress without falling apart. And it permits us to hear diverse viewpoints without taking them personally, without automatically reacting and antagonizing others.

Who is Behaviorally Mature?

People who are behaviorally mature are those who have become emotionally separate from their family of origin. This does not mean that they are estranged or alienated from them. It means that they have taken responsibility for their own behavior rather than *reacting* to their parents' anxieties by mimicking or rebelling against their parents' way of dealing with differences.

Maturity—the balance of thinking and feeling—cannot be taught at Harvard Business School, nor can it be learned in the markets of Wall Street. Its roots are planted firmly in the system of family relations in which all of us play a critical role. Children who grow up in behaviorally mature families are more likely to be behaviorally mature themselves.

The relationships of behaviorally immature people are in jeopardy because they don't know how to settle their differences. Their marriages often end in divorce. That's why more adults of divorce also divorce. It is not the propensity to divorce that is passed on; it is the immature behavioral patterns that led to the divorce.

When divorce occurs, the way family members relate to each other doesn't usually change. It is like heart bypass surgery. The surgery, like the divorce, is only the first step. If you don't reorganize the way you think and change the way you behave, the problem won't go away. What this means to you, the adult child of divorce, is that your long-term response to your parents' breakup depends mainly on two things:

- *The "behavioral" maturity of your parents in settling their differences, which, through the years, made their imprint on you*
- *The degree to which you, as a child, became the focus of and reacted to your family's conflict*

People with lower levels of maturity tend to wander in a "feeling" world. They don't distinguish feeling from thinking, and they can't tell the difference between fact and opinion. Loving and being loved by others is the focal point of their lives, and often they will be excessive in their attempts to garner love and approval.

Julie, for instance, would buy extravagant gifts, not only for close and distant family members, but for new acquaintances whose affections she wanted to cultivate. Once she gave a new friend a round-trip airline ticket to London; another time she catered a wedding reception for a woman with whom she had worked for only seven months. Julie was not wealthy and, in fact, earned little income herself. It was her husband Brian who, while he sometimes objected, financed her quest for love. He too focused on being loved and was afraid that if he protested too much, she would stop caring for him.

People like Julie and Brian are so sensitized to the disapproval of others that they will lie about things they think will upset someone. They feel entirely justified because they don't see what they are doing as lying, just as being emotionally concerned about the other person. And that makes it okay.

Julie admits she is still being influenced by her past. She says she grew up "in the shadow" of her older brother, who became a doctor and went on to become one of the leading radiologists in the country. No matter what Julie did, no matter what concern she showed for her parents, during her youth and as she herself moved into middle age she still felt "second class," as though she were "taking a back seat" to her brother.

Five years after she was married, she had the first in a series of affairs. Most of them were with men, but she also had sexual relationships with two women.

Eventually she and her husband participated in family therapy, but she never revealed anything about her affairs. He suspected, but never asked. Much later she explained that she could not have told Brian because it would have hurt him too much. She never admitted, even to herself, that she was being deceitful. "He couldn't handle it," she argued.

Julie, whose parents were divorced when she was twelve, used to tell friends elaborate stories about her accomplishments. Sometimes it was a nonexistent job, for which she would claim she was making fifty thousand dollars a year.

Sometimes it was the huge sum of money she was inheriting from a distant uncle. Once it was about a Hollywood producer who had seen her in a little theater production and was intent on making her a star. All of her stories contained a kernel of truth: She did have a new job, but was making fifteen thousand; she did inherit money from an uncle—two thousand; and there was no Hollywood producer in her life, just a friend who praised her performance, saying, "You belong in Hollywood."

Most people couldn't understand that Julie believed her own words. As a byproduct of the relationship she had had with her parents and later with her husband, she had lost the ability to separate fact from fiction. Her need for approval was so strong that her capacity to handle disapproval didn't exist.

The Julies of the world may go along unchallenged for a long time in a nonstressful environment. But a major trauma, such as a serious health problem in the family, or a disappointment such as losing a job, can unravel them and trigger a shattering response, such as depression or even suicide attempts.

Intimate relationships in which people tend to be guided more by feeling than by thinking, in which their behavior is almost totally governed by emotional responses to their environment or to other people, are the most vulnerable to behavioral immaturity. Major life decisions are based more on what feels right than on thoughtful reflection about implications.

When behaviorally immature people marry, they often seek to enhance themselves and see the marriage as a way to make themselves "whole people." Forty-one-year-old Mildred, whose parents were divorced when she was twenty, told me proudly that she is only half a person; her husband is her other half. If they marry someone who is more mature, they appear to be more mature themselves; if not, their immaturity becomes obvious. Under stress, without their own inner resources to support them, they often turn to external solutions.

In the past, religion, strong family ties, and society itself, which provided restraints against divorce, mitigated against splintering the marriage. Now divorce often seems the easiest and most acceptable way to end marital conflict. The view is that the marriage is the problem and the divorce is the solution. People who are behaviorally immature are stunned when the divorce doesn't solve anything. The reason is simple: If the person has not changed the way he or she relates to other people, the same problems will surface in the next relationship and the next marriage and may well follow the person through his or her life.

In a world characterized by freedom of choice, behaviorally immature people are at an appalling disadvantage. They are too easily influenced and manipulated by events and people outside themselves, and they seldom make decisions that reflect who they are. Often they believe that independence and maturity are synonymous with rebellion. Doing the opposite becomes their automatic behavior, a behavior that is as binding as blind compliance. Unfortunately there is little freedom of choice for immature people.

In the workplace, where relationships are usually less personal and intense, most people can be more emotionally objective. In fact, the enemies of healthy intimate relationships—blind conformity and acceptance of the beliefs of others—may sometimes be advantageous on the job. Exceptions occur when a job is the most important aspect of someone's life, when tensions in the office get impossibly high, and when a too close, enmeshed relationship with coworkers exists.

Still, adult children of divorce often seem able to do well at work. It is with families and close friends, and especially in trying to develop and maintain intimate relationships, that disaster frequently stalks them. A friend of mine says, when she leaves her office, it is "like leaving my brain behind me."

The critical issue is the ability to master differences between two people in a relationship. In an intimate relationship, it means: How can I remain myself while giving myself to someone else? If you come from a family that wasn't able to do this or who did it by running away from the relationship, you may see yourself as an emotional cripple.

"Borrowing" and What It Means

If you are on the low end of the behavioral maturity scale, you probably do a lot of "borrowing" from the person who is most significant in your personal life. It may be your parent, your spouse, even your child. "Borrowing" in this sense means that you rely on that person to fill in the gaps in your own maturity. It means that you use that person to enhance your own self-esteem.

We all do a certain amount of "borrowing." The commonly used phrase "Behind every successful man is a woman" grows out of this style of behavior between some husbands and wives.

The woman who always defines herself as "John's wife" or whose gratification comes because she is dating or married to someone famous is eventually going to find herself running on empty.

Similarly, the person from whom you are borrowing eventually feels used up. A man who is a successful architect, for instance, but depends on his wife to be everything else—the child caretaker, the housekeeper, the appointment maker, the bill payer, the shopper, the gift buyer, the vacation planner, the social secretary—eventually will have a wife who feels she has given so much of herself that she is no longer a person.

Borrowing has a lot to do with the way people relate to

each other and the way they release their anxiety. And it often has a seesaw effect on a marriage.

The relationship can be calm and wonderful one day and stormy and isolated the next. The couple is exquisitely aware of these highs and lows but doesn't usually understand much about the behavioral style that generates them.

More mature men and women don't need to do as much of this kind of "borrowing" because they have a more substantial sense of who they are and have more choice about whether to react emotionally and impulsively or thoughtfully and reflectively. They can more easily maintain long-term relationships or, in dissolving them, do so in a more thoughtful way. Those who are less mature are more likely to develop relationships based on feelings. They are also more likely to become involved in a relationship or to end it because they *react* rather than reason.

The Behavioral Maturity Quiz

To get an idea of how behaviorally mature you are, ask yourself the following questions. Take the time to think about where on the scale you would place yourself. Be sure that you answer the questions honestly even if it hurts or feels embarrassing. Awareness of the way you tend to act is your first step toward achieving behavioral maturity. After you have answered the questions, ask your spouse or the person with whom you are having an intimate relationship to rate you on the same scale.

	Never	Rarely	Sometimes	Often	Always
1. In my daily life I distinguish between fact and opinion.	1	2	3	4	5
2. I accept opinions different from	1	2	3	4	5

	Never	Rarely	Sometimes	Often	Always
mine and don't feel persecuted and violated.					
3. I have an open mind when I talk with others about controversial subjects.	1	2	3	4	5
4. I allow others the freedom to express their opinions to me.	1	2	3	4	5
5. I listen thoughtfully to what others have to say to me.	1	2	3	4	5
6. I change my mind in the face of new and different information.	1	2	3	4	5
7. I continue to think and do not get emotional when someone criticizes me.	1	2	3	4	5
8. I am aware of how I generally respond to emotionally tense situations. For example, I know that I always bristle when my mother makes suggestions to me.	1	2	3	4	5

	Never 1	Rarely 2	Sometimes 3	Often 4	Always 5
9. I am able to recognize when I am thinking about an issue and when I am feeling emotions.	1	2	3	4	5
10. I have enough self-control to choose whether I respond to my thoughts or to my feelings depending on circumstances.	1	2	3	4	5
11. In arguments I try to resolve the difference or convey my beliefs rather than seek agreement or approval.	1	2	3	4	5
12. I quickly return to my normal activities after a period of stress.	1	2	3	4	5
13. I function as an independent person even though I am emotionally connected to my family.	1	2	3	4	5
14. I remain emotionally connected to my family even while I	1	2	3	4	5

	Never	Rarely	Sometimes	Often	Always
function as an independent person.					
15. I fulfill myself as a person even while I am maintaining an intimate relationship.	1	2	3	4	5
16. When I dissolve a relationship, I do it in a thoughtful, nonvindictive way.	1	2	3	4	5
17. When I don't express my feelings because I believe I will hurt someone, I am likely to develop physical symptoms —i.e., headaches, high blood pressure.	1	2	3	4	5

Note that the categories on the scale are in reverse order for the following four questions.

	Always	Often	Sometimes	Rarely	Never
18. I try to change people over to my way of thinking.	1	2	3	4	5
19. I blame others for what goes wrong in my life.	1	2	3	4	5
20. I blame myself when I get into	1	2	3	4	5

	Always	Often	Sometimes	Rarely	Never
trouble with others.					
21. I do things mainly to get other people's approval.	1	2	3	4	5

The higher you scored, the more behaviorally mature you are. This self-assessment quiz is not intended to be a research instrument, but the results should help you understand yourself and your reactions better. Your purpose in taking it is not to compare your score with others but to help you identify styles you have that may be getting in the way of fulfilling intimate relationships.

CHAPTER FOURTEEN

Find Your Family

Being married is a lot like playing on a football team. You have to learn to be a team player without sacrificing yourself and your individuality. This is as delicate a balancing act as that done by the Flying Wallendas—and just as formidable. Marital partners who can accomplish it stand a good chance of having marriages that will survive and thrive. They can usually deal with differences in a reasonable and responsible way. For those who don't, a shattered marriage is more likely.

Adults of divorced parents often tell me about the *symptoms* that they believe led to the divorce.

"My dad beat my mom so she left him."

"My mom had an affair, so the marriage broke up."

"Grandmom came to live with us and things went downhill from there."

But they don't usually have a clue about *what led to those symptoms*. It reminds me of the patients with congestive heart failure whose ankles are frequently swollen. They come to the doctor asking that their ankles be taken care of. The problem, of course, is not their ankles. It is their heart that needs attention. In physical medicine, that seems quite clear. But in psychiatric medicine the road from cause to effect is often a blurry one.

Looking at your family patterns and the way your family deals with differences can help you make the connections. Examine them in terms of your own life to see how you perpetuate these patterns—by repeating them or rebelling against them.

Families often handle differences in these ways:

• **By avoiding them or distancing from them.** Husband or wife may avoid their differences by pretending they don't exist. Susie, for example, may distance herself *physically* from her husband whenever they have differences. She may slam the door and go around the corner to her best friend's house for a few hours. She may go on a shopping spree and send herself flowers. She may leave home for a weekend until her emotions have settled down. Or she may leave and never come back.

Geraldine locks herself in her bedroom with a pot of coffee, a book, and a box of chocolate chip cookies, not speaking to her husband or anyone else for two days.

The problem with physical distancing is that it accomplishes nothing. Geraldine may not be speaking to her husband for forty-eight hours, but she will be thinking about him and their relationship problems all the time. Susie may storm out of the house and absent herself for a weekend; but in her mind is a continual replay of the incidents that precipitated her leaving. All the time a spouse is away—in another room or another city—he or she is focusing on *his* thoughtlessness, *her* rudeness, *his* clumsiness, *her* insensitivity. Anger and resentment build, but the problems remain.

Sometimes a person will distance himself *emotionally*.

Jeff will continue reading the newspaper while his wife tells him about the man who ran into her car that afternoon. Anita will talk on the telephone with her best friend for three hours every night while her husband watches television. Gail will stay up until three cleaning her house, knowing that her husband will be asleep by the time she gets to bed.

Two of my patients, Heidi and Rick, had been married for three years and worked in the same building, in adjoining research labs. When they had an intense disagreement, they could work side by side for weeks without talking to each other. Once they kept it up for two months. Heidi called it their time of "cold storage."

People who distance or avoid each other typically feel that attempts to communicate are futile. They feel they have lost the ability to reach each other and find it easier to avoid "hot" issues that they know will instigate conflict. They are really avoiding their own discomfort with the sensitive subject and the reactions they know it will provoke in them. People who distance become frustrated and upset, and if they are behaviorally immature, they will see the problem as belonging entirely to their husband or wife. Often they complain of loneliness even in the presence of their spouse because they have no one with whom to share feelings and ideas.

Sometimes husband or wife will become acutely aware that his or her style is to distance, and will try to engage his spouse. He may bring her flowers; she may prepare his favorite dessert. But where husband or wife is behaviorally immature, this technique may lead to greater distancing. If the engager persists, the pattern may switch to open conflict, a style described later in this chapter, followed by periods of distance to calm the intense anxiety. The person who has been unsuccessful in trying to engage his spouse may find another way to relieve his frustration and loneliness. It may be focusing on a child, becoming overly involved with work, or having an affair. As you read the stories of Richard and Jerry later, you will see clearly the distancing patterns in their families.

Couples who avoid or distance become emotionally disconnected and estranged from each other. They are the people who often say that they just "grew apart."

• **By Adapting to Them.** Adapting means modifying yourself to obscure the differences between you and another person. For example, if you ask this kind of couple, "How do you settle arguments?" they say, "We don't have any." The reason they don't have any is that one person suppresses his or her feelings.

It may be over something simple, such as,

   He: "Shall we have dinner in or out tonight?"
   She: "Oh, I don't care. Whatever you want."

Or it may be over something as significant as whether a child should be raised Catholic or Jewish. The husband may say, "It really doesn't matter. Whatever my wife wants."

All of us adapt to some extent. And more behaviorally mature people continually make compromises in their marriages to resolve differences between them and to control anxiety. Two-sided adapting, where each partner compromises in different situations, works well.

But marriages where the same person always adapts are often characterized by one spouse who underfunctions and another who overfunctions. The background of the one who underfunctions is that he or she is accustomed to allowing others to make decisions for him; the overfunctioning spouse often grew up in the role of family decision maker, the one who set the pace for others in the family. In these kinds of marriages feelings are often smothered to the point where a person hardly recognizes he has them. Sometimes one person adapts in the interest of harmony. It may be a woman who saw her mother and her grandmother as the peacemakers in the family and who slips easily into that role. This kind of person often loses the capacity to feel and may retreat into isolation.

But the person who does the adapting most of the time is the one who eventually feels swallowed up in the marriage. It is this person who is likely to become dysfunctional by retreating into drugs or alcoholism or depression. I have heard people like this say, "I had to get out of this marriage. My self simply disappeared."

Sometimes they don't know what it was that made them snap. A twist of fate, a button pushed, a nerve exposed. The awakening is probably gradual but may feel and look sudden. But the person affected knows that something must change or he or she will suffocate.

The story of Murray and Felicia, which you will read later, is an example of an underfunctioning mother who, after divorce, became unable to care for herself. The fallout in such situations is that children are often pushed into "parenting" role reversals that they resent.

- **Open conflict.** In these families there is lots of arguing, lots of blaming each other. Verbal abuse is common and physical abuse often erupts. Husband, wife, or both may have drinking or drug problems. And adults of divorce often say that they grew up against a backdrop of anger and hostility, where the parents' dissatisfaction with the marriage was obvious and explosive.

  While most adults of divorce I have seen, no matter how healthy their current relationships are, would have preferred that their parents stay together, children from violent families don't feel that way. Where their sleep was interrupted with shouts and insults, where they cringed in a corner while their dad shoved their mother across the room, where they lived each day in fear, these children were relieved and hopeful that life might be better for them after divorce.

Open conflict is both a symptom of tension and a mechanism to manage anxiety and gain equilibrium. It happens in all marriages; the critical issues are its severity, how often it occurs, the kinds of issues that trigger it, and what the outcome is. Most people feel better, for instance, if after conflict some agreement occurs and there is a period of forgiveness. In fact, during those times many people report that their marriages take on a new vitality. Even their sex lives are better.

However, when the conflict comes often, when it is precipitated by minor issues, when unresolved conflicts from the past (that are emotionally but not logically related to the current problem) keep surfacing, when the flaws of the other person become the focus of the argument, it is less likely that the conflict will be resolved. Blaming the other person, even when some of that blame may be well founded, is a simplistic technique that usually escalates the argument.

In these cases a third party—the police, neighbors, lawyers, crisis services, or children taking sides—often becomes involved. The child whose job it is to keep the conflict from getting out of hand is often deprived of the energy he needs for his own growth and development. The cases of Sally and Buddy, which you will read later, are examples of this behavior pattern.

· **Focusing on someone or something else.** You may have heard the word "triangle" applied to family relationships. As marriages deteriorate, as relationships between husband and wife become too intense and conflicted, the person who feels the most emotional discomfort moves away and connects with a third person or thing.

The triangle that he or she creates is a way of calming distress. It allows the relationship to stabilize without changing and can often dilute the tension between husband and wife. They now have another issue or a third person on which they can focus.

Think back to your parents' marriage. Try to identify the kind of triangle they might have created as their marriage was crumbling. Was it a triangle outside the family—usually an extramarital affair or an important social network that your mother or father may have turned to to take the pressure off their relationship with each other? Was it a triangle within the family? Perhaps with in-laws, or with one of your parents allied with his or her mother or father? Or was it the most common triangle—the one that involves two parents and a child? Most important, was that child you? We'll talk more about this later in Part Three, "Breaking the Cycle."

But for now, you should understand that when parents focus too much on a child, it is usually an expression of their own behavioral immaturity. It is probably a characteristic that comes across several generations and results in adults who lose the ability to survive independently.

Parents who focus on their children too much often do it by being overly positive or overly negative. In the one case, they have trouble setting limits for their children and believe that nothing is too good for them. This is as much a handicap to children as is the parent who continually worries about them for real or imagined reasons and doesn't allow them to become independent. Children whose parents "love them too much" may become adults who can't survive without unconditional approval from everyone. And the children who never learned independence may have trouble functioning without their parents' day-to-day guidance.

All families do some of the things described here. Everyone adapts and argues and avoids and sometimes focuses on other things and other people when tension is high. That's okay when those behaviors have a calming effect and reduce the anxiety that accompanies the need to settle differences. But the overuse of one style of relating usually settles nothing. And the too-frequent use of all the styles is a certain sign of either behavioral immaturity or chronic stress. Either results merely in a predictable increase in tension and leads to the kind of dissatisfaction with marriage that is the forerunner of divorce.

When family stress is low, behavior patterns are more subtle; when anxiety increases, family style becomes glaringly obvious. To figure out the kind of style that predominates in your family and whether one pattern leads to another, consider the kinds of events that created stress in your home as you grew up. They may include:

- celebrations—birthdays, holidays, graduations, weddings, births, Bar Mitzvahs
- vacations
- visits from extended family members
- mealtimes
- discussions about certain topics such as religion, education, politics, money, sex, children
- how household responsibilities should be defined and allocated

Against that backdrop, ask yourself these questions, *first about your mother, then about your father.*

1. Did she ignore stressful issues?
2. Did she deal with stressful issues by changing the subject or becoming involved in another activity?
3. Did she get quiet?
4. Did she leave the room or the house?
5. Did she present the facade of a "perfect marriage" to outsiders?
6. Did she bring up sensitive issues such as sex, money, or in-laws?
7. Did she become frustrated easily?
8. Did she complain of feeling lonely in her marriage?
9. Did she use alcohol or drugs?
10. Did she develop a mental illness such as depression?
11. Did she accuse your father of being inattentive to her?
12. Did she make overtures toward your father that he rejected?
13. Did she shy away from expressing differences of opinion?
14. Did she make all of the important decisions?
15. Did she make few or no decisions?
16. Was she moody?
17. Did she become overly absorbed in her work?
18. Did she blame your father for all that was wrong with the marriage?
19. Did she have physical symptoms such as nausea, headaches, insomnia?
20. Did she discuss your father's shortcomings with others, but not with him?
21. Did she discuss his shortcomings with you or your brothers or sisters?
22. Did she ask you or your brothers or sisters to intervene?
23. Did she take her anxieties out on you?
24. Did she turn to relatives or friends?
25. Did she have an affair?

26. Did she urge the children "not to upset" their father?
27. Did she snap at the slightest provocation?
28. Did she provoke arguments over minor issues?
29. Did she scream or swear a lot?
30. Did she threaten suicide?
31. Did she get physically violent?
32. Did she cry a lot?
33. Was she an angry, hostile person?
34. Did her presence create tension?
35. Was she manipulative?
36. Did she have her own friends and social network that specifically excluded your father?

Because there is so much overlap in every family, it is not possible to assign a style to each answer you have given. However, the first seventeen questions pertain more to the patterns of distance and adaptation; the balance have more to do with open conflict and focusing on someone else. You should be able to see how one pattern (and its flow into another) characterizes each of your parents and their relationship with each other and with their children. Your responses to these questions and the information you will learn about yourself and your family in Part Three, "Breaking the Cycle," will help you identify your family style and see how it is carried, usually unaware, through the generations.

CHAPTER FIFTEEN

———/———

Divorce,
Anxiety, and Maturity

When divorce occurs, people who would have been considered mature under ordinary circumstances usually regress. While it may be obvious to everyone who knows them that they are behaving immaturely, they are not aware of it, nor can they often help it. Divorce is so stressful that it turns healthy people into dysfunctional people for varying periods of time.

When people feel anxious, they veer more to the feeling side of the thinking/feeling spectrum. Anxiety destabilizes people and pushes them to focus more on the relationship and its problems than on themselves and their responsibilities. As you identify the patterns in your family, you will see that your family used and probably continues to use more than one way to resolve its conflicts. But you will find that one style often takes over. And you will soon see the part you play in your family scenario.

Laura and Mark: Avoiding, Distancing, and Open Conflict

Laura's parents, both in their seventies, tried to find excuses not to visit her and her husband Mark. "Whenever we went there, we didn't know what to expect," Laura's mom told me. "Sometimes she wasn't talking to him. He would be tripping around the kitchen nervously, talking to us and acting as though nothing were wrong. But I know my daughter, and I could see from her body language and her tight lips and her clipped responses that something major was going on.

"I don't remember it happening until they were married about ten years," her mother said. "But after that it was always the same. She was either silent or they were arguing. I wasn't sure which was worse."

Laura and Mark had gotten married when she was twenty-three and he was twenty-four. They met through Laura's older sister, Marjorie, who was married to a well-known real estate entrepreneur. Marjorie was a successful graphics designer in demand by agencies and business firms for her innovative style. She and her husband Larry had twin sons, three years old, who already were reading from second-grade books, holding adult conversations, and showing unusual poise. They were the oldest grandchildren and were adored by everyone in the family, especially Laura, who showed them off to her friends, took them to museums, the zoo, and the beach, and lavished on them expensive clothes.

Laura's family was close with aunts, uncles, cousins, and grandparents visiting frequently and socializing together. When she married, her family embraced her husband, a chemical engineer, as it had her sister's.

At the time, Laura, who had a bubbly and friendly personality, was a museum tour guide who was well liked and seemed to enjoy her work. In their first six years of marriage she and Mark had three daughters who, while not as precocious as Laura's nephews, were bright, inquisitive, and pretty children. Laura loved her three little girls but felt a private sadness, a sadness she denied even to herself, that she did not have a son.

About ten years into the marriage, Laura remembers that she began to feel restless and smothered. She talked about going to law school, investing with a friend in a tony San Francisco beauty salon, studying Eastern culture. In the end she took a job as an executive secretary for a clothing manufacturer.

It was around this time that she began finding a lot of fault with her husband and children. Michelle was sloppy. Robin didn't study enough. Naomi was lazy. She accused Mark of taking no responsibility in their marriage for anything except earning money. She was the cleaner, the clothes washer, the shopper, the bookkeeper, the social director. "All he wanted to do was sit around and watch television and be with me and the kids," she told me. "If I planned a trip, we went. If I cooked a meal, he ate. If I rearranged the furniture, he liked it. But he didn't initiate, he didn't plan. It drove me crazy."

Laura admits now that Mark tried to respond. He washed all the clothes, made the children's doctors' appointments, cleaned the house. She was the envy of her friends, who kept saying, 'If only my husband did a tenth of what yours does. . . .' But it wasn't enough. After three years of therapy, Laura now concedes that no matter what Mark had done, it probably would not have been enough. "The truth was I just fell out of love with him. I lost respect for him. He was too wishy-washy and didn't have much pizzazz. I guess I really wanted him to be famous and wealthy and a great golfer like my brother-in-law. So I picked on everything. I was just so unhappy, and I needed a different kind of husband, one who was more interesting, who would make me feel better about myself."

Laura's style was, alternately, to vent her feelings by screaming and throwing pots around the kitchen, then to distance herself emotionally from her husband and children. During those times there was no conversation and the air was thick with tension.

"We would sit at dinner, and Mom would just serve us without saying a word," remembers Michelle, the oldest daughter, now twenty-eight. "Sometimes she would eat with us. Sometimes she would eat later. Dad tried to act as though nothing were wrong. He would say, 'Naomi, do you want more salad?' 'Robin, you're not eating. Don't you like spaghetti anymore?' 'Michelle, what did you do in school today?'

"She would always be mad at all of us for every little thing. And then after a few days of the silent treatment, she would say, 'Let's talk. We have to communicate.' Except the only communicator was her. She had her opinions and there was no room for any of us to say anything. So we didn't. We just listened and went out with our friends or up to our room or something. I guess she thought she accomplished something. I don't know."

"The one lesson I learned growing up," says Naomi, "was that you don't tangle with Mom because you can't win."

Laura and Mark's marriage was characterized by a combination of "distancing," "open conflict," and "adapting." Laura's failure to communicate not only moved her away from her family emotionally but distanced her children from her, their father, and from each other. Everyone learned that the way to deal with conflict was not to deal with it, to retreat into their own activities, to wait for Mom to calm down and for the immediate crisis to subside.

Laura distanced herself physically and emotionally by turning to a series of affairs, some of them with her husband's friends. Her children watched a lot of television when they were young, escaping into the world of others.

As they grew older, they lived separate existences from each other and from their parents, even though they occupied the same house.

Naomi avoided problems at home by joining drama groups in junior high and high school. She stayed at school as late as possible rehearsing for plays. Robin turned to photography and spent long days and nights alone in her basement darkroom. None of the children had strong relationships with friends.

Mark, meanwhile, focused on his work, which took him out of town frequently. He stayed away longer than he needed to; when he returned, it was almost always to an angry wife, sullen and moody because she felt saddled with the responsibilities of the home and children during his absence.

The cycle continued. More screaming. More pot throwing. More silence. More distance. More trips. More affairs.

Laura and Mark were divorced when the children were in their early teens. The divorce was bitter and angry and ended up where the parents stopped communicating about everything, including the children. Neither has remarried. Now, fourteen years later, they still do not speak.

When Divorce Occurs . . . and Problems Remain

In this case, the divorce solved nothing. Relationships among the family members remain strained. The children cannot mention the name of either parent to the other. Both their mother and father complained to them about each other and are still accusing the other of breaking up the marriage. Most important, neither has gone on to build new and nurturing relationships for themselves.

"I don't see where the divorce accomplished anything," says Michelle. "Neither my mother nor father has changed, and the way they act keeps getting in the way of their relationships with other men and women. They just can't see it that way. But the way I look at it, they might as well have stayed married.''

Michelle admits that she, too, has problems with relationships. "I went with one guy for a couple of years and I thought I really liked him. We liked doing the same things and I counted on marrying him eventually.

"But at one of my friend's twenty-first birthday parties, I met a few other guys that I liked, and I began going out with them. I kind of liked that. No commitment. A different guy every weekend. No one to keep tabs on me. No one to answer to. No one to tell me to hang up my skirt or do the laundry.

"I don't think I'll ever marry. Maybe I'll live with someone for a while. But I don't have any faith it would last. I wouldn't want it to.''

While none of the daughters was focused on by either parent, they all learned from their family the styles of distance and avoidance. Friends and family members complain that the girls are remote and that they have difficulty communicating with them. None of the women is interested in marriage; all tend to move in and out of superficial relationships. Among the three, only Robin is concerned about her failure to connect with people. She is in therapy and is just beginning to see that her family's style of distancing does not have to be hers.

Marilyn: Their Divorce Solved Nothing

Marilyn, the woman we described earlier, whose mother left home to pursue a relationship with a rock star, had a similar experience. She laments that the divorce of her parents did not solve the problems that existed between them. Her mother continued to blame her failed marriage on her husband. He was too boring. Too staid. Too clinging. She needed excitement, stimulation, parties, and dancing. They were, she kept saying, "a bad fit.''

Her father protested that he was a good and kind husband, a loving father; he earned a substantial income and was readily willing to socialize with family or friends. He conceded that he had few interests outside of his family and his job and that he probably was "not the most exciting person to live with." The divorce, however, changed nothing. The happiness Marilyn's mother sought continued to elude her. And her father did not take advantage of the opportunity to pursue new interests.

In the beginning her mother's first boyfriend, Steve, was all of the things her mother said she needed. They amassed a wide circle of friends, entertained a lot, took classes in photography and practiced transcendental meditation. But within a year, it all blew up. And Mom was right back where she started from, unhappy and blaming Steve for not living up to his promise. Subsequent relationships proved no more successful.

Father, on the other hand, settled down to a quiet, uneventful life. He dated three or four women, but each time the romance fizzled for precisely the same reasons his marriage had failed. Women complained that he was too intense with them, too smothering, and he seemed to have no life that was important to him outside of their relationship. He kept talking about going back to school, about joining a gym, about playing golf again, but in the end he leaned back in his overstuffed leather recliner and watched reruns.

Each of Marilyn's parents continues (twenty-one years later) to defend himself or herself and heap responsibility for the demise of the marriage on the other. But neither of them has found a satisfying life. And neither of them has examined, with honesty or clarity, his or her role in the breakup.

In terms of Marilyn's growth, her parents have set a poor example. I believe that the people who get through divorce well are those who have gone beyond the idea of "winners" and "losers." They have advanced past blame and admit how each of them contributed to the downfall of the marriage. With this done, each of them has been able to go on to a better life, one that gives them more happiness and satisfaction.

No matter how painful a divorce is for children, as they grow up and acquire a better balance of reason and emotion, they can accept it more comfortably if they see how it has resolved problems, if they can see that their parents have made better choices the second time around. Those choices do not necessarily need to include a relationship or subsequent marriage but should reflect a more fulfilling and meaningful life. Where that has happened, the children can often emerge with a healthier view of themselves and of what the future can offer. Where it has not, where the husband/wife problems persist, they remain part of the children's problems as they grow up because, in essence, the divorce has solved nothing.

Conflict and Cooperation

All of the family styles I have described—avoiding and distancing, focusing on another person or thing, adapting or volatile conflicting—imprint children's minds with relationship styles that influence their future behavior.

However, differences between people are not avoidable. Indeed, life would be boring without them. And conflict is not always marked by heated anger, hostility, bitterness, and violence. Conflict, in fact, often has its pluses, bringing about productive change and resolution of problems.

In some marriages, husband and wife believe that the most effective resolution of their problems may be divorce. But even when that happens, children do not need to suffer.

Some parents, including those with stormy levels of conflict, can separate their roles as parents from their roles as spouses. These are the parents who are mature enough to recognize that their hated spouse is also the beloved parent of their children. They are the parents who can keep the conflict where it belongs—between them—and prevent it from focusing on their children. They are the parents who can cooperate with each other without feeling compromised.

Conflict that blames the other person, that undermines the other person's self-esteem, is too personal to allow any kind of resolution. It brings about hostile and heated reactions that cannot help escalating the discord. On the other hand, people who recognize that there are differences between them, even irreconcilable ones, but do not attack each other personally, can resolve their clashes more amicably.

There is a difference between saying to your wife, "I'm divorcing you because you are not a good wife for me, but I recognize that you have good qualities" and saying "I'm divorcing you because you are a bad person."

A study by Kathleen A. Camara and Gary Resnick of Tufts University reveals that the social behavior of children from both divorced and nondivorced families seems to be related to how their parents manage conflict and whether they can work together cooperatively as parents. When parents can push past anger, animosity, and accusations, their children stand a better chance of coming through the divorce in sound mental health. Two years after the divorce, the researchers found, these children were less aggressive, had higher self-esteem, and got along better with friends.

Surprisingly, the intensity of the conflict between the parents did not *always* predict their degree of cooperation about their children. Often, where conflict was low and cooperation was expected to be high, it was not. And sometimes parents who were unable to forgive each other for such piercing bruises as extramarital affairs and physical violence were able to work out cooperative communication around their children, who remained a common concern.

While this study looked at children just two years after their parents' divorce, I believe that the results persist. I find that children carry into adulthood the debris of their parents' unresolved relationships. Where parents are still openly critical of each other, where they remain prisoners of their anger, where they are always trying to "get back" at their spouse, children grow up handicapped in their abilities to negotiate personal relationships successfully. They often bungle attempts at intimacy and have an appalling inability to see a world outside of themselves.

Many have become so practiced in concealing their feelings that they don't know how to engage in the give-and-take of an intimate relationship. This is especially true for a child who had to stifle his or her affection for the other parent in order to please the parent he lived with.

Sometimes that child develops a "please the gatekeeper" mentality. He has learned that the person (usually the custodial parent) who controls the basics—love, food, shelter, activities, nurturing—has a lot of power, and he is terrified of tampering with that. Those same feelings often determine how he manages intimate relationships. He sees his love interest as the power broker and he is not able to express his own feelings freely and appropriately. There is too much risk, the ultimate one being the loss of the relationship.

Others employ different tactics. They may distance themselves, physically or emotionally, because that's how they have learned to survive tense times or emotional pressure. They may try to manipulate the other person if that is the technique they have come to rely on. They may create situations that will nudge someone they care about into rejecting them. Or they may do the rejecting before someone else does it first.

However they express it, the legacy handed down by their parents continues to put relationships with intimate partners in jeopardy. Ghosts from the past don't stay buried, and relationship patterns travel with people, cropping up inopportunely with unwelcome consequences.

Children who never see parents work out serious disagreements often come to recognize that they have grown up disadvantaged. I have frequently heard troubled adults say, "I don't know how people resolve personal conflicts because I never saw my parents do it. I've never seen a normal, healthy relationship between a man and woman up close."

Divorced parents, on the other hand, who recognize that they were not suitable mates for each other but continue to treat each other with respect, teach their children productive ways of settling differences and free them to move on in a healthy way with their own relationships.

PART THREE

Breaking the Cycle

CHAPTER SIXTEEN

———/———

Becoming Free

As we have seen, the effects of divorce can be profound. As an adult child of divorce, you have had a shattering experience that has undermined your ability to trust for a long time to come. You are, perhaps, feeling disconnected from your roots since access to relatives diminished. And you certainly have had to juggle a web of complex relationships including step-this and half-that, and carve out new ways of connecting to both of your parents. Even more important in the long run, you have had to contend with a family style that existed before the divorce, during the divorce, and after the divorce while your family reorganized. It is a style that was often immature and damaging and became even more exaggerated during the painful process of divorce when everyone's maturity level took a turn for the worse.

It is hardly surprising that you will have been affected emotionally in ways that will always stay with you. That doesn't mean, however, that you are doomed to repeat your parents' mistakes and are destined to have the fallout of their divorce trail you through life. It does not mean that you must suffer through poor choices in partners and participate in failed relationships.

You may not be able to change your parents. But with awareness and certain guidelines you can change yourself. You can learn how to develop and maintain meaningful and happy relationships.

The key is the extent to which you can extricate yourself from your parents' problems and become emotionally independent of a family style of relating that does not work for you.

How do you do it?

First, you have to identify what that family style is and how you are still reacting to it. It is like having to learn the kinds of emotional nutrients you have been absorbing all of your life and recognizing the effect they have on you.

All of our families have their own characteristics, but it is surprising how few of us, without consciously looking for them, know what they are. And without knowing what they are, where they come from, or, indeed, that they exist in the first place, it is not possible to change our own behavior patterns.

This scavenger hunt into your past may not feel good at first, and you may wonder why you need to do it. But before long you will start to see how powerful family feelings and behaviors linger and influence your intimate relationships now. Lightbulbs will go off in your mind as you say to yourself, "But of course. Why didn't I see that? Why didn't I make that connection?"

An ideal place to start is with your parents' courtship and marriage. In most cases they cared enough about each other to have made the decision to marry in the first place. And somewhere along the way the fire turned to ice. You need to know how and why that happened. These four issues are often good barometers:

- Communication
- Criticism
- Credibility
- Time together

Communication. Marriages that end in divorce usually go through stages. One of them is a move away from open communication and an energizing exchange of information to closed communication and a listless exchange of information.

For example, in courtship and early marriage, when two people are trying to learn about each other, there is usually a lot of shared information about all kinds of things—personal (how I feel about my mother), professional (how I feel about my work), religious (how I feel about God), and emotional (who I am). Both man and woman are struggling to learn whether they can be soul mates for life.

This openness is easier to accomplish in the absence of a commitment such as marriage. If it doesn't work, if there is too much conflict, too much anxiety, too many differences, the relationship can always end.

Once the decision to marry has been made, the picture changes. Now there is a commitment, one that most people want to last. It becomes more difficult to introduce sticky issues that may threaten the relationship.

But during the first years of marriage there are still so many differences to resolve. All of the rituals and traditions of two families need to be blended and worked out. Some are critical. Will we have children? When? Who will work? Who will cook? When do we visit the in-laws? Others are less monumental, but no less traumatic. Do we open the presents Christmas Eve or Christmas Day? Do we go dancing or to the movies? Who takes the clothes to the cleaner? Who makes sure we don't run out of toothpaste?

Because settling differences always generates anxiety, husband and wife begin to choose the issues around which they will take stands. And communication, during the first year or two of marriage, usually becomes somewhat less open than it was during courtship.

During the next several years a style of communication emerges that is a blend of both partners' original family patterns. Sometimes, with luck, therapy, or insight, that pattern leads to an acceptable way of communicating, one that fosters stability and satisfies the needs of both husband and wife.

Often, depending on family style, it doesn't. And the spouses move further away from each other, talking about fewer things, expressing fewer opinions, exchanging less meaningful information, avoiding unpleasant or controversial issues or constantly fighting about them.

Criticism. During courtship and early marriage, there are attempts to understand your partner's behavior and keep criticism to a minimum. But as the marriage settles down and partners stop trying so hard to please each other, they often begin to blame the other one for problems.

"If you had remembered to call the plumber, we wouldn't have had a flood in the bathroom."

"If you had insisted she do her homework, she wouldn't be flunking Spanish."

"If you hadn't wanted to have a baby, we wouldn't be in this financial mess."

Sometimes the blame is articulated. Sometimes it is smothered. In either case, the pattern becomes blaming the other person instead of accepting appropriate responsibility yourself. And it corrodes a marriage.

Credibility. A relationship often deteriorates because one or both partners lose trust in the other. His or her behavior is no longer predictable, and he or she can't be relied upon to be sensitive to the needs and concerns of the other. Sometimes this happens when the husband or wife becomes involved in extramarital affairs. Sometimes it comes with more innocent lies about smaller issues.

"I worked late at the office." Later he learns that she went out dancing with friends.

"I've given up gambling." She finds pari-mutuel tickets in his jacket pocket.

"I'll meet you at nine thirty." She doesn't show up until eleven.

"I always tell you the truth." He confesses, a year later, that he has been bisexual since he was twenty-two.

Credibility suffers when one partner tries to manipulate the other, when he says things he doesn't mean, when she tries to get a competitive edge. One of my patients, for instance, convinced her husband that they should rent an apartment in New York where they could enjoy weekends of theater and museums. He was overjoyed until he learned, a year later, that his wife was arranging to leave the marriage and had planned that the apartment would become her permanent home.

Another patient asked her husband to take a karate class with her, fully knowing he would not be interested. A friend revealed that her invitation was a ploy. At the time she extended it, she and another lawyer in her firm had been enrolled in the class for two weeks. Karate every Tuesday was a prelude to a late-night rendezvous in his apartment.

Time Together. During courtship and in the first months of marriage, couples spend as much time together as possible. They share activities, try to develop an interest in their partner's hobbies, and enjoy exploring the world as a team. This togetherness becomes tempered with time, of course, but it is a danger sign when husband and wife are no longer interested in being together and in sharing activities, when she can't wait for him to go on a business trip, when he tells her to do the things she wants to do with a friend instead.

Deteriorating marriages are often marked by partners who move in different social circles, have totally different interests, and take separate vacations. They become strangers to each other and eventually there is no marriage.

The importance of all of this for you, the adult child of divorce, is that your family style—avoidance, adaptation, conflict, or focusing on someone else—determined the course of all of these critical issues.

And it is the way these issues—communication, criticism, credibility, and time together—are played out that fortifies or chips away at a marriage. Moreover, that same family style dictates how *you* are likely to deal with those issues as they evolve for you in your intimate relationships. If, for instance, you tend to distance yourself from your partner physically or emotionally when you disagree, you will end up with poor communication, a certain mark of a deteriorating relationship.

You need to understand better the situations, the words, the behavior from others, that trigger reactions in you. And you need to break the cycle by changing those reactions where they originated—with your parents.

Some people are unable to make this journey into the past alone. For them, working with a therapist may be an appropriate way to begin. He or she will help you identify your family style. Working together, you can see the ways in which you are still reacting to that style, perhaps by repeating it, perhaps by rebelling against it.

At some point you will have achieved enough insight into your past, into your multigenerational history and the part you played in it, to be able to go back to your parents and ask them to talk with you about their own courtship.

Why?

You need to get information about your past that is not accessible to you without them. As a child, you may have been aware of the way your family behaved, but you couldn't see and probably still can't see that that behavior is part of a predictable pattern that makes your family unique, that gives it its own special stamp, the stamp that you imprint on your relationships now.

In order to change that pattern, you must get a balanced view of both your parents. You need to stop seeing one parent as the victimizer and the other as the victim. Until you do, you remain entangled in a triangle that paralyzes your ability to pursue relationships in a satisfying way.

There are fixed times, universal times, in the lives of all families—courtship, two or three years after marriage, birth of the first child, the last child leaving home—when people are forced to come to grips with differences. Knowing how your family handled them will allow you to see the way communication and credibility deteriorated between your parents. You will be able to recognize that communication breaks down because it is regulated by family style. It doesn't help to urge people to "communicate better." If they could, they would. It is their family style that has to change. That's what you need to work on.

Why is their courtship important to you?

Learning about your parents' courtship can often give you clues about their divorce and why it occurred. I believe that courtship patterns are similar to divorce patterns; people get married the way they get divorced. Those who have tempestuous courtships marked by oozing love and scintillating moments will, if they divorce, usually wrench apart bitterly, painfully, and punitively. Falling in and out of love are accompanied by the same degree of intensity—only the direction is different.

Ask your parents these questions:

How did they meet?

How long did they know each other before they married?

Can they remember being in love?

What attracted them to each other?

What was their parents' reaction to their decision to marry?

Did they know each other well before they married?

Did they talk about important issues, such as differences in religion, their ideas about having and raising children, how they felt about *their* parents?

What was the environment in the family when you were born? Ask about the contentment level of the family at that time. Had there been recent deaths, births, marriages? Were both parents happy in their work and personal lives? Was your birth planned? Ask those same questions about your brothers and sisters.

When do your parents remember falling out of love?

At what point(s) did they stop communicating with each other?

Did they start blaming each other for problems in the marriage? What kind of problems? When did that start?

What would they say caused their eventual divorce?

Do they feel the divorce solved their problems? Do you think it did?

What kind of relationship do they have with their own parents? How did their mother and father relate to each other? How did they resolve differences?

What kind of relationship do they have with their siblings, aunts, uncles, and cousins?

As you gather this information, you will begin to identify the kind of family you come from, how it handled differences, and why.

You will be able to see more clearly whether your family is one that conflicts . . . or adapts . . . or avoids . . . or, most important for you, focuses on someone else.

Then you need to see whether that someone else is you.

CHAPTER SEVENTEEN

———————— / ————————

Where You Fit In

Where do you fit into your family's behavior pattern? How did your parents involve you as you were growing up? How did you react? How are you still reacting?

All children are affected by discord in their families. But often it is one child, more than others, who is caught up and entangled in family struggles. Sometimes it is a child with a chronic illness such as a congenital heart condition, or a disability such as a permanent limp resulting from an automobile accident. It may be the firstborn child or the last. Sometimes it is simply the child who, because of his or her temperament, responds most emotionally to the parents' problems.

In any case, it is this child on whom the parents focus their anxiety. They treat him or her mainly based on their own needs and anxieties, without being aware of the child's needs. That child becomes the family "scapegoat." When the parents' tension escalates, they calm themselves by shifting their attention to the child.

A number of intriguing studies, particularly by Dr. Salvador Minuchin, a pioneer of family therapy, professor at the University of Pennsylvania and New York University, and author of *Families and Family Therapy* and *Institutionalizing Madness,* show that many children with intractable asthma or diabetes develop actual physical symptoms when a family conflict occurs.

In these families the child's physiology is so tuned in to the tension between parents that as soon as it happens, the child gets anxious and develops symptoms associated with the illness. The child with asthma begins to wheeze. The child with diabetes experiences elevations in blood sugar. Then the parents unite around the child and avoid their own problems.

This kind of child grows up unconsciously feeling that this is his or her role. That he or she is needed to maintain the family system. When the family's real conflicts cannot surface, everyone lives in a chronic state of stress.

When divorce occurs in a child-focused family, it is likely that the child will continue to play the same role throughout the divorce and afterward. He or she will be more caught up in the divorce than his brothers and sisters, and over time his or her sense of self-identity will become more entwined in his relationship with his parents. His emotional autonomy will be seriously damaged; he will be less able to rely on himself and will have poor self-esteem.

Sometimes these children never leave home. Sometimes they leave and pretend to grow up. Some quickly substitute another family for their own. What they do is regulated by the amount of anxiety they feel about becoming a responsible adult.

It is this child who, as he or she grows up, has the most difficulty with intimate relationships. Let us see why.

If your parents' anxieties and conflicts were processed through you, you tended to become more "relationship-oriented" than "task-oriented." This means that your energy was diverted from the job of growing up and dealing with your own stages of development. You became invested instead in your parents and their problems. As your parents' anxiety increased, your relationship with them centered around mutual worry and concern. And your parents continued to turn to you as a way of seeking comfort and reducing their own turbulence.

The more entangled, intense, and emotionally reactive you became to your parents' difficulties, the more your life became governed by feelings—theirs and yours—and less by rational thinking and reflection. The more your parents put you in a compromising situation and urged you to take sides, the more enmeshed with their problems you became, and the less freedom you had to develop your independence.

Take Nancy, for instance. Nancy is the oldest of three sisters and a brother and had always had a close relationship with her mother, who grew up as an only child. To Nancy's mother her oldest daughter was the sister she never had. While she loved all of her children, Nancy was clearly her favorite. She was a brilliant student, was popular with friends, and had an easygoing, pleasant disposition.

When her father had his first affair, Nancy's mother turned to her for comfort. Nancy was then thirteen. "What shall we do?" her mother pleaded, immediately drawing Nancy into the problem between her and her husband. Nancy got the message. She felt it was her responsibility to find an answer.

That night she interceded. She waited up until midnight when her father returned from his job as banquet manager of a large hotel. She confronted him about his affair. He cried. She cried. And he promised her he would stop seeing the other woman.

Nancy's father had two more affairs before he filed for divorce. Each time, Nancy ran interference. The triangle was clear—Nancy and her mother against her father.

When the divorce was final, Nancy felt she had failed, that she had let her mother down. But she continued to be the family mediator. She, not her mother, was the one who called her dad when the support check was late, when her sister Betsy broke her leg skiing, when there was a fire in their house. Even after she became an adult and moved out on her own, she carried her family role with her, protecting her mother and scolding her father. It took almost a year in therapy for her to see that she continued this pattern in her relationships with men.

As an adult, you are still reacting to the scenario of your childhood. It is most apparent when you try to negotiate intimate relationships of your own. Because you have not emotionally separated from your family, you are still acting out the anxieties you have absorbed at home and playing the roles prescribed for you by your parents.

Your ability to be behaviorally mature is seriously impaired because you have not learned how to separate thinking from feeling. And you are less able to separate *your* thoughts and feelings from those of close family members. The way you behave is almost totally governed by your emotional reactions to your environment or to other people. You have a poor sense of who you are and, in many ways, you may be an emotional appendage to the relationships around you.

You need to find out whether you played that role in your family and how reactive you were—and still are—to the destructive position in which your parents placed you.

Jennie, for instance, was the youngest of three sisters. Her father was a workaholic who believed that his job was to earn a living and his wife's job was everything else. Jennie's parents spent little time together, although they did take family vacations and give big holiday parties. Jennie's mother, a quiet, accommodating woman, was thrilled when her oldest daughter expressed an aptitude for tennis, a sport in which, as a teenager, she had longed to excel. She encouraged Jennie to take lessons, practice every day, and enter matches.

As her marriage deteriorated, Jennie's mother shifted her energies to Jennie and her tennis. She went to every match, became the assistant coach, and traveled with the team. Jennie's tennis became her lifeline. And Jennie became responsible for maintaining it.

Even when she realized that she did not want to be a professional tennis player, she felt that she couldn't stop. Her mother wouldn't tolerate it. Her mother counted on her, not only to be a tennis champion, but to be enthusiastic about it.

When Jennie was twenty-five and in a relationship with Danny, she became bulimic. She says that her relationship with him was "inadequate," as had been two previous relationships, and that she felt tremendous pressure and responsibility for the course of the romance.

She felt it was her job to keep Danny happy. Even if it meant that she had to go skiing when she hated the cold. Or had to cancel an important appointment at work because he wanted to leave town early. When they had an argument, she chided herself because she was convinced it must be her fault.

After a year in therapy, Jennie could see the pattern. She could recognize that her role at home as she grew up still tagged along with her.

"Of course," Jennie says now, "I thought my job was to make the most important person in my life happy. First my mother. Then Danny. I didn't think much about what would make *me* happy. I just reacted the way I had done all my life. I had so much free-floating anxiety that I didn't know what to do with. Bulimia gave me an out—it gave me something concrete to be anxious about."

After several weeks in therapy, Jennie began to understand that bulimia had been just a substitute for tennis, that Danny was just a substitute for her mother. Because her relationship with her mother was organized around tennis, it was natural for her to develop something—the bulimia—around which she and Danny could organize *their* relationship.

Once Jennie recognized the similarity, she began to pick up her own behavior patterns. About eight months after she began therapy, Jennie went home to Charlotte, North Carolina, to talk with her parents.

She says that it has been painful and that she sometimes leaves her parents' home frustrated and angry. But she believes that she has made a good start toward a healthier, more honest relationship with them. "I've just taken the first step," Jennie says. "But now that the connections are clearer to me, I think I can begin to short-circuit them."

CHAPTER EIGHTEEN

———/———

Putting It Together

When you are able to put together your new insights about your own behavior patterns and the information you have received from your parents about their past (which is also *your* past), when you have been able to figure out the kind of family you come from and can see the extent to which you were drawn into your parents' problems, you can begin to let go of that role. It is a role that may have worked for you and your family as long as you lived at home. But as soon as you began to separate from them and form your own relationships, the reactive patterns you carried with you were as destructive to you as they were to them.

As you let go, you will be able to create a more emotionally independent life for yourself and be freer of the legacy handed down to you by your parents. That freedom will also allow you, perhaps for the first time in your life, to become closer to your parents. You will be able to react more calmly with them around emotionally charged issues, feel relief from longtime tensions, and develop a healthy, mutually fulfilling relationship with them. Doing that will also be a giant step toward establishing a more satisfying relationship with your intimate partner.

Do not expect it to be easy. For one thing, your parents may be reluctant to answer your questions. Particularly if your family style is one of avoidance or distance, sharing personal information may be threatening and uncomfortable.

How you encourage them to do it will tell you about *your* personal style. Do you give up? Do you persist? Do you argue? Do you get angry and leave? Do you find other ways to get the information you need? How do you settle this difference between you and your parent? The information you get from your parents and the activity around your getting it will provoke an emotional reaction from you. You will become anxious. And so will they. It is guaranteed to feel uncomfortable at first.

You may wonder: Why am I doing this? Isn't the point to *decrease* anxiety, not to stir it up? Yes, eventually. But first you need to resurrect some of the reaction processes that are deep within you, unrecognized, but that are damaging your ability to develop closeness.

In some ways it is like desensitizing yourself, the way people with phobias are treated. If they are afraid of heights, they stay off elevators. If they panic at going outdoors, they stay at home. But they do it at the expense of a healthy, vital life. When they are exposed, gradually, to the very things they are afraid of and recognize that their fears are without foundation, they can overcome the phobia. In the same way, if you recognize the way you express anxiety, then change that way, those around you will have to change their behavior too. And you can begin to make real progress toward more fulfilling relationships.

If you discover that you cover anxiety by always talking, try listening. If you are a "distancer," try moving closer. If you have always talked to your mother, approach your father. Taking the opposite position is not a magical quick fix. But it will allow you to experience a relationship in a different way.

Understanding the way your family worked is the first important step. But it is not enough. Eventually understanding has to be coupled with action. The value of going back, of talking with parents and grandparents, is that it is an action step. It forces you to do something with the insights you have gained through therapy, to put them back in the place where they occurred. As you talk, your emotional responses . . . and theirs . . . will start to make sense because of the new perspective you have. Your ability to react less emotionally, more calmly, to them will make all the difference.

It will also help you see more clearly the way you tend to react when dealing with your parents on an adult basis. Because you are provoking reactions deliberately, they will become more obvious to you. Armed with new information and knowing what to look for, you will begin to "catch yourself" and your parents reacting in familiar ways. You've always done the dance. Now you are learning the steps.

How well you recognize those steps, how well you become aware of your own "emotional reactivity," will determine your ability to change.

First, you need to change the way you react to your parents. As you do, your parent(s) will undoubtedly become upset. Your new reactions destabilize the status quo. What your parents will really be telling you, without realizing it, is, "Don't change. We want you to be the way you were"—even if the way you were doesn't work for you.

Elva's father, a controlling man in his early fifties, had always made the decisions in his marriage to Elva's mother. Because Elva's mother was an alcoholic, the triangle that was created was Elva and her father allied against the mother. But when Elva asked her father to answer her questions about his past, he refused to talk to her. He said he had remarried and that his life with her mom was a blur to him, a time that he preferred to forget. He told Elva she would be better off forgetting it too.

Unable to persuade him, Elva decided to talk to her grandmother, her father's mother. Until then, Elva had never visited her grandmother alone. Her father always planned the visits, when they would occur, how long they would last, and what they would do. When he learned from his mother that his daughter was traveling to Milwaukee to see her and that Elva hadn't consulted him about her decision, he became agitated and anxious. Something was happening that he couldn't control. The triangle was shifting.

His reaction was anger and a warning to Elva that what she had done was not acceptable. Elva's reaction was the temptation to do what she had always done when her father became upset . . . to be compliant, to cancel the visit. But because she had provoked her father's response, she could see more objectively what was happening. When she defied her father, when he felt out of control, he got angry. She was afraid of losing his love, so she retreated. That was the way it had always been. This behavior successfully impeded communication between them, and as a result Elva and her father didn't know each other very well.

Elva could see that she repeated the same behavior with men. She could see, for instance, that she did the same thing with her boyfriend, Sonny, that she did with her father. Sonny kept talking about the importance of "togetherness" in a relationship. What he meant was that Elva and he should always agree to "do it his way." When she didn't, he got angry. Unable to tolerate that, Elva would suppress her own feelings and back off. She *adapted*.

But doing that made her angry. She was angry a lot. But she didn't communicate her feelings to Sonny. If she did, maybe he would leave her. It had been six months now, and

Elva could see that communication between her and Sonny was not good.

The incident with her father, before she ever met with him or her grandmother, before any questions were asked or answered, had already helped her see the connection between her past and her present. She could identify, clearly, that her own emotional reactivity was triggered by a relationship pattern that mimicked the one she had with her father.

CHAPTER NINETEEN

———/———

Safeguarding Your Marriage

As the adult child of divorced parents, you already know that you are at greater risk of divorce yourself. If you were the child on whom one or both of your parents focused during their marriage and divorce, and you are still reacting to that, your risk is even higher. And if you don't have a clue as to why your parents' marriage failed, you may be headed for trouble in your own. That's why it is especially important, at the time you are developing an intimate relationship that you hope will lead to marriage, that you seek help yourself. If you have never done it before, it is an appropriate time to talk with a therapist.

You wouldn't hesitate to take a mammogram if you were at high risk for breast cancer. Or to consult an electrician if the wiring in your house were frayed. You should not hesitate to take the steps that may strengthen your own relationship and prevent your own marriage from unraveling.

With the help of a therapist trained in marital and family relationships, you can develop a new perspective about the way you relate to the intimate person in your life and develop a timetable for the important step of going back in time with your parents.

You should ask yourself a few critical questions about yourself and the person with whom you are contemplating spending the rest of your life.

Why are you marrying?

Why do you want to marry *this* person?

Why does he/she want to marry you?

Are you primarily uniting against a common enemy, your respective families?

Is your spouse-to-be someone else's victim? And are you marrying to save him or her?

Can you identify the patterns each of you displays in your relationship?

Is one of you an "emotional distancer" and the other an "emotional pursuer"? Does one of you want to talk things over, while the other wants to avoid talking?

Is one of you always accommodating to the other?

Are you or your partner always "giving in" instead of communicating your feelings and airing out an issue?

Is either of you afraid of commitment?

Are you afraid of being betrayed?

In all instances, a probe of the past will help you understand that your own style of relating didn't spring up in isolation. You will learn about yourself and your family, and you'll find connections you never dreamed of that are influencing your behavioral style today. Family secrets and forbidden topics, important for your growth and your freedom, will be revealed. And you will be able to enter a relationship with less anxiety and more confidence that it will work.

Raising a Family

Because the birth of a child is so pivotal a point in people's lives, it forces a confrontation with differences and a search for ways to resolve them. How well you do that will depend on how thoroughly you understand the family style you came from, your own emotional reactions, and the kinds of situations that trigger them.

If you haven't probed your past before, this is a good time to begin. You might want to do it against the backdrop of these important child-rearing issues that place stress on a marriage:

How will you handle differences of opinion about how your child should be raised? Suppose one of you wants public school and the other demands private school? Suppose one of you thinks Santa Claus and the Easter Bunny should visit and the other doesn't? Suppose one of you thinks weekly visits to grandparents are essential and the other thinks they are a waste of time?

What about feelings of jealousy that might arise because of the child's demands?

Will you feel overwhelmed by the additional responsibilities of parenting? How will you manage?

Will you overcorrect for the deficits in your own upbringing? If you weren't allowed to play after school, will you allow your child to play until midnight? If you couldn't have dessert until you finished dinner, will you allow your children to eat anything they want? If your parents left you with babysitters too often, will you always stay at home with your child?

Issues of overcompensation should concern someone like Ronnie, the psychiatrist who spent so much of his life searching for his father. Ronnie has said, "Everything I do in my life is for my sons. I want them to have from me what I missed from my father." That's fine as long as it doesn't get too intense, as long as the marriage doesn't get so heavily focused on the children that it prevents husband and wife from developing a sense of who they are.

Issues around raising a child provide fertile territory for conflict. But you need to remember that you are in control of the behavioral messages you give your children. The perpetuation or alteration of family patterns—good ones and harmful ones—is up to you. Your children will absorb them the same way you did. What do you want them to learn?

CHAPTER TWENTY

———————/———————

Children of Divorce
Grown Up

The men and women you will read about in the following chapters are at various stages in their search for fulfilling intimate relationships. They experienced their parents' divorces at different ages, a few even as adults. In one case the parents have been separated for thirty years but are not yet divorced.

In some cases the divorce was a cooperative one in which the parents were able to make the best interests of their children a high priority. Other situations were rife with tension and conflict, and children became the pawns in a punitive divorce. Some had close relationships with their noncustodial parent; others rarely saw that parent. Some had strong support systems among family and friends; others felt isolated and alone. In some cases there were remarriages and the complexities of stepfamilies; in others the parents remained single.

You will see examples of all of the family styles we have described, and as you read the stories of adult children of divorce, you will find parallels in your own family. You will be able to identify the behaviors that feel familiar to you.

Most important, you will see that many adults of divorce are not destroyed by their parents' breakup. The key issue is whether their parents have demonstrated for them effective and cooperative ways of resolving differences.

Each of the following chapters describes an adult of divorce and his or her current dilemmas about relationships. It looks backward to his growing-up experiences in his original family, defines the style that characterizes that family, and draws the connection between the past and the present. Finally, integrating what has been learned in earlier chapters, it suggests what that person can do to turn his or her life around.

These specific situations may not totally mirror yours, but they will give you a framework within which you can consider changing your perspective.

No book can give you magically all the answers or, overnight, reverse patterns that have built up through a lifetime. But this can be an enlightening beginning. With determination, courage, and fresh insights, you can take the first steps toward rich and rewarding connections.

PART FOUR

Siblings of Divorce

CHAPTER TWENTY-ONE

---/---

Same Divorce, Same Parents, Different Views

When I talk with brothers and sisters about the divorce of their parents, I sometimes wonder whether they are describing the same family. Johnny says his father is warm and caring; his sister Mary says that the same man is distant and detached.

Irene insists her parents were always "indifferent" to each other, while her twin brothers, who are four years older, portray the same mother and father as having been devoted and loving. Their marriage broke up, they said, because they grew apart in later years.

Based on the dramatically different ways siblings react to their parents' divorce, it is clear that each is viewing—and responding to—the family through a different lens. This happens because every child grows up in his private, unique environment, which may be totally different from that of his brothers and sisters.

Children enter the world under different circumstances. The parents who were ecstatic when their son was born because life was going well for them may have been down in the dumps by the time their daughter came along three years later. Her birth may have followed the loss of a job or the death of a grandparent. The mood in the family will influence the feelings and behavior of the child.

Birth order matters, too. Parents respond to their first-born differently than to their sixth child, and children who join a family with brothers and sisters enter a different environment than the child who comes first.

Some children are temperamentally more compatible with their parents than others. And it is no secret that parents often have favorites, whether or not they admit it.

All of these things contribute to the role a child plays in his or her family. We have talked about the child through whom the parents play out their differences, the child whose job it is to compensate for deficiencies in the marriage. It is this child who, singled out from his brothers and sisters, often becomes the repository of family emotion when divorce occurs. It is this child who is likely to be most reactive to his parents' divorce. And to be most impaired in his ability to form and sustain intimate relationships. Nowhere is this more evident than in working with brothers and sisters who come from divorced families. The details in the two cases that follow dramatically illustrate how the same divorce affects children in the same family in different ways.

CHAPTER TWENTY-TWO

---/---

Murray and Felicia:
"Mom Was There". . .
"No, She Wasn't"

Murray's Story

Murray, twenty-nine, works in his father's printing business in San Francisco. He is good-looking and articulate and says he has few problems in life. He describes himself as strong, competent, and well adjusted. It is just this relationship with Mariana, a television producer, that is giving him sleepless nights.

Murray and Mariana have been living together for sixteen months. Mariana is intelligent, independent, self-assured, and highly respected by her colleagues. She has strength and solid convictions, everything Murray admires in a woman. They have fun together. In fact, Murray admits that Mariana is the first woman with whom he has been able to express a softer side of himself. "I need to do that to maintain the relationship with her," he says.

Still, there are a few things about Mariana that bother

Murray. He says if he had to place a bet on the survival of their relationship, he'd bet against its lasting.

"I met her at this cocktail party, and I kind of liked her. She's nice-looking, but not great-looking, not like a model or anything. But I asked her out and we had a very romantic evening. We went for drinks, we ate, we went dancing and in the car on the way home, she kissed me; it was instant chemistry. The next morning I dropped everyone else I was dating.

"I've been with her ever since. But I don't know if I should marry her or not. I have to determine—is this the woman that I want to spend the rest of my life with? On the one hand, the chemistry is irrevocable. There is nothing better than hearing her say, 'I love you.' And she's been super with me when I've been down. She tells me, 'You have to do this and you have to do that.' I like that strength in a woman.

"But on the other hand she doesn't offer me a lot of things I respect in a marriage, in a family, in a home. She can't cook, she's not the greatest cleaner in the world. She doesn't do the little soft, maternal things that maybe I would like. She is self-centered and demanding. And she lacks style. Not class, but style.

"Besides, my father is always right about everything. AL-WAYS. *He* knows me better than *I* know me. And he says, 'If you want to marry this girl, you have my blessing. But I don't think she is the right girl for you.'

"That's a big roadblock for me. You know you go through these years of battling with your father. You want to feel as though you know better than he does or at least that you're equals. But you know something. We ain't equal. He's better. My father is the smartest man I've ever met. When he says, 'My boy, this isn't the girl for you,' you pay attention."

Murray's parents were divorced when he was thirteen and his sister, Felicia, was ten. He remembers his early years as wonderful ones with parents who were openly affectionate, dancing in the kitchen and holding hands as they walked down the street.

But he remembers, too, a turning point when everything changed. Their relationship became what he calls "blasé." They began to sleep in separate bedrooms, and for almost four years their relationship was distant and unloving. "There was no joy in our house anymore," he says. Then came one big argument, complete with screaming and the banging of doors. When Murray and his sister returned home from summer camp that year, their parents had separated and they and their mother moved into a new house. "It was a done deal," he said, "and there was nothing I could do but just accept it."

Murray says his mother is weak and that he has no respect for her. She has always been too emotional and offered him unconditional, uncompromising love, love without limits and guidance. He still pictures her standing at the door crying when his camp bus picked him up. He was seven then.

"My mother is a loser," he says. "She has no self-esteem. She only does things for other people, never for herself. It is as though she is a nonperson. She let me down. She provided no direction. She was no guiding light. Other people might see a mother as being that warm place where you put down your head. But I don't see it that way. I wanted a mother I could respect, not someone who cries every time you walk out the door, not someone who needs to be taken care of all the time and who is a basket case without her own agenda in life."

Murray smiles broadly and says, with pride, that he identifies with his father, who is a high school dropout and worked his way up to become the owner of a substantial business. He understands why his father divorced his mother and feels as though Janice, his father's second wife, is his "real" mother. She is "smart, opinionated, and she lets you know if she doesn't like what you have to say. But she is also soft and maternal and caring and a buddy and a friend. Janice," Murray told me, "is perfect."

Murray says that he doesn't know precisely why his parents divorced and he doesn't care. He knows that his mother's parents were also divorced, but he's not sure why either. His grandfather's alcoholism may have had something to do with it. He has no contact with his mother's family and disdains his mother's inability to take care of his grandmother when she was old and alone.

Even though his father was the youngest of five children, neither he nor his father sees any of them. Murray insists that none of that bothers him. When his parents were divorced, he was taken to a psychiatrist, just one time, a psychiatrist who told him to take all of his "bad" feelings and problems, put them into a black plastic bag, and dump it in the ocean. Murray obeyed and says that since that time he has felt no frustration, no tension, no guilt, about his parents or their marriage. "I don't carry that baggage."

Baggage from the past, however, is not that easy to discard. And it is with intimate relationships that Murray's buried baggage, the baggage he tossed into the sea, has surfaced.

Before Mariana there was Gretta. Murray met her at college and found her "exciting, attractive, popular, well connected in terms of sororities and party invitations." They went together for two years and Murray thought he might like to marry her. But his parents (father and stepmother) didn't think he was ready to settle down.

Then came Lucy. Murray says she was beautiful and had lots of spunk, just the kind of woman he needed. But when she began to talk about marriage, he backed away.

The same thing happened with Melanie. "She was everything I want a woman to be," Murray said. "Funny, vivacious, very successful, religious, but not overly so. And she was talented. She was a cosmetics consultant. She invested her money wisely and I really respected her judgment. She also taught me how to laugh, and I loved us being a fun couple. But I couldn't see myself marrying her. She had no style for dress—the wrong color combinations, the wrong shoes, the wrong image. And with all her achievements, she wasn't strong enough for me. She lacked individuality. So I left her because I didn't want to have a permanent relationship with her.

"I don't understand why I keep finding weak women, the kind that fold right into a man. I know I'm no day at the beach, but I'm willing to wait until I find what I want."

"What do you want?" I asked.

"I want what my dad has. I want that kind of woman, just a younger version. I have been fortunate so far, I guess, in that I haven't gotten hurt. I've always been the one to make the decision to get out."

Murray is what I call "emotionally underdeveloped." He is not aware of his feelings, or what lies behind them, and does not know how they influence the way he behaves with women.

The roots of Murray's behavior can be traced all the way back to his grandparents. His mother, who came from an angry, conflicted marriage with an alcoholic father, moved into her marriage determined to keep peace at any price. If the price required her to deny her own needs and feelings, so be it. She was compliant with her husband, allowed herself to be absorbed by him, and was totally dedicated to her children, smothering them with unbridled and undisciplined love.

His mother was and still is on the low level of the maturity scale and had no balance between thinking and feeling. This pattern eventually turned her into a highly dysfunctional person who couldn't take care of her own needs. Her self-esteem was poor, and she and her husband did not relate to each other maturely on an emotional level. She was a classic "no-self" who relied on others to define who she was. During her marriage, the only "self" she could be was a mother. She focused on Murray, which is not unusual because he was her firstborn and he is male.

Murray became extremely reactive to the intensity of his mother's focus and dependence on him. He responded by rebelling and eventually distancing himself from her physically and emotionally. It was the only way he felt he could define himself and reach for some autonomy.

His father became his hero, the man who could do nothing wrong, the man who married the perfect woman, the woman he is seeking but can't seem to find.

Murray's relationship with his parents figures heavily in the kind of women he chooses. They must not be weak, as his mother was. But once they demonstrate independence and self-assurance and do not provide the "maternal" characteristics he wants, the characteristics his father's wife Janice has, he backs off. Then there is Dad to deal with. Murray's choice in a mate must please his father. He is so dependent on Dad's approval that he cannot take the chance of disappointing him. One parent is already emotionally lost to him; he can't afford to lose the other.

No wonder that intimate relationships provoke anxiety he doesn't even recognize. It makes him, at the point the relationship becomes intense, begin focusing on the woman's flaws. Those flaws loom large and give him permission to do what he is skilled at doing—cutting himself off emotionally. The prospect of involvement with a woman who has her own needs and emotional demands is too frightening. He doesn't see that his search for the "perfect" woman is an intellectual one, not a balanced one.

Because Murray has no appreciation of the process that led to his parents' divorce, he has no clue about how relationships work. He is stuck with the notion that his mom was the "bad" person and his father the "good" person. He does not recognize that even the father he idolizes is not perfect and, in fact, contributed to the breakdown of his family.

As a child, the emotional distancing from his mother and his substitution of stepmother as his "real mother" may have helped him survive. But as an adult, it is impeding his intimate relationships. He is still reacting to the gushing emotionality of his mother the way he did when he was a child. He is still overwhelmed by it. As a result, he distances himself from women the way he did from his mother.

No matter how "perfect" a relationship seems, he keeps it at arm's length by setting up conflicts and finding faults. He drops women from his life the same way he dropped the little black bag into the sea. It is a built-in mechanism, a response to his anxieties about personal relationships. And he does it without understanding or even being aware of it.

Murray never witnessed a balanced, comfortable relationship between his parents as a role model. And as much as he insists that it is his father's present marriage, a marriage he wants to emulate, that influences him the most, it is the unresolved issues in his parents' relationship that are driving his life.

Murray believes he is independent. The reality is that he is still paralyzed by the need for his father's approval, still convinced that Dad is always right.

He is having the same trouble with boundaries that is the pattern in his family. He wants so much to be like his father that he doesn't know where he begins and his father ends. Like many people I see, Murray is intelligent, articulate, and sophisticated, but so bruised in his early years that his emotions are stunted.

Murray needs to see that he is involved in a triangle—he and his father united by a negative view of his mother, by mother as an outsider. That same triangle develops when Murray is involved in a relationship with a woman. As much as he thinks he loves the woman, he must nitpick at her deficits so he and his father can preserve their closeness in the way they always have—united against someone else.

Murray has to find a way to make his father less of a presence in his life and to disengage himself from the need for his father's continuous approval. He must develop the capacity to appraise his own needs. He can do that only by learning how his father got to be so powerful in his life and understanding that his intense disdain for his mother is contributing to his anxiety about relationships.

I suggested that he try to find out how the relationship between his parents deteriorated. He might ask his father: "Why did you marry Mom in the first place? How did your marriage go from being loving and caring to hostile and critical? What's the difference between your first and second marriages? How much of it is you? Why don't you have more contact with your original family?"

When Murray is able to see his mother in a more neutral way, he may be able to talk with her. At first, such conversations will probably reactivate his old biases. But that's okay. It is important that he observe something about his reactions to his mother because it is those reactions that determine the way he behaves with women.

Until Murray can get a more balanced perspective on his parents' marriage and divorce, he will continue backing off when an intimate relationship gets uncomfortably close.

Felicia's Story

Murray's sister Felicia sees her parents' divorce differently. Felicia remembers that her parents sat her and her brother down at the dinner table and explained that their marriage was not working out well, and that divorce would be best for everyone. She describes her father as being diplomatic but said he had no effect on her life at that time. "He thinks that he was a wonderful father and was always there for me, but I only remember him not having anything to do with my life," she says.

She describes her mother as coming from a difficult family, with an alcoholic father and a mother whom she did not respect. For fifteen years she was married to Felicia's father, who was reasonably successful but who degraded her and was not supportive of her. Her mother, Felicia says, was a "wonderful mother," always home after school, always having lunch on the table when she came home at noon, and doing everything a housewife with two children does. "Her children were really her life," Felicia says.

Felicia believes her parents separated because "my mother didn't grow as much as my father did. She's really vulnerable. She has talent. She is creative and writes poetry and is wonderful with other people's children. There are kids aged eighteen and nineteen in the neighborhood where we lived who still call her 'Mom.' I guess that's why it's so hard to respect her. She has qualities that she could use, but she doesn't. When I look back, I can't see how my father was able to be married to her."

While Murray, Felicia, and their mother moved to a new house after the separation, Felicia said it was not traumatic for her because the neighborhood was the same and she did not have to change schools or even take a different school bus. Like Murray, she remembers weekly visits with her father. First her dad came alone on weekends and took her and Murray to "exciting places for young kids." Later he came with the woman he eventually married. "At first I didn't like it. I kept asking, 'Is this woman going to be here all the time?' But my mom didn't seem to feel threatened by it and she never pumped us for information about what was happening in my dad's life."

Felicia's mother, however, became even more helpless after the divorce. She couldn't discipline her children, she couldn't control their comings and goings, and she and Murray were having a lot of problems with each other.

"It wasn't a very happy environment," Felicia remembers. But when my father asked Murray if he wanted to live
with him, he said he did. I felt neutral. Even though I was
close with my mother, I didn't mind leaving. Maybe underneath, though I loved her to death, I really knew that she
wasn't an adequate mother."

After going to live with her father and his new wife,
Felicia and her brother saw their mother infrequently. They
were too young to drive and their mother "couldn't get in a
car and be on the clogged California highway." She did call
often and sent hysterical letters to Felicia. "But for some
reason I developed the ability to be upset and then just
forget about it. I'm not sure it's a good trait, but . . ."

Felicia says despite the good memories of her childhood
with her mother, she does not respect her now because she
has been unable to take charge of her life. "But unlike my
brother, the good parts of growing up with her have not
disappeared for me. She is still my mother.

"I always bring my boyfriends to meet her and they all
like her. She likes them too. Anyone I would bring to her
she would love because if she thinks they love me then she
loves them. Her approval has no bearing on anything.

"Everyone [all Felicia's boyfriends] thinks she is very
normal, very happy, very loving. But that's only on the
outside. I have to explain privately that this is really not
who she is. I'm honest about it. It is part of who I am. I'm
not happy about it, but I'm not embarrassed either. Still it is
my biggest problem. This is my mother. Am I going to
follow this path?"

Felicia recognizes that her mother considers herself a
victim. "My mother sees herself as someone who got the
bad end of the deal, someone who is always taken advantage of, someone who has been giving her whole life and
feels she has never received anything."

Although Felicia understands and supports her father's
leaving her mother, she admits that if "God forbid I end up

with the problems she has, I would want someone who wouldn't abandon me. My father doesn't understand my mother, but he is trying to help me, in the ways he can, piece together why she is the way she is now—helpless, unable to maintain friendships and to function."

Felicia is convinced that her family's problems did not develop because of her parents' divorce. "People concentrate so much on the divorce and I keep finding it's not the divorce at all. I have no trouble with that. It is the whole family style of living.

"I don't want to be like my mother. I don't like the way she is. But I can also see the characteristics in my father that I'm not comfortable with. He has been dominant with both Murray and me. We both think twice before we do something different from what he says—Murray more so than I. It's as though he [father] was totally right and she [mother] was totally wrong.

"I think it is important that you understand your parents. My brother doesn't even want to talk about it. But I think that if I understand my mother and father, I have a better chance of understanding myself."

Felicia has had several relationships with men that have ended for "natural" causes. School was over. The summer was over. Someone moved away. For the past two years she has been going out with a man close to her own age. He too comes from a divorced family and is cautious about moving into a permanent relationship. "He wants a perfect family," Felicia says.

"I want a man who is successful, and someone who wants a lot of family around him, someone who would be there for me. I look forward to having children. I want my kids to have a better life, be more educated and more aware of the options out there.

"I do have the normal conflict of a woman of the nineties. Do you work and have a family or do you not work and have a family? My mother was there for us at home and she was a very good mother and my father divorced her. I think I need to be more independent than my mother. A man has to respect a woman and I don't think they respect a woman who is a housewife.

"On the other hand, I think the best thing for children is to have somebody there for them, not a maid or a nanny, but a mother. But basically my theory is that if you want to make a relationship work, you can make it work."

Felicia's chances for successful intimate relationships are considerably higher than her brother's. She had the same advantages he did—a loving stepmother with values she respected who took her mother's place early enough in her life to make an impact and a father who made his relationship with his children a high priority.

But Felicia has a more balanced view of her parents' marriage. She can appraise the flaws and the assets in both parents and can distinguish which parts of them she would like to incorporate or discard in herself. She understands that her mother is inept and unproductive, but sees the role her father played in creating and perpetuating that pattern. Despite her lack of respect for her mother, she still has fond memories and does not have to plow through life impeded by anger and contempt of her.

While Felicia is closer to her mother, sees her more often, and responds to her more sympathetically, she is actually more emotionally distant from her than her brother is. Her brother is still reacting because he was caught more tightly in the marital triangle. It is not just that he rejects his mother or needs approval from his father. He is caught between the two of them. Felicia can view it more objectively and be less reactive to it.

It is a difference that grows out of the way their mother focused on her children. Murray was the object of her intense attention. He was the one whose departure on the camp bus made her cry. He was the one who needed to put physical space between himself and his mother in order to grow emotionally and survive.

As we said earlier, sometimes mothers relate to their male children the same way they did to their husbands. In this case, Murray's mother expected him to take care of her just as she expected her husband to do. The demands she made on him were too burdensome, beyond the capacity of a young boy. He was too young, in fact, to say to his mom, "This is not appropriate." He did the only thing he could— he backed away.

He is still backing away when he comes too close to intimacy. He is still controlled by a past that imprisons him. His freedom will come when he makes the painful but necessary journey into his past, a journey that will help him understand—and change—his present behavior.

CHAPTER TWENTY-THREE

———/———

Alice and Joyce,
Edward and Carol

These are four siblings whose parents were divorced twelve years ago when Alice was twenty-one, Edward was seventeen, Carol was fourteen, and Joyce was nine. Edward and Carol are stumbling through life while Joyce and Alice are enjoying or moving toward happy, healthy relationships. Why?

Alice is married, has a three-year-old daughter, and says her marriage is loving and fulfilling. Joyce, her youngest sister, is a sophomore at college with plans to go on for a doctorate in English. She says that she wants to get married, but not right away. She believes that she must be a complete person—emotionally and financially—before she considers an alliance with a man. It is a three-step process, she says. You stabilize yourself. You have a sense of completeness. Then you look for someone you might want to marry.

On the other hand, their brother Edward says he does not want a permanent relationship with a woman. At twenty-eight he says he can't envision himself getting married, but if he does, it would be with the clear understanding that it might not last. He doesn't think marriages can survive beyond ten years with the same person.

Meanwhile, in a way that is typical of the men described by Alan Booth and his colleagues in "The Impact of Parental Divorce on Courtship," he dates many women, moving quickly from one to the other. He chooses women to whom he feels superior, then grows bored with them.

He is now seeing Rebecca, a massage therapist. "Dad doesn't like her," Edward told me. "He thinks she is cheap and loose and not very intelligent. That's probably true. But I think I may marry her," he said. "Just for a little while, just to see the look on Dad's face."

Carol, Edward's younger sister, is having similar trouble with intimate relationships. Throughout college she became involved with men who abused her physically and emotionally. She describes herself as being "clingy and needy" and is hoping to meet a man who will love her and make her feel "complete." She suffers from periods of depression and is afraid she will turn out to be a street person. She blames her problems on her parents' divorce.

Joyce told her older sister, "*My* parents got divorced too, and I don't look at the world the way you do."

Edward and Carol were born into the family at the time of greatest turmoil. They became the focus of their family's conflicts. Joyce and Alice, luckily, escaped that role.

Actually, Alice could have been at the highest risk because she was the oldest daughter and there were serious problems in the family early in her life. She was two months old when her grandmother (her mother's mother) committed suicide; her mother could have focused on her for comfort and continued to relate to her too intensely as she grew up.

Alice's mother, however, is a sensitive and incisive school counselor, who was acutely aware that she might lean too heavily on her daughter. She made a conscious effort not to, knowing that it would impair Alice's growth and development. As a result Alice was able to keep herself out of family conflict before the divorce, during its process, and afterward. It was a role that felt comfortable to her because she had grown up with it.

"It was not that I wasn't hurt by their divorce," Alice told me. "But I had always been encouraged to live my own life and not become overly involved in my parents'. I didn't see myself having a lot to do with their conflicts or their divorce. It was their lives. I loved them both and after twenty-one years I believed they both loved me. I was able to be supportive to them but still go on with my own life."

Joyce, the youngest child, was not the focus of family problems either. Youngest children are often spared that role because children born earlier have already assumed it. And because Joyce was only nine when her parents divorced, she doesn't remember a lot of the fighting between them. She was more involved, she says, with the lives of her brother and sisters than those of her parents. Edward and Carol became the vehicles through which their mother and father played out their conflicts.

The marriage was one where all four family styles—conflict, adaptation, distancing, and focusing on a child to avoid important issues—were overused. The children were aware for a long time that their parents were having problems about money, about sex, about jobs. For a long time their mother *adapted* to her husband, who was a moody man with a short temper and rigid rules about the way life should be lived. He often made his point with his fist. He was a *distancer,* concerned more about his job as a computer consultant than he was about spending time with his family. He felt that earning a living was *his* job. Everything else was his wife's province. He and his children rarely talked to one another about anything other than their schoolwork.

Their mother thought about divorce for a long time and

was determined to initiate it as soon as she was financially secure. But when her husband became more violent, she knew she couldn't wait. The day he dislocated Carol's arm in a skirmish about a friend's party, she knew the marriage was over.

The children were assured that it was not their fault. Their parents emphasized that it was a problem between them and that they would do their best to keep the family emotionally intact despite the divorce. The children would have access to both their mother and their father and would continue to see grandparents, aunts, and cousins on both sides.

However, Edward and Carol continued to be the children most caught up in family struggles. Edward often interceded to protect his mother and sisters from his father. As Mother pulled further away from her husband, she moved closer to her son. In retrospect she realizes that even when he was twelve, she was dealing with Edward more as a peer than as a child.

After the divorce Edward became seriously depressed, and for a long time he refused to have anything to do with his father, whom he saw as responsible for the divorce. Because he grew up overly aware of his mother's emotional needs, he became emotionally needy himself, driven by his feelings, and unable to be thoughtful, the way his sisters Joyce and Alice were, about how to develop relationships.

While Edward angrily ran interference during his father's physical outbursts, Carol saw her responsibility as keeping peace in the family. She would gently chide her father about his moods and his violence. And she learned how to distract him by telling him about her dancing lessons or what she had learned in school that day. She felt as though she were the stabilizing force in the family, the one whose responsibility it was to calm the waters.

When the divorce occurred, she was shattered because her stability depended on the family's integrity. She saw the split as her failure. At first she became quiet and withdrew from friends and from others in the family. Her mother was relieved when, a year later, she showed renewed interest in her classmates and resumed some of her former activities.

For the next several years and through high school, her mother was confident that Carol had turned the corner. Her schedule was busier than ants at a picnic and she spent little time at home. Her mother didn't know then that what looked like "adjusting" was really "distancing." Carol was removing herself from an environment that made her too sad. She began seeking refuge in daredevil activities such as motorcycle riding because they relieved her anxiety. If she could be successful taking risks, maybe she would survive. She purposely drove her car off the road and sustained minor injuries to test her boyfriend's love for her.

The crowd she moved with was fast and loose, her relationships with boyfriends short-lived and chaotic. At sixteen she began experimenting with drugs. This pseudoindependent behavior, marked by poor judgment and no limits, was the way she responded to anxiety about her parents' marriage and divorce.

In this family Alice and Joyce understand that they are at risk but have given thought to how they want their relationships to be and are able to work at it. Edward and Carol, however, are still prisoners of the past. They are still reacting to their parents, still putting themselves in the middle of destructive situations, and are victimized by their own behavior. They have the advantage of having sisters who view their parents' marriage differently than they do. The four children need to talk together about the role each of them played in their parents' marriage and divorce, and think about how that influences their choices in intimate partners.

Edward must recognize that it probably will be difficult for him to have a stable relationship with a woman without resolving his relationship with his father, from whom he is all but estranged. He must find out, for instance, if he wants to marry the woman he now lives with *only* to provoke his father.

Edward's uncle, his mother's brother, has a stable, secure marriage, and Edward could benefit from spending more time with him and his family. He could learn about the give-and-take of a healthy relationship. And before attempting to approach his father, he might talk with his dad's relatives —his two brothers and three sisters—to learn how his father grew up and why they think his marriage failed.

Carol is still behaving like the victim, still carrying the burden of her failure to save her parents' marriage. Talking with her mother, her aunt, her sisters, and her father would help her understand that she is still allowing herself to be defined by relationships with other people. Any perspective she could get about how she came to be the most victimized child in her family and how she continues to perpetuate that role could help her. When victims become aware of how they participate in what happens to them, they can begin to make changes. Until then, they walk around with the attitude that "the world is against me." As long as they feel that way, they will be unable to participate in satisfying intimate relationships.

PART FIVE

Sons of Divorce

The stereotypical behavior of both boys and girls becomes more pronounced as the maturity level in a family declines, as it always does during and immediately following a divorce.

In earlier chapters, you have seen that the behavior of boys and girls differs in this time of upheaval. Boys tend to:

- be more aggressive and show more anti-social behavior
- feel more insecure and have low self-esteem
- have trouble controlling their impulses and frequently become hyperactive
- have a rocky relationship with their mothers and have trouble identifying with her anguish and pain
- frequently retreat into isolation

Boys who have a poor or no relationship with their fathers suffer a severe blow to their self-confidence and may go through life searching for Daddy. Sometimes a good relationship with a stepfather can fill the gap.

As boys of divorce grow older, one of the major problems of those less "behaviorally" mature is their inability to acknowledge and express feelings. Sharing feelings is not a characteristic encouraged in boys so they have little practice. In intimate relationships, which are so rooted in the balance between thinking and feeling, they are at a distinct disadvantage.

Keep this information in mind as you read the stories of Brent, whose anxiety about commitment destroys his relationships; Richard, who, against the odds, emerged with a strong marriage; Jerry, who doesn't know what feelings are; Russell, who comes from a family where secrets were a way of life; and Buddy, whose first marriage has failed and who is timid about trying it again. You have a front row seat at their family dramas, and you are likely to see significant parallels in your own lives.

CHAPTER TWENTY-FOUR

————/————

Diane and Brent:
Come Closer . . . Move Away

Brent, forty-five, came to see me because serious problems had developed in his relationship with Diane, the thirty-six-year-old woman, divorced five years earlier, with whom he had been living part-time for two years.

Diane, a political speech writer, and Brent, manager of a women's apparel shop, had apartments within a mile of each other. Most of the time they lived together at her place, but a couple of times a week and occasionally on a Sunday Brent would go home.

Both of them were feeling anxious about making their relationship more permanent. Diane said she felt ready to marry Brent and wanted him to give up his apartment. She wanted to have a baby but wouldn't do it unless they were married. Still, she admitted that the thought of permanence scared her. Brent, on the other hand, backed off physically when they talked about wedding plans. After they argued, Brent would storm out of the apartment, often not returning until three or four in the morning, while Diane

walked the floor agitated and angry. Brent admitted that he
was out seeking other women. His interest in them was not
necessarily for sex, just for fun—dancing, drinking, or simply flirting.

Then there was the money issue. Diane earned twice as
much as Brent. She was also better organized and a better
planner than he was. She took care of her clothes and her
car and paid attention to detail. Brent's salary was adequate, but he was thinking of changing careers, and Diane
would probably have to support him partially, at least for a
while.

She didn't mind when it was a vacation or the theater or
something that would benefit both of them. But she did not
want to support what she called his "irresponsibility."
When, for instance, his car was vandalized on a downtown
Detroit street because he ignored warnings to park it in a
garage, Diane refused to contribute to the repairs.

The cycle was: Diane would criticize; Brent would become tense and go to other women; Diane would get angry
and feel rejected; they would argue more. And when they
thought about marriage, both of them became anxious.

After I met with each of them alone and together, it
became clear to me that Brent and Diane were both hos-
tages of their earlier family relationships. Brent's parents
were divorced when he was five, after a ten-year-long marriage marked by high conflict and little cooperation. His
parents argued, criticized each other mercilessly, and were
physically violent. Brent remembers the police coming to
stop their fights. On those occasions he would run up to his
room, shut the door, and crush the pillow over his head to
drown out the sounds of their screams.

His mother remarried quickly but treated Brent the same
way she had treated his father. Although he showed early
talent in art, his mother ridiculed his drawings. She wanted
him to get better grades, be more active in sports, and be
more attentive to her. When he tried to discuss a problem

with her, she turned him away; she couldn't tolerate the idea of any deficiency in her son.

Brent would then turn to his father, who reassured him that he was okay. His mother resented the time he spent with his dad and frequently told him, "You're just like your father." Brent always felt anxious about this loyalty struggle he had with his parents.

Brent's mother, even today, tries to cling to him in an unhealthy way. Although he sees her twice a month and talks to her every week, she is not satisfied. She tells him he is "like all men, insensitive and uncaring." She still devalues him. Why doesn't he see her more? Why isn't he making something of himself? Why isn't he married? Why doesn't he earn more money?

Brent is having trouble distinguishing Diane from his mother. When he and Diane argue—about anything—he feels demeaned and personally attacked. He responds in a way familiar to him, by turning to someone else who will bolster his sagging self-esteem. He is really saying, "If you're unhappy with me, at least someone else is not."

Diane also comes from a family of divorce, characterized by a highly dysfunctional mother who became an alcoholic. As with many such families, Diane grew up never knowing what would happen to her next. Sometimes her mother physically abused her; other times she hugged her. Her older brother protected her at times, then sexually molested her while their mother looked the other way. She became confused about relationships and what you can expect from them. If the same people who love you also abuse you, what does that mean?

Nonetheless, like many daughters of divorce, Diane seemed to do well for a long time. She earned high grades in school and had a stoic quality about her that suggested a maturity beyond her years. She saw her role as taking care of her mother and consciously tried not to react to her mother's erratic behavior. But this kind of overfunctioning, as we have suggested earlier, often has repercussions. In Diane's case, she married a man who was as dependent on her as her mother had been. He was unable to hold a job and Diane ended up supporting him. He was moody and Diane felt as though she had to "walk on eggshells" to keep him from becoming agitated.

But she didn't see that her role in her marriage had been a replay of her role in her original family, a family that was still orchestrating her life in spite of the fact that she moved away from her mother's city and was visiting only once a year.

I was convinced that Diane and Brent loved each other and wanted to form a permanent relationship. But they had to learn that their reactions to each other had nothing to do with money or sex or flirting; these were merely the vehicles through which they expressed their anxiety.

Diane contributed her part to their contentious relationship because of her earlier experiences. Her style was to overfunction and take care of Brent just as she did with her mother and first husband. But after a while she resented doing that, and so did Brent. They would argue. And he would leave to find another woman.

Diane believed that Brent loved her, but his flirtatiousness felt abusive. She was back to her beginnings where she wondered if the people who love you always hurt you. Her anxiety escalated and her relationship with Brent deteriorated.

As soon as I realized that there was more anxiety than substance to these conflicts (a typical scenario), I decided to talk with Brent and Diane separately, but in front of each other. I didn't want a three-way conversation that would lead to conflict. I wanted Diane to hear the conversations between Brent and me, but I did not want to involve them in an exchange that would be unproductive. As Diane listened, she would learn a lot about Brent and why he behaved the way he did. She would then be able to work on her reactions.

When we talked about his affairs, for instance, Brent's insecurity became evident quickly. Diane could see that the issue was not that he didn't love her, but that he was so anxious about their relationship. That understanding recast the whole picture. For starters, it allowed Diane and Brent to recognize that the problem was the anxiety, not the other women. Diane could also see that she helped make Brent anxious because she was constantly urging him to be different—be more responsible with money, get a better job—just as his mother had done.

Diane and Brent are still in therapy. They are working toward the time when they can go back to their families for more information and a new look at their past. Meanwhile, their relationship has become calmer. Diane is no longer as critical of Brent, so he feels less anxious. And he has begun to recognize why his behavior—turning to other women— is offensive and unacceptable to her. Since they have become tuned in to their own and each other's behavior, they are making progress toward their mutual goal—to be married and have a family.

CHAPTER TWENTY-FIVE

—————/—————

Richard's Story: Against the Odds

Sometimes a person's family history is so littered with unresolved issues and so complicated by the web of relationships we described in earlier chapters that the chances of a healthy intimate relationship seem remote indeed. But for a variety of fascinating reasons this is not always the case.

Consider Richard, the boy who consoled himself with rock music after his parents' divorce.

Richard comes from a family where there have been two divorces for each parent. He has had two stepmothers, two stepfathers, and assorted stepsisters, stepbrothers, and cousins. After his parents' breakup, he had serious behavior problems for many years and spent a lot of time alone, experimenting with drugs and battling with his mother. When he was seventeen, he met a woman his age, fell in love, and was determined that his relationship with her would be one that would last. It has—for the past fifteen years. Let us see why.

Richard and his wife, Paula, have what both of them call a

rich and loving relationship. They have three children they adore, enjoy a host of friends, and are working on building closeness with their original families. Yet Richard admits that something he can't explain gnaws at him. Maybe it is just his exquisite awareness that he is the adult child of divorced-more-than-once parents. Maybe he wonders how much his family history will impose itself on his life. Maybe it's his concern about his wife and the effect her tangled family background will have on them.

Unlike many of the people I see, Richard talked knowledgeably about his original family and seemed aware, from the start, that he must make peace with himself by digging into his past.

Richard remembered his early years with his parents as happy ones. He remembered feeling close to his mother and father and spending a lot of time with them, gardening and swimming. But he also remembered that his dad had what his mom called a "temper." In retrospect Richard conjectures that his mother, who was raised in a family where it was not acceptable to express emotion, probably didn't know how to deal with that very well. She and his father argued behind closed doors where she tried to calm him down and keep peace for the sake of Richard and his sister.

The problems between them escalated when his dad began to make more money as manager of a restaurant chain. His father wanted to spend it on beautiful things and a luxurious lifestyle. His mother agreed to move to a spacious suburban house but was uncomfortable with their new Mercedes and dresses with designer labels.

Then his dad opened his own glitzy gourmet restaurant and found suddenly that his money and power made him attractive to women. "And it was the sixties," says Richard, "where the rules were looser."

Soon afterward Richard's father told him that he was moving out. He didn't tell him why, just that it had something to do with money. And Richard says that he was not aware for a long time that his father had been having an affair with a family friend. Even after the friend left her husband and moved in with him, even after they were married, Richard didn't realize, until years later, that she had anything to do with his parents' breakup.

Nonetheless, Richard continued to worship his father and constantly sought his approval. Since his mother had asked his father to leave, he blamed her for the divorce, and his relationship with her was stormy throughout his childhood and adolescence.

He kept telling himself that he benefited from the divorce. He had weekends with his father in his downtown apartment together with his sister, his two stepbrothers, and his stepsister. "It was a party down there," Richard says. "We ate Chinese food together, went to the movies, and took neat vacations together. We were this *Cheaper by the Dozen* kind of crowd."

While Richard's mother, Abby, never criticized her former husband, Richard's father denigrated her at every turn. He called her "square" and said she was living "with a bag over her head." Richard usually supported his dad, mainly because he so urgently wanted his approval. "I was angry, but I never let my anger be directed at my father," he says. "He was loud and quite judgmental, and I had learned that he could just pick up and leave. I felt that our relationship was fragile, and I didn't want to lose him for good."

So Richard's rebellion was with his mother, whose love he never had to earn or doubt. When she remarried, two years after the divorce, Richard was at the peak of his defiance. He hated their "square, suburban" house, he hated her new husband and his two daughters. In his words, he "walked all over his mother, ran wild," and thought a lot about being older and running away from home. He wouldn't let his stepfather discipline him. "I kept telling him, 'You're not my father.'"

Richard was a loner through adolescence, having only one good friend with whom he smoked pot and cut school. He stayed up late at night and slept most of the day. When his mother's marriage broke up seven years later, Richard blamed himself. He thought his outrageous behavior had caused the rupture in their relationship.

When I asked him if he understood, now that he was an adult, why his mother's second marriage was unsuccessful, he couldn't remember anything specific. It had more to do, he told me, with their very different styles of relating to each other and dealing with marital conflict. His mother wanted to talk; her husband tended to retreat. The more she pressed him, the more stressful it became. Finally they parted.

At about the same time Richard's father and his wife announced that they were divorcing. His father had been having affairs almost from the beginning of his second marriage. "I remember being very upset about that," says Richard. "I had adjusted to the way things were, and now what I thought was permanent was temporary. It made me very sad."

Richard, meanwhile, was not the Casanova he perceived his father to be. He was afraid of dating and of girls and says he didn't feel "worthy" of their attention. He feared being rejected, and didn't know that his father had felt the same way for much of his life.

Then, when he was seventeen, he met Paula, a year older, with whom he felt instant closeness. Over a pitcher of beer they shared their sad stories. Her father had committed suicide when she was only one year old. Her mother was pregnant with her younger brother at the time. Five years later she remarried and gave birth to Paula's half brother.

Paula didn't like her stepfather much but has fond memories of her childhood nevertheless. She was close to her mother and her mother's "warm and wonderful" family. Her grandparents, her mother's parents, had come here from Europe in the twenties, built their own home, and were romantic, enchanting people. When Richard met them, he loved them as much as Paula did.

In that first conversation they had with each other, Paula asked Richard what he believed in, what he wanted for himself. He responded that he wanted "moments that last." She said she wanted the same thing.

Richard and Paula spent the next six years together in a cohabiting relationship. There was one breakup during that time, but they came back to each other, recognizing that they were both intensely committed and wanted to marry and have children.

Richard kept telling me how determined he was to make his marriage last "through all time." He feared that for some reason he wouldn't be able to control, he would repeat his father's behavior, and he was terrified of not being a good husband and father. He wondered what makes some people stick to a marriage while others drift from partner to partner.

Richard, of course, has reasons to be apprehensive. In his chaotic past are the ingredients for disaster in intimate relationships. Two marriages for each parent. A struggle for his father's love and approval. The high-voltage acting out that boys in care of their mothers often exhibit after divorce. Failure to become attached to the stepfather he lived with for seven years. Guilt that he had been responsible for his mother's second divorce. A rocky, rebellious adolescence. A love-at-first-sight relationship, at seventeen, nourished by mutual past tragedy. His history, you might say, is ominous.

Richard needed to recognize why, despite his fierce allegiance to his marriage, the issue of commitment is laced with so much anxiety for him. He needed help to work out some of the still unresolved problems in his life, including awareness of the kind of family he came from and appreciation of why his parents' marriages didn't work, so that he could feel more relaxed about his future.

Richard's anxiety is rooted in those unresolved relationships with both of his parents. And that anxiety, even after a successful marriage of eight years, is still troubling him in *his* most intimate relationships—the ones with his wife and his children. Richard realizes, despite feeling as though he is an adult, that he becomes a child again when he is with his parents. His instincts are to criticize his mother and to try to impress his father. Why?

Richard came from a family characterized by an *adaptive* mother and an *emotionally distant* father. Mom was the one who absorbed blame and didn't do much about it. Dad wouldn't deal with emotions at all. That was Mom's job.

This *adaptiveness* didn't work well for Richard's mother during her marriage and didn't help his relationship with her afterward. After the divorce, for example, Richard's mother seemed to do all the right things. She took good care of Richard and his sister. She waited two years to marry and had a husband whom even Richard describes as a kind and gentle man. She didn't deride his father or create loyalty struggles that often complicate the lives of children of divorce. And she tried to be supportive, even when Richard was at his most rebellious.

Why then, did Richard have so many problems with his mother? Why was it she, not his father, against whom his outrageous behavior was directed? Why was he not critical of his father's irresponsible conduct? And why is it his mother, even today, whose love and support he takes more for granted?

The relationship between Richard and his mother is one that I have seen often. When Father leaves, especially when another woman is involved, it would seem that children would sympathize with their mother. Instead they often, consciously or not, feel angry with her. It happens because Mother is usually the person responsible for the way the family functions. Mother gets the breakfast, calls the electrician, decorates the house, takes the children to the doctor. When divorce occurs, Mom is still seen as responsible.

No matter that Father is the one whose behavior precipitated the split. No matter that he found new interests. No matter that they argued all the time. It is Mom's job to keep the family together. When she has not been able to do that, the children often blame her.

In this case Richard's mother even carried the responsibility for maintaining the connections between Richard and his father's family. "My dad was always embarrassed by his roots," Richard says. "He was status conscious and always concerned with social climbing and the 'way things look.' He more or less walked away from his family, which was working class."

After the divorce Richard saw his father's family only through his mother's continued connection with them. Ironically, if something went wrong with those relationships, he could unconsciously hold his mother, not his father, accountable.

Mom absorbed blame throughout the marriage and didn't do much about it. She didn't even explain to Richard the reason his father left home. So blaming Mom was easy because she didn't defend herself or fight back.

Then, too, Richard knew that his mother's love was there . . . and unconditional. She was the logical person at whom he could discharge his anger and sadness.

Dad's response to anger, based on experience, was to climb into his Mercedes and run away, find other people who were more attractive, buy new clothes. It is big-time adolescent behavior in a successful, professional man. Had Richard acted out against his father, had his father become angry at him, he might have abandoned him the same way he did his mother. Richard couldn't afford to take that chance.

Richard is still carrying around a lot of guilt about his

relationship with his mother, guilt that could be diluted only with better understanding of the dynamics between them. Partly because of his mother's tendency to be stoic, to withhold information about her own feelings that might be painful to her children, Richard and his mother don't talk much about the difficult issues that create tension between them. Any anger Richard feels toward his mother, especially about the past, is still bottled up inside him, mingled with guilt and confusion.

He hasn't been able to do much better with his father. Only recently was he able to confront him with his anger about a specific incident. Richard and his family spend every Thanksgiving with his father. It is their time together and it is meaningful and precious to Richard.

Last year Richard asked his father if he and his third wife wanted to have Thanksgiving dinner at his home. He would invite his father's sister and her family. Richard liked the idea of "one big happy family" and was pleased when his father agreed.

Thanksgiving arrived, but his father did not. He called to say that something had come up. And Richard was devastated.

"There I was with my father's sister and all of my cousins and I really wanted to be with my father," Richard says. "I was very angry with him and we barely spoke until that Christmas. But we got together at Christmas because holidays are important to me. It took a long time for my father to admit that he had done something wrong. He admitted he was being selfish, but he underestimates how important he is to me."

Despite his discomfort about important aspects of his past, Richard is more fortunate than most men with a background as tangled as his. Significant pluses in his life have allowed him to make a commitment to an intimate relationship while others like him are still floundering.

He remembers his predivorce family as loving and close,

so the impressionable childhood years were nurturing for him and helped him develop the image of the kind of family he wanted for himself. Unlike Murray, whom we described earlier, he was not the focus of his parents' problems—that role fell to his sister, who is still inordinately troubled and having difficulty organizing her life. And while he is still strongly connected to his parents emotionally, he has managed to recognize that he is different from them. He does not need to do what they would do. He can act in ways that feel comfortable to him.

For instance, when his father urged him to see other women during his brief breakup with Paula during their courtship, Richard was able to say, "No, that's you. It is not me. It is not what I want to do."

This is testimony to the value of continued contact with parents. Children have the chance to make changes in their own lives by seeing their mothers and fathers, not through the eyes of children, but as adults, and to see how they want to be the same or different from them.

Richard recognizes that roots and staying in touch with the past are important to his growth. In persisting in his relationship with his father and extracting information from him, he has become aware that his father distances himself from pain and discomfort. He walked away from his original family because he was ashamed of them; he walked away from Richard's mother when they couldn't deal with their differences; he left his second wife and suggested to Richard, during those muddled moments of his courtship with Paula, that he leave her.

Richard has always had, even during his most turbulent adolescent years, at least one good friend with whom he could talk and discuss problems. And he has not lost his extended family. His aunt, his father's sister, describes him as "her favorite nephew," and his grandmother (his mother's mother) talks proudly of his accomplishments on Wall Street. His mother and her husband baby-sit for his chil-

dren, and he stays involved in family celebrations and rituals. While he and his father have not resolved their relationship, he did not have an "absent" father, a father with
whom there was no contact. And he did not allow the cutoff
of divorce to continue between him and his father.

His long cohabitation with Paula before they married
speaks too to the strength of their commitment. It is unlike
the two- or three-year-long live-in relationships that are
often proving to be commitments not to be committed.

"For me, commitment meant that you stop weighing the
value of the relationship every day," Richard told me. "The
relationship becomes a given. You know how important it is
for you to be together and you don't analyze it. You just
relax and give it its best chance for survival."

Although Richard did not talk about it and perhaps has
never thought about it, I could see parallels between his
relationship with Paula and his parents' marriages. His
mother's and father's marriage ended after seven years.
Both of their second marriages ended after seven years as
well. Paula and Richard did not marry until their relationship had survived for almost seven years.

Is that significant? I think so. Neither of his parents made
it past the "seven-year itch." I think that on a level below
consciousness Richard was saying to himself, "Let's see if
we can make it seven years, and then we'll get married."

It isn't something you're aware of, but it is like having a
father and a mother who both died when they were fifty-
five. You wonder if the same thing will happen to you.
Richard may have been, without knowing it, driven by the
notion that if his relationship with Paula lasted longer than
his parents' marriages, it was viable and solid. Family patterns often repeat themselves in mysterious and subtle
ways.

Richard now needs to express his feelings more honestly
to both his parents. He needs to know more about why
their marriage failed. He needs to get a more realistic per-

spective on his family history and know how it is still influencing his behavior. Most important, he must reexamine his attitudes toward his parents, particularly his mother, and he must get to know her better. If he is insensitive to her, there is the risk he may, without realizing it, repeat that behavior with his wife. Once he understands more clearly his reactions to both his mother and his father and changes the ones that are no longer productive, he will be free of much of the anxiety that makes him uneasy about his marriage.

Richard and his wife have to be careful not to become overly anxious about their children. His mother once told him, "I think I was too much of a mother and not enough of a wife." He has to guard against behaving the same way.

Richard and Paula were united by an intense preoccupation with a common past. Each of them had lost a father, albeit in different ways, and their hunger for permanency drew them together. On the first date they talked about the most intimate things, giving their meeting a unique excitement and intensity. They must be cautious not to allow that intensity to flip over onto their relationship with their children. If the comfort in their relationship with each other is based on concern over a third thing (which is what made it so consuming at the start), they must not let that third thing now become their children.

Children pick up their parents' anxiety. It is important for them to feel, as they grow up, that they are well cared for and loved. But if they sense that their parents are constantly worried about them, that they are overly anxious about them, problems can result. Children who experience this kind of parenting often grow up reacting to their parents' anxiety rather than acting in ways appropriate for themselves.

Richard and Paula are conscious of these risks and are determined to avoid them. Because they communicate honestly with each other and are persistent about reaching into the past to interpret and resolve current dilemmas, I would predict for them the "moments that last" that they want so much.

CHAPTER TWENTY-SIX

––––––––/––––––––

Jerry:
The Ghost of
the "Emotionally Distant Family"

Jerry doesn't know, even now, why he and his wife, Doris, were divorced five years ago. They are still good friends (even though she has remarried), they still care about each other, and he still thinks that had they worked at it harder, they might have stayed together.

They have remained friendly with each other's family, and when Doris visits her mother in South Dakota, she and her husband stay with Jerry's brother. Jerry has dinner with her at least once a month and calls her on the phone every week.

When I talked with Jerry, he seemed passive and somewhat helpless, as though he were more a spectator in his divorce than a participant. He said that while he had pledged not to divorce the way his parents did, when it happened, he absorbed it and it was okay.

Jerry is a thirty-eight-year-old chemist, personable and respected in his community. He plays tennis, enjoys his nieces and nephews, is always invited to friends' homes for

Thanksgiving, and goes home (to South Dakota) every Christmas. He says he is content, but he knows there is something, a certain vitality, that is missing from his life. The last woman he dated told him he was like a sponge. He wasn't sure exactly what she meant.

When I asked him to think about why his marriage fell apart, he said, "I wish I knew. I thought I was doing the right things. We hardly ever fought about anything. I always encouraged Doris to be free to do whatever she wanted to do. If she wanted to go out with friends and I preferred to stay in and read, it was all right with me.

"I liked the aloneness. And I think she liked the freedom. Maybe too much. We did a lot of things together at first, but that began to change. And one day, after we had been married four years, she said to me, 'I'm sorry, but I don't think I'm in love with you anymore. I have the greatest feelings for you, but I don't think it's love.'

"We talked about it for about three or four days and decided on a trial split-up. We would see what happened. If we missed each other, felt we did love each other and wanted to be together, we'd come back. If not, that was that."

Jerry and Doris never lived together again. "It seemed we didn't love each other so much, and I didn't want to hold her back. If there had been kids, there never would have been a question about divorce because we would have been absolutely comfortable living together. We might have even grown to love each other again."

In talking with Jerry I saw clearly that he was acting out his family script. He was thirteen when his parents divorced. He remembers his family before then—he, his older sister, and two older brothers—as being close and doing lots of things together—fishing and playing baseball and picnicking—things a working-class family from a small town could afford.

His dad had what Jerry described as a "short fuse." He

frequently accused his wife of "fooling around" with other men, and occasionally he smacked her. "I don't think he hit her very often," says Jerry, "although I do remember a couple of black eyes. A few times he threatened to kill her, mainly when he had been drinking—which he did a lot— but I don't think he would ever have gotten to that point."

When Jerry learned that his parents were planning to divorce, he felt relieved. But he and his sister and brothers never talked about it with one another. Or with their parents.

"I guess we were all embarrassed a bit. And in our family no one talked much about anything. We felt close because we did things together, but we never talked about our feelings. I remember thinking that the divorce should bother me, but it didn't. I remember thinking that I should be crying, but I wasn't. I think I just decided that there wasn't anything I could do to stop it, so I just wouldn't focus on it."

After his parents' divorce, all of the children lived with their mother, and Dad took an apartment in the next town. But he came to visit often and, as far as Jerry can remember, he was always welcome in his mother's home. He would have dinner with the family once a week and on every holiday. Sometimes Jerry's father cried and said he would like to try again, but his mother was firm. He could come for dinner, but he could not move back in. There was no fighting, no arguing. "Sometimes I wondered how that could be," Jerry told me. "They couldn't be married, but they could be friends. I didn't understand it."

When he was eighteen, Jerry wasn't sure what he wanted to do with his life. He took a few courses at a community college, flipped hamburgers at McDonald's, and scoured science magazines cover to cover. When he met Doris, he was still floundering. But she literally put a college application in his hand and instructed him to "do something with

your life." So he did. He went through college and graduate school, earning his Ph.D in chemistry.

After graduation Doris wanted to get married. They had,
after all, been dating for eight years. Jerry says he would
have been as happy to stay single, and doesn't know, even
in retrospect, whether he was afraid of making a commitment. "But Doris was upset," he told me, "so I said, 'Okay,
I'll get married.' "

Jerry didn't see that he was mimicking the same kind of
"adaptive" reaction typical of both his mother and his father at different times in their marriage. For eighteen years
his mother had adapted to her husband's abuse and drinking, pretending that it wasn't important and protesting that
it didn't bother her. Inside she knew he was a "pussycat,"
she said.

She insulated herself by returning to school, finding a job
as a cashier in a local bank, and eventually working her way
up to be an assistant vice president. But until the year
before she and her husband separated, no one in the family
mentioned his abusive behavior. "I guess we took our cues
from Mom," Jerry says now. "It was just something we
didn't talk about."

When Jerry's mother finally decided she had had
enough, her husband became the adaptive one. He did
nothing to dissuade her. He said he wanted to stay in the
marriage, but made no suggestion that they try to work at it
or that he would be willing to change his behavior. He knew
that his wife had reason to divorce him, and he placidly
accepted her decision.

"Doesn't that sound familiar?" I asked Jerry. "Isn't that
what happened to you? Your ex-wife told you to go to
school, so you went. She said she wanted to get married. So
you did. She said she wanted to be divorced. So you did
that, too."

Jerry acknowledged that he was the kind of person who

usually "goes with the flow." When his wife began spending more time away from home, he didn't question it. When she became anxious about their marriage, he picked up her anxiety and reacted to it by agreeing to a divorce. He began to see that he adapts to other people's experiences and, despite his intelligence and professional achievements, doesn't seem able to think for himself on a personal level. It is as though he is a nonperson. His feelings and beliefs don't stand on their own. They are always subject to the influence of others. Jerry is what I have referred to earlier as behaviorally immature; he does not have an appropriate balance between thinking and feeling. He allows events, rather than his own convictions, to dictate his behavior.

Jerry patterned his postdivorce relationship with his wife on what he saw between his parents. His mother and father remained friends even through his father's final illness, during which his mother visited him every day in the hospital. Jerry's friendship with Doris and her new husband and his continued contact with her and her family are rooted in familiar soil.

Most significantly, perhaps, Jerry wears the badge of emotional distance that characterizes his family, a badge plainly visible to everyone but him. When his parents' marriage broke up, he didn't talk to anyone about it. Unlike most children of divorce, he didn't recognize it as a crisis in his life; he just absorbed the tension without realizing it. During his own marriage, he behaved more like a roommate than a husband. When he admits that children would have kept the marriage together, he is really saying that his wife would have been so involved with the children that he would not have needed to be emotionally available to her. He could have remained the provider, been a peripheral member of the family, and maintained the emotional distance that felt comfortable to him.

He remembers that his marriage ended quietly with no

bickering and that he continued, willingly, to pay for his wife's apartment until she remarried. When the divorce decree arrived in the mail, he says he read it but felt nothing.

When his marriage finally disintegrated, his pattern of emotional distance continued. For a year he did not tell his family that he and Doris no longer lived together. When they would call asking for her, he would say merely that she was "out." He only admitted that he and Doris were separated when his sister became suspicious.

Even after that no one in his family asked him how he felt, nor did he volunteer any information. He knew his mother felt badly because she and Doris had been good friends, but she never discussed it with him.

Over time Jerry has begun to see how his past is still dictating his behavior. He can recognize that he has been a "good guy," going through life directed by other people. Jerry knows that he is going to have to be more in touch with his feelings and be less of an emotional stray before he can develop an intimate relationship with anyone. "I keep thinking that in some ways I like being alone. There is no one to intrude in my life, no one to compromise with. But down deep I think I really want to share my life with someone and have someone to grow old with. If I can just loosen up a little and meet the right person, I would probably jump in with both arms and legs and be very happy about it."

After Jerry had been in therapy several months, I suggested that he reconnect with his family and his social network of friends in a way that would establish a new closeness with them. Because he had been distant for so long, it was not realistic to expect that he could talk with them about emotionally significant issues right away. That would be "jumping in" too soon and would be unproductive. It was important, first, that he become a more significant and visible part of his own family. He could begin by engaging in "planned communication" with his brother, his sister, and his mother and being conscious of regular contact with them.

Almost as an assignment, I asked him to call his sister, brother, and mother regularly and write to them often so he could become more a part of their everyday lives. He was also to participate in important family events such as weddings, graduations, and holidays. If he couldn't be there, he was to send a gift or a telegram or make a phone call to let them know he cared. And he was to be in touch with family members before and after the event.

Jerry himself put together a list of family birthdays and anniversaries and tracked them on a calendar so he would not forget to acknowledge them. In these ways Jerry could tell his family that he had a commitment to it. His participation and interest in his siblings and their families would energize his relationships with them and ultimately, would energize him so that he was not an emotional zero.

I warned Jerry that he might encounter resistance. His family members might be angry—distancing by a close relative often breeds anger—and indicate that they didn't want him to get closer. They might have the attitude: "You've been outside so long, why are you back now? And now that you are, what do you want us to do about it?"

Jerry's spontaneous reaction would be to cut off, to retreat into the distance he knows so well. I asked him to be aware of that reaction, of the behavior that feels natural to him when people do not embrace him. But I asked him to smother those instincts and not to run away.

I had cautioned Jerry against "jumping in with both feet," as he put it. People like Jerry, who are emotionally distant, are likely to be impulsive and highly reactive when they try to reconnect with people. It was usually to avoid this kind of intensity that they distanced themselves in the first place. But extremes in behavior often drive people away. And Jerry must relearn this lesson in his own family where it all began before he can move toward a healthy, intimate relationship of his own.

CHAPTER TWENTY-SEVEN

———— / ————

Russell:
"Why Am I Destroying My Life?"

Russell came to me because he felt overwhelmed with problems that he said had turned his life upside down. He showed me his journal, in which he had written, "What a way to destroy a life! Once I was an extrovert, organized and very social. Today I am an introvert, obsessed with my own problems."

Russell is a well-known attorney, with clients throughout the United States and in foreign countries. He is recognized as a tough bargainer and a challenging opponent in the courtroom. Russell, thirty-three, told me that in his private life, however, he is a "wipeout." For five years he lived with Sophia, a charming, affectionate woman who owned and managed two posh restaurants in Chicago. As soon as Sophia suggested that Russell give up his apartment and move in with her, he became nervous but could think of no good reason to refuse. Instead of working on his relationship with her, he sought opportunities to travel more on business. Two months later he began having an affair with Marla, a Florida woman who was an exotic if somewhat neurotic nightclub dancer.

Because Russell's work demanded a lot of travel, he began to live what he calls a "schizophrenic existence," ricocheting between Sophia in Chicago and Marla in Miami. Each woman believed she was the only one in his life. And Russell says he felt no guilt.

After six months Sophia became suspicious and confronted him. He denied that there was another woman in his life but became so agitated that he began to confide in friends and colleagues. When he thought about leaving Sophia, he sobbed. But it didn't stop him from being magnetically drawn to Marla. It eventually became the only thing he could talk about, the only thing he could think about. Each time he visited Marla, he saw Sophia in his mind. When he returned to Chicago, his heart was still in Miami.

In his journal he wrote, "This is my first crisis. I have never had to leave something behind. I need to know why I'm having so much trouble. I feel my problems with these two women are symbolic of something much deeper. . . ."

Russell, of course, was correct. His problems could be traced back to his grandparents and to the style of *avoidance* and *distance* that characterized his family. Russell knew, for instance, that his mother's parents were divorced when his mother was eight and her brother was eleven. He knew too that his grandmother had remarried and died several years afterward. And that his mother's older brother died a year later.

Russell knew, too, that their deaths were something that the family did not talk about, that they were forbidden secrets from the past. He did not know that both deaths were suicides and that his mother blamed the suicides on the divorce of her parents.

His mother, a psychiatric social worker, married when she was forty. Her husband, an economics consultant, came from a large, happy family, the kind his mother wanted to be part of. They agreed that they would have one child and dedicate their lives to him. His mother wanted to make up for her own unhappy childhood, and his father, having come from a joyous family, wanted to pay, through his child, what he considered his debt to society for having given him so much happiness.

Russell was born a year after they married. Six months later they divorced; the contrast between his father's close family and his mother's absence of family ties caused too much tension between them.

Russell's mother, an attractive and competent woman, remarried immediately, and Russell was raised by his stepfather. Until I brought his mother in to join us in therapy, Russell did not know that his stepfather was not his biological father. His mother confessed that she thought it would be too painful for him and saw no purpose in revealing that information.

Russell remembers his early life as being a maze of parties, friends, relatives, and what seemed like endless entertaining. His mother, in an effort to keep the peace in the family that was so important to her, rarely offered an opinion about anything. It was clear that even when she disagreed, she suppressed her feelings to maintain harmony.

But as far as Russell could remember, his parents never talked to each other on an intimate level and never resolved any differences between them. His mother just accommodated to whatever her husband wanted, and substituted a dizzying social life for the intimacy that would have enriched her marriage.

Meanwhile she saw her job as protecting her son from pain and anxiety. When there was a problem, however insignificant, between Russell and the man he thought was his father, she intervened and kept them from settling it together. She said that raising Russell was "her job." Her husband didn't understand children. As a result Russell grew up distant from his stepfather and helplessly dependent on a mother who managed his emotional life for him.

Russell's mother didn't allow him to go to anyone's funeral because it would be too traumatic for him. He never visited his grandparents' or his uncle's graves. He never saw his biological father, and his mother did not tell him when his father died. Russell was nineteen at the time.

I wasn't especially surprised when I learned that Russell had been keeping secrets from me too. In our fifth session together he revealed that he had married Sophia just before initiating his affair with Marla. None of their friends knew about it; neither did his mother. He knew his mother and Sophia didn't like each other, and he wanted to spare his mother the pain of knowing that he had married her.

Russell acknowledges that he counts on women to be like his mother—to compromise their feelings and please him. He also expects them to take care of him emotionally the way his mother did. His mother did all of his feeling for him and didn't expect him to deal with intimacy on his own. She helped him become a good student and competent in working with large groups. But he is anxious about intimacy because he doesn't know what to do with it. It is easier just to walk away.

Sophia is demanding that he get to know her better and she wants him to reveal himself and discuss his feelings. He has no experience doing that.

Marla, on the other hand, is willing to do what his mother did, protect him and even think for him where relationships are concerned. But he wants more from marriage than that. He knows that his mother has not been happy, and he is angry with her because she never speaks out for what she wants. He doesn't want to be like his mother, but he doesn't know how not to be.

When Russell talks of not being able to leave anything behind, he is referring to his family of origin. His is the classic case of a child-focused marriage where the anxieties

of his mother, who never came to terms with her parents'
divorce and her mother's and brother's subsequent suicides, were centered on him. By insulating her son from
pain, she is able to avoid her own.

Russell is still reacting to it, angry at his mother on one
level but unable to extricate himself from her emotionally
on another. He is her flip side: she takes care of emotions
for everyone else and Russell gets everyone else to take
care of emotions for him. He needs to begin taking responsibility for his feelings instead of relying on others to do it
for him. And he needs to work with his mother to unravel
the secrets of his past so they don't continue to cast shadows on his life.

On the plus side Russell did not have some of the problems that plague children of divorce. He was not subjected
to the "web of relationships"—stepparents, stepsisters,
stepbrothers—that complicate the lives of most children
whose parents split, then remarry. And he was so young
when his mother remarried that he never had to deal, as he
was growing up, with the divorce that occurred between his
biological parents. There was no issue about visitation
rights, custody, or an absent father (that he knew about) to
add trauma to his life.

But divorces—his grandparents' and his parents'—have
trailed him, because they and their legacy were not acknowledged and worked through as a part of his family
history. Russell had no opportunity to struggle through
relationships with people who could have helped him know
who he was.

The reason for his grandparents' divorce—she found her
husband in bed with another woman—was a taboo subject.
And Russell was a man without a past, without continuity,
without a backdrop against which to examine himself.

While Russell knew intellectually that his relationship
problems with Sophia and Marla had their roots in his
mother's relationship with him, he needed to experience

that pattern where it began. He started meeting with his mother once a week to talk about her childhood, encouraging her to share her feelings so he could begin to understand his own.

I suggested that he talk to his mother about Sophia and Marla even though he knew it would make her unhappy. I told him to ask her how she dealt with men when she was dating.

Did she ever experience the feelings he is having?

How did she decide when a relationship was over?

How did she decide that she wanted to get married? And divorced?

How did she deal with doubts about herself?

As I had warned Russell, these meetings with his mother resulted initially in a reenactment of old family patterns. Russell's mother, instead of talking about herself, shifted the focus to her son. She offered him advice, made it clear that she would try to "heal" him, and told him how much she was worried about him. At first Russell allowed her to do that. It felt comfortable and it felt good. But after a while he became frustrated and he could see the pattern. He wanted his mother to talk about *her* feelings. She kept focusing on *his*.

The parallels in his own relationships with Sophia and Marla became remarkably clear. When his relationship with Sophia became too intense (as his did with his mother when he asked her to reveal her feelings), he withdrew and headed for Marla, who would comfort and take care of him. Just as Mom did.

Russell is starting to see that Sophia's complaints about him are valid. She doesn't know who he is because he doesn't know who he is either.

Russell knows he has just begun. He has asked to see pictures of his father and wants to know more about him. He wants to meet his father's sister and her children, who live in Phoenix. Meanwhile he tells me he recognizes that

Marla was merely a "prop" for him and that he is beginning to feel less tense and more committed to his relationship with Sophia.

He showed me the most recent entry in his journal. It was a letter to Sophia.

"Dear Sophia," he wrote. "I love you, but I hate you for forcing me to look inside myself. It is painful and I have no experience doing this. My mother kept me from feeling because she did it for me. All my life I have known where I was going. Now I have to begin to learn who I really am. Please stay with me while I try. . . ."

CHAPTER TWENTY-EIGHT

———— ⁄ ————

Buddy: The Second Time Around

Buddy's parents divorced when he was thirteen. He was divorced when he was thirty.

Sally was divorced when she was thirty-one. Her parents filed for divorce six months later.

Now Sally and Buddy, after living together for two years, have decided they want to marry. They want to have children and build a cohesive, close family, unlike the ones they came from. They are united in their goals but consider themselves losers. They have no confidence that they can achieve the kind of marriage they want.

Buddy is perplexed. He thought he knew what was wrong with his parents' marriage. And he entered his own marriage with Karyn, his first wife, prepared to live differently than his parents had.

Sally's parents were together when she married for the first time, but their relationship was tempestuous and fragile. Like Buddy, she thought she had learned from her parents' mistakes. She was shocked when, after two years of marriage, she and her husband agreed they were not meant for each other.

Buddy and Sally were afraid it would happen again. No matter how determined they were to build a strong marriage, neither Buddy nor Sally was convinced that they could do it. After all, they had already tried once—and failed.

Buddy is one of three children. He has two sisters: one, a year older than he, and one, a year younger.

Buddy remembers his childhood as chaotic, explosive, and full of conflict. His parents rarely agreed about anything and blamed each for everything from the leak in the bathroom plumbing to the war in Vietnam. He said he felt as though their separation would be a relief.

It wasn't. After the divorce, all of the children stayed with their mother for almost two years. But Buddy says that his relationship with his mother was a replay of the chaos and arguments that had plagued his parents' marriage. As I explained earlier, after divorce mothers often treat their sons the same way they treated their husbands, and in so doing foster the same kinds of conflicts.

The children had little to do with one another. Each expressed his or her misery differently. Buddy screamed and slammed a lot of doors. His older sister spent a lot of time with friends and was at home only at mealtime. His younger sister and mother seemed close for a while, but when she turned seventeen and began to date, problems erupted between them. Their parents agreed that it might be better for all of the children to live with their father.

"When I lived with my mother, I couldn't concentrate on anything and I really didn't care," Buddy says. "I felt disconnected and we had no family to speak of. We never saw my mother's relatives, and my dad's family lived far away. So I felt as though I were floating in space, with no roots. I felt as though my mom was always picking on me and nothing I did could ever please her. I used to see other kids who seemed to be part of happy families, doing things together. I felt deprived and angry. I was happy to move in with my father."

Buddy's father had wanted to become a college professor, but his family could not afford his education and he became a high school teacher instead. He very much wanted his son to be what he could not, and he encouraged him to study and think about an academic career.

"Maybe it was because I finally felt someone cared what I did," Buddy told me. "Or maybe the goal of being a professor was something real I could hang on to. Or maybe it was just that my dad and I got along better and our home felt stable for the first time I could remember. My grades rose from *D*'s to *A*'s and I found myself on the honor roll."

Four years later his father remarried and had another child, a son. Then everything changed. Despite his father's attempts to be attentive to him, Buddy felt very much like an outsider in what he considered this new family of three.

"We lived in the same house—my sisters, the baby, my dad and his wife and me—but I might as well have been living on an island alone. My sisters and I, instead of becoming closer, seemed to go our own ways, and we lived separate lives in our own little boxes. When I came home from school, I would go into my room and close the door. I might not say a word to anyone until dinner."

Buddy talks about feeling stranded and isolated, unable to share his feelings with anyone. He envied the warm, noisy families he saw around him and longed to have that for himself one day. Meanwhile he found his solace and safety at school. There he achieved high grades and became active in extracurricular activities. He was star of the debating team, won a scholarship to college, and went on to graduate school.

When he was twenty-four, he met Karyn and they married after a brief, intense, four-month courtship. Buddy was attracted to Karyn, a petite redhead, and drawn to her

family. She was one of four children, all closely involved
with each other. They lived in the same city, talked on the
telephone every day, saw each other on weekends, and
spent every holiday together, including birthdays and anniversaries.

It was a dramatic contrast from the fragmentation of his
own family. This was the kind of family Buddy had dreamed
about, and he joined it eagerly.

For a while it worked. He felt nourished by the closeness,
supported by the loyalty, and strengthened by the unconditional love his wife's family brought to him. There was,
however, a downside for which he was unprepared. Karyn
was so enmeshed with her family that she did not know how
to build a separate, intimate life with him.

It was not an issue until she became pregnant. When she
learned she was going to have a baby, she told her mother
and sisters before she told her husband. "That didn't feel
right to me," says Buddy, "but I told myself that that's the
way it sometimes is in close families. And that was, after all,
what I had wanted. Wasn't it?"

After the birth of the baby, a daughter, their relationship
as a married couple fizzled. Karyn was constantly visiting
her mother, talking with her sisters and brothers, and hov-
ering over the baby. There was no time left for a husband.
Then Buddy was offered a prestigious teaching position in
another part of the country. Karyn accepted the move without protest but found she was irritable and unhappy with
the separation from her family, on which she was so dependent. She and Buddy began to argue. Some days their
three-room apartment almost burst with the sounds of
high-pitched voices, screams, and accusations. Other days
it was silent without a word spoken between them. Their
telephone bills soared as Karyn spent hours on the long-
distance line.

"I used to get this déjà vu feeling," Buddy told me.
"Whenever we argued or gave each other the silent treat-

ment, I relived my parents' marriage. That's exactly what they did. Exactly what I promised myself I would never do. We were growing further and further apart. It was almost as though I were a helpless bystander watching my marriage go down the drain."

When he came to see me, he knew that he could not enter a second marriage before he understood what had gone wrong with his first. But he did not have a clue to the scenario that now seems simple and obvious to him.

He was so eager to embrace a family different from his own that he did not take the time to know Karyn as an individual before they married. He could not see and at the time probably didn't care that she was an emotionally immature woman who literally never left her parents. As long as she lived near them and was entwined in their lives, she was able to function. Without them she felt vulnerable and unprotected.

Buddy married too early. He was not sufficiently mature in his personal relationships to assess what he really wanted for his future. He leaped from the sterility of his own family into the tantalizing passion of Karyn's. The stability that had eluded him in the past was seductive. And he bought the package blindly.

I helped him to recognize that *closeness* in families is not synonymous with *enmeshment,* that even the most devoted family members can be emotionally separate from each other and free to build their lives with their spouses and children.

In Karyn's family people were not expected to separate. In the case of her brothers and sisters, each of whom married someone who didn't mind, perhaps even revered, that lifestyle, it worked out all right. Had Buddy not been transferred to another area, had he not cared that his wife was more involved with her family than she was with him, their marriage might have worked too.

In their case, though, the birth of a child signaled the

rapid demise of the relationship. It is not uncommon. A husband and wife, even those with limited emotional maturity, frequently can manage an intimate relationship with each other. Their marriages looks successful—until a child is born. It takes a lot of emotional maturity to juggle another intimate relationship. And a child born to an emotionally immature couple often marks the start of serious problems. Even when they don't understand the dynamics, people intuitively know that a child will test a marriage's strength. That's why there is so much anxiety connected with having children. As Buddy says, "Once we had a child, we no longer had a marriage."

Children often respond to their parents' behavior patterns in two ways: They repeat them or they rebel against them, aggressively trying to be different, to live differently. *Both kinds of behavior are potentially destructive because they are based on reactions to the past and to other people.* Repetition and rebellion are opposites sides of the same coin; both represent bondage, not freedom. For behaviorally immature people, freedom of choice is an illusion.

Freedom comes when people separate their needs and their responses from those of their parents. No matter the choices they make—some may be the same as their parents, others may signify a sharp departure—they should occur because an individual feels comfortable with them, not because he or she is playing out the past.

Buddy still dreams of a close, warm, and nourishing family. But he is no longer willing to be seduced by that image without considering the other things that are important to him in a marriage.

Unlike Buddy, Sally's parents stayed together for nineteen years. However, their marriage, like Buddy and Karyn's, began to unravel as soon as their first child, Sally's older sister, was born. With each additional child—Sally and her younger sister, Martha—the marriage became more a backdrop with the children and their mother as the major players.

Sally's mother is the youngest of four siblings, none of whom was particularly successful. She came out of that family determined to "make something of my children." From the day they were born, she began to mold them into the competent, professional women she wanted them to be.

Today Sally is a bank president, her older sister is senior partner in a prominent accounting firm, and her younger sister is a surgeon. Sally describes her mother as a blend of pushy and domineering with her children, but subordinate to her husband, a highly paid management consultant.

In fact, Sally's mother allowed her husband to make decisions about everything except the children. He decided where they would live, which vacations they would take, how they would furnish their house and spend their money, and who their friends would be.

"I think my mother tolerated it because it didn't really matter," Sally says. "Her primary goal was to raise three high-achieving daughters. As long as Dad didn't interfere with that, anything else he wanted was okay. When he did try to have some say about us, that's when the trouble started."

Like Buddy and Karyn, Sally's parents argued about their "child-focused" marriage. Sally's father wanted more energy devoted to him. Her mother wanted him to be more invested in the children. Sally remembers conflict escalating in the marriage and reaching its highest pitch each time one of the children was leaving home.

After all of the children were gone, her parents had nothing left but a conflict. So they divorced.

In the meantime Sally had quickly climbed the ladder of success her mother had constructed for her, but she was struggling with personal relationships. She lived with a man for two years through a stormy and unstable alliance. But they decided to get married anyway, hoping that the marriage would save the relationship. It did not. Sally had never seen her parents solve personal conflict, and she didn't have the remotest idea of how to solve her own. Neither did her husband, whose parents were divorced when he was ten. After eighteen months they made a mutual decision to go their own ways.

Sally recognizes that she is inflexible, much like her mother, and that she doesn't know how to confront differences and work them through. Like her mother, she ignores issues that she doesn't consider critical, but won't bend about others that are meaningful to her.

"I didn't like the way my ex-husband left the bathroom," Sally told me. "He wouldn't dry the sink and he'd leave the toothpaste open and his wet towel hanging over the door. It would make me crazy. But I ignored it because there were more important things to argue about. For instance, my work schedule. I traveled at least seven days out of every month. He didn't like it. I wouldn't stop doing it. For me there was no compromise. We argued all the time, but we got nowhere.

"I wonder now if we were really arguing about my travel or whether it was the sloppy bathroom we never talked about that made me so unwilling to compromise. If I tolerated his mess, maybe he shouldn't be so picky about my travel."

Sally and Buddy learned a lot about themselves through looking back at their parents' and their own first marriages. While they very much want a baby, they don't want the baby to usurp their relationship with each other. Sally knows she is at risk for practicing the same level of addiction to a child that her mother did, and Buddy, through his experience with Karyn, is exquisitely aware of how the advent of a child can strain a marriage.

In fact, they talk a lot about who will take this baby, yet unconceived, to the baby-sitter each day, how much night work each of them will be able to do, and how the baby will fit into their busy lives. They talk about the appropriate level of what they call "babyhood," meaning the level of devotion to a baby. Sally is making it clear that if a baby is in their future, she is not having it alone.

Both recognize that an unbalanced investment in a child is not only bad for the marriage, it is bad for the children. They may become skilled professionals, such as Sally and her sisters, but they are impaired because they have not been exposed to a marriage that is attentive to the needs of each parent as well as those of the children.

It is unfortunate that it took a failed first marriage for both Sally and Buddy to help them see their noxious family patterns. But against that backdrop, the awareness it has given them, and with continued communication with their families, I believe that they can achieve a satisfying and happy marriage.

PART SIX

————/————

Daughters of Divorce

Like boys, the stereotypical behavior of girls tends to become more pronounced when the family is going through a period of stress and the maturity level of all its members plunges.

You have learned, in earlier chapters, that during and immediately after the divorce, girls tend to:

- identify with their mothers and show sensitivity to and compassion for them
- become supercompetent, taking care of their mothers through depression, looking after younger siblings, and doing household chores
- relate well to adults and have meaningful friendships
- appear to have adjusted well

Their relationship with their mother often takes a turn for the worse when the girls move into adolescence and begin dating. Or it may happen even sooner if the mother remarries and her daughter resents her stepfather.

The importance of a girl's relationship with her father cannot be underestimated; it is from this relationship that she learns, or fails to learn, how men think and behave and gets a sense of her femininity.

As they grow up, girls, particularly those who have had poor or no communication with their fathers, often have trouble with heterosexual relationships. Sometimes, as in the case of Carolyn, whom you will meet in the next chapter, they can't control their emotions. Sometimes, as in Vicki's case, they choose the wrong men. Or like Tammy, they can't sustain a relationship.

You will also be reading about Ginger, who doesn't want to make the same mistakes as her parents; Vivian, who believes that relationships are not meant to last over time; Sheila, who says she can never trust anyone; and Donna, who despite a good marriage lives in fear of being betrayed. As you read their stories, think about yourself and which patterns feel familiar to you.

CHAPTER TWENTY-NINE

Carolyn:
"I Never Feel Good
About Myself"

Carolyn comes from a family that has given her an overdose of all of the immature family styles we talked about earlier. There is extreme distance juxtaposed with choking closeness. Her family is violent, chaotic, and dysfunctional, and it includes an alcoholic father whom she seldom sees. At thirty-three, Carolyn is still the object of intense child-focus by her mother.

She understands clearly the reasons for her parents' breakup, and she knows how she became the target of her family's problems. She sees the patterns that are at play in her family. Nonetheless she is not able to use that knowledge to improve her own relationships with men. Despite her considerable achievements in school and in her career, she feels she is worth nothing, and her low self-esteem drives her into highly intense but ultimately destructive personal relationships.

Carolyn is convinced that her life will never include happiness with a man. "I have been told that I antagonize men," she says. "I have been told that I am too clingy. That I'm too needy. Or I'm not needy enough.

"I know I'm emotionally unstable. Sometimes I make nice-nice with people and never say how I really feel. Sometimes I'm like a lunatic. I scream and scream and overreact. If I have a confrontation with someone, I cry. I cry a lot.

"Anger? What do I do with my anger? I'm never angry," she says, self-mockingly. "It is frightening. I sometimes feel something that might be anger. But I never know what it is until it builds and builds and turns into rage. Then I'm out of control."

Carolyn has a high-powered job as a financial analyst. She sailed through college with a 4.0 average, was graduated Phi Beta Kappa, was first in her class and head of her sorority. Before graduation she was solicited by several of the country's premier brokerage houses.

She is known as a dynamo in her field, smugly independent, meticulously organized, and unbearably efficient. Her friends find it incredible that her private life is in such chaos, that she is tortured by thoughts of growing old alone and lonely. And that she is totally unable to transfer her logic and competence from her professional to her personal life.

Carolyn recognizes her problems with an insight that is clear and penetrating. She says, "In academics, a career, in volunteer work, I'm A–OK. When it comes to family, sex, life, relationships—even with girlfriends—I'm a zero. I know that there are many people like me who kick ass in the professional world and cry themselves to sleep at night."

Carolyn knows that she places herself in destructive relationships. She knows that she begins a relationship feeling slightly scornful of the man and determined to maintain emotional distance from him. And that the minute she lets down her defenses, the minute she begins to care, her stance switches from strong and independent to demanding and needy.

"Men have told me that one month I'm one way and the next month I'm completely different. I know that as soon as I get involved with a man, I wait for the other shoe to drop. So I create a situation where he will leave. I push and I antagonize. It makes him crazy and we always break up."

Carolyn's parents were divorced when she was nine after a violent, blustery marriage marked by screaming, cursing, and physical abuse. Carolyn says she was never abused, but her mother and father fought with their fists. In between the violence, there were some peaceful times when her father, who was an alcoholic, would hug her and play with her. "When I smell alcohol now," Carolyn says, "I still feel my father hugging me."

Within six months after the divorce her mother brought a new man home and told her children—Carolyn and her three brothers—that he would be staying. So would his four children. "They got married and I got four instant sisters," Carolyn says. "One moved into my room, and the others shared all of my things. My mother was trying so hard to mother these girls, to win their approval, and I was jealous. I kept thinking, 'What about me?' "

Life for Carolyn became even more chaotic. Her mother's second marriage was, in some ways, more conflicted than the first. There were custody battles on both sides and bitter envy between her father and stepfather. Each demanded that she denounce the other, and visitations were a nightmare.

"I knew some divorces where the parents were civil to each other. But I was scared every time my father dropped me off at home after visitation. My father and stepfather would get into a fistfight. My stepsiblings would start screaming at my father. They hated him. Then my mom would start yelling. I felt as though I had to run for cover."

Like many children of divorce, Carolyn felt a sharp sense of split loyalties. Her father wanted her to side with him, against her mother; her mother wanted the same thing.

"When I was with my dad, I wanted to agree with him so he would love me. To defend my mother was to alienate my father. Then my mom would get angry because I was not defending her enough. It was a free-for-all."

Carolyn couldn't wait to get away from home for college in California. She was certain she could discard her past and make a new beginning. It didn't work. At college she became promiscuous and gained a reputation for being loose and easy.

"People think that kids are resilient and that they bounce back after their parents divorce," Carolyn says. "But that's not the way it happens. The problems follow you like the scent of a perfume you can't wash away. The kind of stuff I went through lowers your self-esteem, and that leads to all kinds of problems. I have never seen long-lasting healthy relationships between adults, and I don't have the vaguest idea how to have them myself. I never made the connection."

After college Carolyn continued to have a series of draining relationships. There was Willie, who showered her with gifts and flowers and kindness. At first she resisted his overtures and made it clear that she could "take him or leave him." But the minute she started to care, she became a different person—clingy and immature, doubting his love, constantly demanding reassurance that she was the most important person in his life. The relationship ended after four months.

Then there was Ben. Ben told Carolyn she was special and he loved her more intensely than he had ever loved anyone in his life. The trouble was that Ben was engaged to Vyette and would be married in four months. No matter. Carolyn continued to see him because "he was stroking me all the time, feeding all of the needs I had for so long. It didn't matter that he was playing me like a violin.

"I never felt as though I deserved to be number one in anyone's life anyway. This whole crazy scene, the emotional highs and lows, the instability, the bizarre nature of our relationship, felt like home to me. I knew it was wrong, but I couldn't stop.

"When you grow up in a chaotic home, chaos is all you know. There is something addictive about it. That's the way you feel comfortable. So when you're in a relationship that is stormy and troubled, you feel like you're swimming in familiar water. You meet someone who is stable . . . and that is foreign territory. My childhood has really done a number on me."

Carolyn can remember no celebration involving her family that has not been marked by turmoil and embarrassment.

"Friends would walk into my house and feel the tension of our blended family. No day was sacred. We have never made it through a holiday yet. It is too stressful, and my stepfather can't handle social behavior. My college graduation was a nightmare.

"We were in a restaurant after graduation. All of my peers were there. And it was me, my mom, my stepfather, and his daughters. All of a sudden my mom and stepfather started arguing loudly. Everyone was looking at us. Then he got up and blustered out of the restaurant and locked himself in his hotel room. Here I am, graduating with the highest honors and my parents aren't speaking to each other. All of us are sobbing and everyone is trying not to stare. I have lived with this kind of pressure all my life. No matter how well things are going, I always wait for something to spoil it."

Carolyn describes her relationship with her mother as very close. "We look alike and we think alike. But Mom feels guilty about me, and she tries to advise me about relationships. She says she has done this to me, that she never showed me anything better. She is compulsive about not wanting me to feel her pain. She'll say to me, 'You sound too needy when you say that to him.' Or 'You go too fast.

You'll scare him away.' Once she took notes on the back of an envelope about what I said to a guy that I shouldn't have said."

Carolyn grew up with no supportive people in her life. Her mother's father was killed in an accident when she was a toddler. His wife, Carolyn's grandmother, was mentally ill and later died of heart disease. One of her aunts, her mother's sister, died of uncontrolled diabetes when she was in her twenties. And her mother had married at seventeen to get away from home.

When her parents divorced, Carolyn said, there were no more relatives. Connections with her father's extended family dissolved. Her grandmother told her, "I'm not related to you anymore."

In the midst of this isolation, Carolyn had to deal with a father who rejected her, a stepfather who alternately embraced and cast her aside, and a mother who exchanged one volatile relationship for another. There were different sets of rules for dealing with different people, and Carolyn said that at any given time she could have kept a list of people in the family who weren't talking to each other.

"When my mother and stepfather had a difference, they would blow up at each other. There was no physical violence, but lots of obscenities and meaningless threats. Then Mom would want to talk. But my stepfather would stop talking. That was his way of punishing her. So I would watch communication cease while everyone just continued to go on as though nothing happened.

"So I learned not to trust feelings. Your parents act like nothing is wrong. But you know that everything is wrong. So now I check everything. I have no convictions. I don't even trust myself. I almost have to check the color of my underwear. And I'm like a chameleon. I tend to become who I'm around because inside I'm really nobody."

Carolyn has made giant strides in therapy. She knows that her academic and professional achievements are external props that she can count on. They feed her self-esteem . . . but not for long. And they haven't made her feel better about herself.

She knows that she has trouble setting boundaries and can't regulate appropriate distance between herself and a man. She is relationship-dependent. As soon as she begins to care for a man, she puts all of her energy into him and loses focus on herself. This imbalance between thinking and feeling is overwhelming to a potential partner and scares him away.

Carolyn understands, too, that she is too enmeshed with her mother in a way that does not respect limits. Her mother gives her money for her birthday, then tells her how to spend it. She invites her mother and two guests of her choice to lunch, then tells her whom to bring. She admits that every time she leaves her mother's house, she wonders whether she will ever see her again. This is the kind of anxiety a year-and-a-half-old child struggles with. Something is wrong when it is still a problem at age thirty-three.

Carolyn is trying to become less intensely involved with people and to tone down her reactions. I have asked her to contrast her personal and professional life so she recognizes that she has the capacity to behave differently. I asked her: "How do you resolve a difference of opinion at work? How much do you worry about whether your coworkers will agree or disagree with you?" Carolyn says that kind of thinking has helped her. It makes her feel as though within her lies the potential for a less frenzied personal life. She no longer feels she has an inherent defect that she can never escape.

While Carolyn and Jerry, whom I described earlier, have taken different journeys through their lives, they have arrived at the same place. Both of them are products of intense relationships in their families. Jerry reacted by "distancing" himself from his emotions. Carolyn became too emotional and lost the ability to be self-reflective. In the end they both feel as though they are emotional nobodies.

Carolyn's intensity keeps her from sustaining a relationship. She becomes so entangled with people that all she can do is react without thinking. Jerry is as emotional as pablum, reacting to nothing, so his relationships don't survive either.

Carolyn has to learn how to regulate her feelings in the context of a close, personal relationship. While group therapy—where she could become aware of how emotionally reactive she is—could help her, I suggested that her family needs to be her group. She needs to "catch" her emotional reactions with the people who make a difference in her life.

Carolyn has begun to meet with her mother once a week to talk about the past in a calm and thoughtful way without overreacting. "It's hard," Carolyn told me. "I'm so used to jumping in with both feet [the same expression Jerry used]. But I'm determined to stay with it because I don't want to go through life the way I am.

"Right now I have little faith in lasting love. I feel people love me for short periods of time, but anyone who has said he loved me has found it easy to stop loving me. My father. My stepfather. My boyfriends. I think it is a fairy tale that someone will be there for me for a long time."

CHAPTER THIRTY

———/———

Ginger:
"I Don't Want to Make
the Same Mistakes"

Unlike Carolyn's volatile parents, Ginger's family had a civilized marriage . . . and a civilized divorce. Until the day she came home from college to find her father's closets empty, Ginger did not know that her parents were having serious problems. She still doesn't understand why their marriage broke up. She has asked her parents, but neither of them is able to explain it in a way that makes sense to her. Because there is so much information she doesn't have, she feels free-floating anxiety all the time—as though something will go wrong with her life and she won't even know what it's all about.

Ginger is twenty-nine, married, and pregnant with her first child. She describes her courtship as "whirlwind," her marriage as "solid," her career as a commercial artist as "satisfying." There is no reason, she says, why she should be so preoccupied with her parents' divorce, why she should be as nervous as she is that something she can't

control will, without warning, sweep down and turn her
world upside down.

Impending parenthood, for all of us a time of joy and
stress, has made her even more conscious of the fragility
and complexities of human relationships, of bonds that
suddenly break and ties that insidiously disintegrate.

Ginger was twenty-one, a junior in college, when her
parents divorced. She and her younger sister, Gail, were
given no information or explanation, just a lot of tears from
both her mother and father about a marriage that wasn't
meant to be and couldn't be salvaged.

"She doesn't want me there," her father said sadly.

"He just left me," her mother said between sobs.

Ginger was furious that her parents had not shared with
her news that would change her life as dramatically as it
changed theirs; they said they didn't want to disturb her
during exam time.

Her sister, who was living at home, just said, "Dad's
gone. I don't know why." She hinted that their mother had
another romantic interest, but Ginger says she didn't, and
still doesn't, believe it. When I asked whether she had ques-
tioned her mother, she said she couldn't do that. She didn't
know why. She just couldn't. But she thinks about it a lot,
and she uses up a lot of energy trying to unravel the mys-
tery of her parents' split.

"We had a charmed family," she told me. "Wonderfully
close, especially on my mother's side. There were almost
no arguments, and the four of us went to church together
every Sunday. We visited my grandparents—my mother's
parents—a lot, and we didn't hear any arguing there either.
Gail and I were pretty happy kids. That's why the divorce
was such a shock."

In looking back, in trying to dissect the marriage, Ginger
admits that there were clues. Her mother and father shared
few interests except their children. Her dad was a workaholic who brought papers home at night and stretched

them across the dining room table after dinner. There was little talk between him and Ginger; mostly it was Ginger, Gail, and Mom who spent time together.

Ginger's mother, outgoing and bubbly, loved the theater, rock music, and dancing; her father, serious and sedate, preferred golf and card games. As years went by, they spent more time with their own circle of friends than with each other. It was a family that did little sharing of feelings. If there were differences of opinion between her parents, Ginger didn't know it. They never discussed anything other than trivia.

After several months in therapy, Ginger is recognizing that it was not the absence of differences that characterized her parents' marriage. It was her family's style of not acknowledging differences, not confronting them, not seeking ways to resolve them, that was the biggest problem of all. It is a problem that still exists for Ginger and for her parents. And now she can track specific incidents—a series of flashbacks—that puts the family style in sharper focus for her.

When her father was about to remarry, he called Ginger the day before to share his plans. He told her, tearfully, that he wanted her to be at the marriage ceremony. He didn't tell her, and she didn't ask, why he waited so long to call her. Click.

When Ginger was graduated from college, a year after her parents had separated, her dad told her he had been at her graduation. But he hadn't been able to come up to her because he couldn't handle seeing her mother up close. Click.

When her grandfather (Dad's father) died, her stepmother, not her father, called to give her the news. "Your dad's not good at this sort of thing," his wife told Ginger. Click.

When Ginger visits her hometown on holidays, she usually sees her dad once but spends most of the time with her mother.

How does her father feel about it? Does he wish she would spend Thanksgiving or Christmas or Easter with him? "I don't know," Ginger admits. "I never ask. He doesn't say." Click.

When Ginger's aunts—three of them, her mother's sisters—all divorced within three years, no one asked whether there might be any common causes. In fact, no one asked anything, and Ginger does not have any idea why the divorces occurred. Does her mother know? Probably not. But Ginger doesn't ask. Click.

When Ginger became engaged to Bernie, her mother had not yet met him, and Ginger had not even indicated to her mother that she was seriously interested in a man. When she called home to announce the engagement, her mother wondered, "Who is he, dear?" Click.

When Ginger met her husband, she was just winding down a seven-year-long romance with Elliot. But she never called Elliot to tell him she was about to be engaged . . . to someone else. "I think he was shocked, but it never occurred to me to talk to him about it." Click.

This "click" did not come easily. In fact, even after I pointed it out to her, Ginger was stunned that her behavior mirrored her family style. "That's awful," she kept saying. "I can't believe I did that."

Ginger says that when she thinks of her family, she still thinks about the "four of them"—her parents, her sister, and herself. "I like to think of the way we were, not the way we are now. This is a divorce that didn't have to happen. My mom and dad still belong together."

Ginger is still seeing the collapse of her parents' marriage as the collapse of her family, and she finds it exquisitely painful. Actually, the marriage was over long before the divorce occurred. It was only her mother and father's separate social networks that stabilized their relationship enough to keep it together until their children were older.

It is not the divorce that is making Ginger feel so impoverished. It is her family style. She and her sister were young adults when her parents decided to end their marriage. They could have discussed their divorce with her and Gail and assured them that they would not be losing their family. Her father could have attended her graduation without hiding. Perhaps her mother even could have included her former husband in Thanksgiving dinners.

But this is a family that can't deal with pain or loss or face unpleasantness. That's why Ginger's parents are having so much trouble continuing their role as parents. It is why her father can't tell her he would like to see her Christmas morning. It is why her mother can't explain why her marriage collapsed.

Ginger's goal in therapy is to "find her parents." The marriage is over, but her parents are still there. If she can be persistent in trying to reach them, she will get to know them for the first time. The new closeness she will feel will replace some of her pain.

Ginger's tasks include visits to each parent to ask questions about how their relationship deteriorated. She will ask each of them how they experienced important events such as her marriage, the birth of her sister's child, her father's second marriage. How does each of them think the other experienced it? Do they have unresolved feelings? Would they do things differently today?

As her questions provoke anxiety in her parents, she will observe how each of them responds. And she will notice her own emotional reactions. She will have to pay special attention to her family pattern of obscuring communication and avoiding unpleasantness, and be aware of how she participated in it.

As her questions and their answers open up communication, she will gain an understanding of her parents that will result in a different and more satisfying relationship with them. And she will be able to relax more in her own marriage, feeling that she still has a family and knowing that she does not have to repeat her parents' mistakes.

CHAPTER THIRTY-ONE

---/---

Tammy:
"I've Never Seen
a Normal Relationship"

Tammy's parents separated thirty years ago, but they are still not divorced. For most of that time Tammy has been the mediator in her family. When she was young, it was her job to deliver messages from one parent to another. When she grew up, she became their advisor, telling them how to live, where to live, which jobs to accept, and how to take better care of their health. She believes that she will spend her entire life ministering to them and envisions them together in their old age, with her as their caretaker. Meanwhile Tammy, a buyer for a Boston specialty shop, has not been able to form relationships of her own. She chooses men who she acknowledges are "losers" and says that she doesn't think she could have a successful relationship with anyone. "I've never seen people work out a relationship, so I'm not good at doing that. I'm afraid of ending up dependent and alone like my mother."

Tammy's parents separated when she was four and she has little recollection of an intact family. From time to time they would come back together for a month or two, but that hasn't happened in the past ten years.

Tammy's life has been one of never-ending conflict. It had to do with money, with visitation, with her father's girlfriends and her mother's boyfriends. In all of it, Tammy told me, she was the pawn, the go-between. She was the one who had to tell her dad that the support check bounced, who had to ask her mother if she could spend the weekend with Dad instead of just Saturday, who had to tell Dad how disgusting it was that he flaunted his new girlfriend with the dress down to here.

"It wasn't the separations that bothered me so much. It's the way I was used in them. My parents related to each other by putting me in the middle. My dad was painted as the 'bad guy' and I bought that image of him. In some ways I still do.

"But I'm not sure how much of it was an allegiance to my mother and how much anger I felt myself because Dad was the one who kept walking out on the marriage. Even though I'm closer to him today, I can't forgive him for running away and leaving us with a stack of bills and a lot of insecurity."

Both of Tammy's parents have had a series of romantic partners; Tammy has not liked any of them. "Mom chooses men who are nasty to her like my dad was, and Dad picks women who are so dependent that I end up taking care of them too. I talk to both of my parents three or four times a week, sometimes more. They always seem to have some problem they need my help with.

"Now that I'm older"—Tammy is thirty-four—"I can see the problems with both of them. My mother was too dependent, too much of a victim. She didn't take very good care of her own needs. Dad is erratic. And he has a terrible temper. He's not the kind of person you can count on. Still he is not all bad or all good. And the message I get is that even a good man can do bad things and hurt me."

Tammy told me that she very much wants to get married and have a family, that she envies her friends who are settled down with children. But close relationships scare her so she chooses men who are unavailable. Kevin, for instance, was married. He told her that he and his wife had grown apart, but that they "coexist." Tammy decided he was safe. Their relationship ended when he missed her birthday because it was his night to baby-sit.

Lenny lives in Omaha and comes to Boston once a month on business. He is safe too. "I can put him on the plane and send him home. I feel comfortable getting involved with people who don't live in Boston. That way I don't have to commit."

Douglas was her telephone companion. They talked for hours late at night and on weekends, but Douglas was involved with someone else. He kept making promises that his current relationship was nearing an end. When it did, Tammy changed her telephone number.

Tammy says she doesn't want to be victimized but is feeling panicky that she has the "victim mentality." And whenever she mentions a man to her mother, she senses animosity. "Maybe she thinks it will take time away from her. Or maybe she's afraid I'll get hurt."

Tammy represents the extreme in a child-focused marriage. Her mother and father make no distinction between being a parent and being a spouse. In fact, they are only spouses to each other through their relationship with her. Tammy completes the triangle that preserves the stability in her parents' relationship without permitting change, that keeps the marriage intact despite the long separation. Both of her parents depend on her, process their problems through her, and count on her, unconsciously, to keep the family from totally splintering. This has been Tammy's role since childhood, and it has not changed.

All of this puts her smack in the middle of her parents' marriage—where she does not belong. And it does not permit her to grow up and move toward establishing a family of her own.

Tammy's relationships fail for several reasons. She chooses the wrong men—the ones who aren't available—because she is afraid of a long-term commitment. She doesn't know how such relationships can work successfully because she has no examples in her past. And she does not know how to resolve differences without rupturing the relationship. As long as she doesn't get too close, she can't get too hurt.

The emotional architecture of her relationships with men duplicates that in her family. She fits into her partners' lives the way she fits into her parents'. By allying herself with men who are not available, she forms the triangle with which she is so familiar. This time her role is that of the other woman in someone else's unhappy marriage.

She says she wants marriage and a family but doesn't know how to get to that point. She admits that she "feels" her way through a relationship. As long as it feels okay, as long as there are no problems, she stays with it. But longer relationships inevitably produce differences that need to be thought through. That's when Tammy calls it quits.

"I don't know much about how to compromise, and I don't know what to do when he wants one thing and I want another. I figure that's my signal to leave or be left."

Tammy doesn't have the energy or time to pursue seriously her own relationships because she is still expending too much of herself on her parents.

In therapy she is facing several challenges—understanding how she can extricate herself from the family triangle without losing her closeness with her parents; learning that she is not responsible for her parents' happiness; mastering the blend of thinking and feeling that will help her move through the rough spots of relationships; and developing the courage to discuss her past with her parents so she can be free to change her response to damaging family patterns and reshape her future.

An early attempt to talk to her mother about their situation ended in an argument. So Tammy is trying to learn about her past through her mother's younger sister. But setting up a meeting with her aunt has already produced problems. Tammy's mother was threatened by her daughter's attempt to have a one-on-one relationship with her aunt. She felt excluded and sulked. Tammy felt guilty. So she canceled the appointment.

Tammy is stuck because she does whatever it takes to avoid grappling with feelings. Even though she knows how important it is for her to talk with her aunt, she can't tolerate the upheaval it will cause in her family. This is typical of people on the lower end of the behavioral maturity scale. They feel helpless about making change no matter how much it is needed. Once they can stop *reacting* and begin responding to an appropriate blend of thinking and feeling, productive change can take place.

Tammy needs to communicate with her aunt about her mother. She needs to know how her mother's family operated. How did her mother get along with *her* mother? What kind of marriage did her grandparents have? What role did her mother play in the family? Did her mother have trouble dating? What kind of men did she choose?

Tammy will learn that her relationship with her parents is strong enough to tolerate her search into the past, no matter the intensity of their protests. Tammy is a vital link in her family. Her parents may become angry, but they won't cut her off. That will be an important lesson for Tammy. Anger does not need to end relationships. In fact, dealing with anger appropriately can make a relationship stronger.

In talking to her aunt, Tammy can learn a lot about her mother and her family that will be useful in learning about herself. And the time will come when her mother and father (with whom she must undergo the same process) will be able to talk to her directly about issues that concern all of them.

This will be the mark of a relationship that has become "unstuck," a relationship between Tammy and her parents that is more mature. And it will be the beginning of Tammy's freedom to establish healthy relationships of her own.

CHAPTER THIRTY-TWO

————/————

Vivian:

Happily As Long As It Lasts

Vivian's parents prided themselves on their harmonious relationship. They never argued. They had no conflicts. And they would point with disdain to other couples who sparred publicly and didn't have their formula for happiness. They handled their divorce the same way they handled their marriage. Over dinner one night they told Vivian, who was fifteen, and her brother Eric, who was twelve, that they had decided to separate. "Don't worry," they told their children. "Nothing will change except that you will have two houses instead of one. You'll spend a week with Mom and a week with Dad and you'll have two sets of everything, one for each house."

The major problem was that neither Vivian nor her brother was given any reason for the breakup. "Mom told us sweetly that she and Dad just didn't love each other any more. These things sometimes happen," she said. "It was so civil." Today Vivian says she does not believe in marriage and "happily ever after." She says relationships are "happily as long as they last." She does not want to marry and believes that relationships cannot sustain through time.

I have known Vivian's family for more than twenty years. Vivian came to me eleven years ago because she was disturbed about the sudden rupture of her parents' marriage. More recently, she came to me because of Jordan, the man she has lived with for the past seven months. She has no idea whether she loves Jordan because she is not sure what "being in love" means. She enjoys being with him and they are attracted to each other sexually. She would be willing to continue the live-in arrangement they now have.

But Jordan has other ideas. He wants to become engaged and be married before their friends and family, where he and Vivian can pledge publicly their love for each other. Vivian does not want to make a commitment. "That's how people get hurt," she says. "Why not just be happy as long as it lasts? When you have that attitude, the end isn't so difficult."

Vivian is twenty-five and knows that she came from a family where both her mother and father *adapted* too much. Because of their backgrounds (both came from families with high levels of open conflict and some violence) they were determined to have a marriage that ran smoothly. They were dedicated to a life of peace and tranquility where their children would not experience the turmoil and chaos both of them knew so well.

Of course, it was a dream that was destined to shatter. No marriage is without its differences; not dealing with them, pretending they don't exist, doesn't make them go away; it just makes resentment simmer and build until it can no longer be tolerated. Vivian's parents couldn't even identify for themselves just when and where their marriage began to sour. They just know that they never discussed anything remotely controversial.

By the time they decided to divorce, they could identify

specific problems but admitted that they had permitted them to fester rather than stimulate the kind of conflict they had known in their original families. But it seemed too late to go back. It was easier, they felt, to divorce and begin again.

They were as stunned as their children by the demise of their marriage. The conflicts they had struggled to avoid suddenly galloped out of control. Their individual personalities, the ones that each had suppressed through the marriage, broke through, revealing to their children a different and unpredictable mother and father.

After the separation Dad ran a casual household where his children made the rules. There were no guidelines, no discipline.

Mom, on the other hand, through her own therapy, was able to see how her constant adaptation and compromise had destroyed her marriage. So she tried to discuss with her husband her feelings about his laissez-faire style of managing the children. Her challenge was new to him; he responded by arguing with her and complaining to his children about their mother.

Vivian says that initially she drew closer to her father, but admits now that it was a closeness that grew out of the nonconfrontational environment that felt familiar to her. Dad might suggest that she shouldn't smoke so much or drink so much or come home so late, but he didn't press her. He didn't want to make her angry.

Mom, with a new vision about the perils of her earlier behavior, was more challenging. Vivian was not permitted to miss school or violate curfew. Her father seized upon the opportunity to ally himself with Vivian by condemning her mother.

"I felt close to Dad then," Vivian says, "but now I realize that we never talked about anything important. We just bitched together about how difficult Mom was. We always shared information, but never thoughts or feelings. He never told me anything about himself; our conversations were always about somebody else."

By the time Vivian was twenty-one, she felt herself drawing closer to her mother, who had developed into a more mature woman, better able to take care of her own needs without destroying a relationship. Vivian found that she and her mother could argue about their differences, express anger to each other, discuss divergent opinions, and still remain friends.

During their talks she learned that her father and mother, while pretending that all was well through their marriage, were dealing with their differences in their own way. Dad had strong emotional attachments to several male and female friends. Her mother resented the time he spent away from her but never asked questions about what he was doing or why. It is still an issue that no one in the family has discussed. Mom had found her solace in books and painting and revealed to Vivian a folder of charcoal drawings she had made over the years, each one depicting a stage of her life. She and her mother talked about what Vivian describes as "important things"—themselves and their relationships with men.

Now, almost twelve years after the divorce, neither of Vivian's parents has found another mate. Dad is still stuck, not able to break away from his pattern of peace at any price. He says he is not interested in another marriage. Mom, despite her personal growth and increased emotional maturity, keeps getting involved with men who are weak and can't make decisions. She would like to marry again but doesn't want to end up taking care of another man.

Families like Vivian's are masters of denial, a behavior pattern that often masks the tension and lack of harmony in the family. The lesson it has taught Vivian is that relationships are not to be trusted. "Just because something looks warm and fuzzy for a year, for two years, for ten years, doesn't mean it is," she told me recently. "Underneath there are sharp bristles that eventually will come through and hurt you. People are seldom what they seem to be."

Vivian's first weeks in therapy helped her see that she is confused about relationships. She knows that arguing all the time, the way her grandparents did, doesn't work. But never arguing, the style practiced by her parents, doesn't work either.

She admitted that she suffers from poor self-esteem and has no confidence that there is anything she can do to make a relationship work.

"Relationships have a life of their own," she told me. "So I make a minimal investment. Maybe it is self-protective."

I believed that Vivian's lack of self-worth came from too strong a focus on relationships, an area of life in which she felt inadequate. If she could see how her feelings about relationships evolved and at the same time bolster her self-esteem, I believed that her situation with Jordan would become less tense and anxiety ridden.

Since so much of a person's self-esteem comes from maintaining responsible family connections, I suggested that Vivian continue to stay in close contact with her parents and to link herself more with both her parents' extended families. While her mother and father have little to do with their families, *their* distance does not have to be *Vivian's* distance. She can get valuable information from aunts and uncles who can explain such things as how *they* dealt with their parents' conflicts as opposed to the way Vivian's parents reacted.

Vivian's second task was to focus on her own goals. One of them was to complete her doctorate in educational psychology so she could work in a special program for children with learning disabilities. Another was to resume the guitar and voice lessons she had stopped taking eight years earlier.

Four months later, Vivian reported that she was feeling

more relaxed about her relationship with Jordan. A visit to her brother, who moved to Seattle when he was twenty, was an eye-opener for her. For the first time, they talked about their parents' marriage and divorce, their reactions to it, their own relationships and goals. One of their goals, they decided, was to see the other at least three times a year.

Vivian says her new focus on her career and family has taken some of the pressure off her relationship with Jordan. She can see that happiness can come from regular, responsible contact with her family, setting and achieving personal goals, and developing her potential to the fullest. She does not need to rely on an intimate relationship alone to bring her happiness. Her talks with her brother, parents, and other family members have helped her understand more clearly why her parents' marriage crumbled. And she is beginning to believe that the same thing doesn't have to happen to her.

CHAPTER THIRTY-THREE

———————/———————

Sheila:

"I Don't Trust Anyone;
I Need to Take Care of Myself"

Sheila's parents, both administrators of a social service agency, were divorced when she was fifteen. Their marriage was a highly emotional one, with periods of physical violence. Her father was a workaholic, and he and her mother fought about their jobs, sex, money, and the children. Sheila says that her mother was excessively involved in this highly intense relationship with her husband and spent most of her time taking care of him, physically and emotionally. But she never took care of herself. Sheila believes that the combination of a volatile father and a mother who, despite her protests, didn't know how to be attentive to her own needs, ultimately destroyed the marriage. Unfortunately her mother's second marriage changed nothing. Sheila says her mother is fervent in her need to care for other people, but she still hasn't learned how to take care of herself.

Sheila is determined not to repeat her mother's mistakes. She is wary about relationships, doesn't trust anyone to be there for her, and arms herself against becoming even minimally dependent on a man.

Sheila, twenty-seven, is in her last year of law school at an Ivy League university. She came to see me because she was concerned about how to negotiate relationships with men. She was terrified of trusting a man, not because she thought he would betray her but because she was afraid that as she felt more comfortable in a relationship, she would lose the ability to take care of herself. So she always chose men over whom she felt more powerful, intellectually and emotionally. She even selected men who were smaller than she physically. But Sheila found that, as she became more involved in the relationship, she did, indeed, stop looking after her own needs. In one case she remained too long with a man who was physically abusive.

Sheila believes that the important people in her life will always disappoint her. Even her mother, with whom she felt close, let her down because she didn't have the capacity to negotiate with her husband for Sheila's educational needs after the divorce.

"Because she never learned how to take care of herself, in the end she couldn't take care of me either. So I figure I can depend on only one person—me."

Sheila does not expect that she can ever achieve a fulfilling, mutually nurturing intimate relationship. And she has no confidence that a man will ever be able to take care of her emotionally. In fact, her appraisal of men is that "most of them are jerks." She describes herself as having a "profound distrust of relationships."

In looking back at her family history, Sheila could see that the theme of caring for others/caring for yourself has always been an issue in her family. Sheila's great-grandmother had become an invalid shortly after giving birth to her daughter Celia, Sheila's grandmother. Celia spent her life taking care of her mother, then taking care of her husband, who was pleasant but weak and couldn't seem to do much on his own.

It was Celia who made the major decisions and ran the family "her way." But when she became ill, no one was available to take care of her. She had "set herself up," Sheila says. "By never expecting anything for herself, she never got it."

This legacy was handed down to Sheila's mother, who repeated the pattern. No matter how abusive her husband was, no matter how inattentive to her needs, she felt helpless to take charge of herself. Even thinking about it was too painful. When she met the man who was to become her second husband, she saw a way out and took it.

It is clear to Sheila now, after a long time in therapy, that the *behavioral immaturity* in her family was played out through a father who was volatile and violent and a mother who was highly *adaptive* and *adaptable*. The combination created unbearable intensity in the family. To relieve it, to take the pressure off themselves, family members started taking care of other people. Their home was always clogged with troubled aunts, cousins, and neighbors who distracted the family from its own issues.

Sheila admitted that she resented her mother for not having been responsible for herself and for having depended on a man in the wings as a way to solve her problems. Had her mother been more secure, stronger, better able to look out for her own interests with her first husband, Sheila thinks the marriage could have survived.

She sees a lot of similarities between herself and her mother, and that disturbs her. After the divorce, her mother began, almost immediately, to live with the man who became her second husband. When Sheila went to college, she too began living with men. She says it was not a well-thought-out decision, but it paralleled what her mother was doing. Did that mean she was as needy as her mother? she wondered.

When her mother remarried, she was pleased because she believed that Martin, her mother's new husband, was more dependable than her father, and she hoped that her mother had learned more about appropriate give-and-take in a marriage. She thought that at last she would be able to see a healthy relationship between a man and a woman.

She was wrong. Instead she saw *two* people who ended up not being able to take care of themselves or each other. Their efforts, early in their marriage, were so intense they were smothering and produced conflict. When that happened, neither of them knew what to do. So they did what came naturally: they focused their attention on other people.

It was even worse, Sheila says, than it had been in her mother's first marriage. A friend of Martin's, a thirty-eight-year-old woman with a small child, had nowhere to live, and she was invited to move in for a while. Eight years passed, and the woman and her daughter were still there, living in Sheila's old room. When Sheila brought one of her boyfriends home for a weekend, her mother invited him to move in, too, because he couldn't afford his own apartment while he searched for a job. Now, two years after he and Sheila are no longer dating each other, he still lives in her mother's home. Recently a cousin, temporarily out of work, has joined the family for a few months. "She'll probably be there forever," Sheila says. "Just like the rest of them."

"I was happy to see my parents separate," Sheila says. "I was so sick of the fighting and frightened by the violence. But I'm sicker that nothing in my family is any different. The divorce solved nothing. There is just a new cast of characters."

Sheila's current boyfriend, with whom she has been living for a year, wants to get married. He sees living together as a step toward marriage. She does not. In fact, she says if he insists on marriage, she will break off the relationship. Consistent with the findings of the largest study on adults of divorce, Sheila insists that she values a career more than she does marriage but has concerns that as she gets older the rewards of work may not continue to satisfy her. But she does not expect that relationships can last forever, and she does not see marriage in her future. It is a great paradox of relationships that in a family so focused on caring for others no one *in the family* feels as though he or she is being taken care of. It happens because the emotionally driven wish to care for others *has more to do with the needs of the care giver than the realistic needs of the one cared for.* Caring for others is how the people in this family regulate their own anxiety.

Because Sheila is so successful academically and so promising professionally, it is unlikely she will be motivated to do much about her personal life until she is well established in her career. Still, she sees her parents who are professionally successful, but not very happy. And she is conscious of not wanting to end up the same way.

Sheila had a breakthrough when she noticed that the heritage of taking care of others had started to surface in her own professional life. She caught herself becoming overly involved in the problems of clients she served during summer clerkships, and she was able to stop herself.

Sheila had been avoiding contact with her family, hoping that if she ignored her parents and other relatives, the legacy it handed down to her could be ignored. But as she sees more clearly that she shares a behavior pattern with her mother and grandmother, she understands that the opposite is true. She needs to initiate talks with them about it.

The big issue for Sheila is: "I don't feel as though my mother took very good care of me." But that issue is too emotionally charged for Sheila to introduce it right away. She might first talk with her mother and grandmother about why caring for others drains them so much. Then she can approach her mother about her inability to take care of herself with either of her two husbands. A discussion that does not focus immediately on the relationship between Sheila and her mother will be less anxiety producing and will pave the way for the stickier issues to come. Sheila could then explain to her mother how in identifying with her she copies her mother's pattern and feels impaired in her ability to take care of herself.

The revelation by Sheila that she didn't feel well cared for, undoubtedly, will be mind-boggling for her mother, who believes that she abandoned an abusive husband, struggled to put Sheila through school, and focused her life around her daughter. She won't understand how Sheila could have those feelings, and she will probably get angry and hurt. But her mother's response, if Sheila doesn't get so emotional that she closes down discussion, will open the door for productive communication about their family style and how it affects each of them.

Sheila, too, needs to appreciate the part *she* played in that scenario. Perhaps, in her effort to prove her independence, she rebuffed her mother's attempts to take care of her. Did she ever tell her mother what she needed from her? Did she refuse to accept help her mother offered? Was she so anxious about her parents' marriage that she covered it by withdrawing from her mother's overtures?

Sheila should also talk to her father and grandfather. She needs their views about why the women in their lives were so overly responsible in caring for the men. She needs to know what the men did to encourage that kind of behavior.

The usefulness of working out the problems at their source is that the contributions made by all family members surface. And it is easier for change to begin. It is like looking at a roadmap. Once you see the highways and the routes through which they connect, reaching your destination becomes clear. It doesn't mean that you won't get lost on the way, but you have a better chance of finding your way back.

CHAPTER THIRTY-FOUR

———/———

Vicki:
"We Were Such a Nice Family"

When Vicki was fourteen, her cousin told her that her parents, Vicki's favorite aunt and uncle, were getting a divorce. Vicki remembers saying, "I'm so glad my parents are happy and are staying together. Divorce will never happen to them." She can still hear her cousin's quiet response: "Don't say that. You never can be sure." Seven years later Vicki's parents split. "I was shocked," Vicki says. "We were such a 'nice' family. My parents weren't close. They didn't seem to have a lot to do with each other. And I knew that Mom, at least, felt as though marriage had kept her from being a star somewhere, probably in New York. But I never had any thoughts about them being unhappy enough to be divorced. We were big into a good image. It was passed on from one of my grandmothers to my mother to me. Our unspoken passwords were:

" 'I'm a nice person.'
" 'Everyone is nice.'
" 'Aren't I good-looking?'

" 'Isn't everything sweet and lovely?'

" 'Tra-la.' "

Now, four years later, Vicki says that her life is a "total mess." She wanders from one relationship to another, all of them with men who are needy and destructive. As she struggles to "save" them, she has had two mental breakdowns and some days is so depressed she can't leave her bed. She blames it all on her parents' divorce.

In the fall of 1985 Vicki's father reminded her that in three months he and her mother would be celebrating their twenty-fifth anniversary. Vicki was in the midst of planning a party when both letters arrived. The one from her mother, scribbled dramatically on fuchsia stationery, was just one sentence. "Vicki, I love you with all my heart."

Her father's letter, Vicki says, sounded as though it were a classroom essay written in the third person. It was on her father's letterhead and read "as though it needed footnotes. 'A terrible thing has happened. Your parents' marriage is dissolving. They were never passionately in love . . .' " As Vicki read it, she felt instant disillusionment. "If my father, of all the saints in the world, can do this to us, then nothing matters. I can do anything I want to. No restraints. No limits."

Vicki's parents, who had known each other briefly in childhood and met again as adults, handled their differences by denying that they existed. Both of them were highly respected professionals—her father a university professor and her mother the vice president of communications at an art institute. Vicki describes her parents as "very liberal, very sixties," very cause oriented, very philanthropic.

"Mom was moody, intense, and ahead of her time. She got zero thrill out of most housewifely duties like going to the grocery store and driving in the car pool. And she felt she had been sidetracked into marriage on her way to a star-studded career as a hotshot public relations executive in New York. She was emotional and dramatic at home, very different from the rational, reasoned, sensible woman she was at work. I never could understand it."

Vicki's father was jolly and less intense, but had a short temper that snapped quickly when he was crossed. He couldn't handle confrontation with anyone; if his wife raised her voice, he left the room.

"Neither of them seemed to take a lot of interest in me or my brother," Vicki said. "We coexisted in the same house. Everything was pleasant, always pleasant, but not close. We were not involved with each other's activities."

The family had moved east from Utah so there was almost no contact with their extended family. "We had some laughs around the dinner table," says Vicki, "but mainly it was like four people each doing their own thing."

Vicki had little discipline, few rules, and no one objected when she began smoking pot heavily when she was fourteen. "It wasn't that they said, 'Okay, go ahead,' but they never confronted me. My father did his thing—he buried his head under a sand dune. Mom gave up on me early. It was massive denial of me not being Miss Nice."

As Vicki grew older and prettier and boys began to notice her, she ached for her parents to pay more attention to what she was doing. They never discussed sex with her and didn't seem to be concerned about how she dressed or what was happening in her life. If she came home at four in the morning, her dad would mumble, "Oh, you're awfully late getting home," then look away. Her mom said nothing.

Through high school Vicki earned a reputation for being "easy" with boys. At fourteen she had her first sexual experience. After that it was one boy after another. When one of them finally called her a "slut," her fragile sense of self-esteem was thoroughly crushed. "I beat myself up and kept allowing people to treat me badly because that's what I thought I deserved."

She was heavy into drugs, smoking pot several times a

day—before lunch, after lunch, and always before bedtime.
She lied all the time. "I had a lie for every occasion," she
told me. Her relationship with her mother deteriorated and
they fought a lot.

"She did confront me a little bit," Vicki recalls, "but she
didn't constructively try to discuss much or even punish
me. She would just say she couldn't believe I was wearing
that dress that made me look like a tramp. Or how could I
do such a lousy job of cleaning out the refrigerator? We
fought as much about whether I did the laundry as we did
about my doing drugs."

Vicki says her parents' divorce put her over the edge. She
resented her father for giving her mother no chance to
discuss their problems or to try to resolve their differences.
She bristled because he handled the divorce with the same
nonconfrontational style that had marked his behavior in
the marriage.

"He even waited until I was away at college to tell my
mother . . . and me. Not only that he was leaving, but that
he was marrying his assistant. He said he waffled back and
forth about the decision, but when he decided to make it,
he did it all by himself. It was the ultimate humiliation."

Since that time Vicki has been involved in a series of
lethal relationships with men—men her friends warned her
against; men who were certain to devastate her. Each of
them has left her feeling "hollow," as though "my gut was
pulled out." There was Troy, who was dating her for a year
. . . but living with someone else the entire time. There
was Henry, whom Vicki calls a "lowlife." He didn't work
and he slouched around Vicki's apartment drinking beer,
watching television, and going for days without showering.
Charles was "weird and different. I kept thinking that one
day he'll ask me about myself or tell me I'm pretty or want
me to meet his friends. I begged for his attention. And I
never got it."

But Ellis was the one that nudged Vicki into her last

breakdown. "He was an advanced alcoholic whose mother had committed suicide a month before we met. She took an overdose of pills and alcohol. Ellis just sat around not paying his bills and looking grungy. He would stand me up every day in the week and I would keep begging him to come back and pay attention to me.

"He was pitiful. But I kept coming back for more. I was out to save him. It was as though if I could focus on saving him, I didn't have to think about saving myself. It was my 'numbing' technique. Once when I had a boyfriend who didn't need to be saved, I didn't know what to do with myself, and I began to fall apart."

After six months of hard work in therapy, Vicki has developed some insights into her behavior. She can now recognize a few of the family patterns she has been perpetuating.

She can see that she grew up in a fantasy world, where her parents were so heavily into denial that they couldn't see her as she was or acknowledge her needs. Vicki grew up persistently struggling to capture the attention of whoever was important in her life at the moment, as attention from her parents had eluded her.

She mimics her mother's highly emotional behavior that was inappropriately focused on her as she grew up. Vicki's mother, for instance, had so little balance between her thoughts and her feelings that she could not distinguish between the significance of her daughter's doing drugs or not doing the laundry. Vicki never learned from her mother how to figure out what is and is not important. As a result she is unable to make the distinction between men with whom she could have a chance at a satisfying relationship and those who will surely mistreat her. It is beginning to dawn on her that she practices the same kind of denial she saw in her parents' marriage and in her grandparents' marriage before that.

Vicki's grandparents (her mother's parents) were much like her own parents. Grandma was emotional and melodramatic. Grandpa was quiet and nonconfrontational. Talking about issues was not permitted.

"I think it may be a Southern thing," Vicki told me. "Jewish and Italian people always seem to be yelling about problems. We don't do that. It just isn't proper."

So Vicki ignored her friends' warnings about her poor choices in men. In fact, she became a skilled weaver of fantasies about how well the current man in her life was treating her, how exhilarating their relationship was. If her parents couldn't tolerate her being less than 'nice,' she certainly couldn't tolerate that in herself either. The scenarios she created were as much to deceive herself as those around her.

Vicki is learning that she defines herself by her relationships, and admits that she doesn't have the faintest idea who she is. She has trouble setting limits because no one ever set them for her. She can't stop lying to herself and everyone else, especially to her parents. "It is so important that people like me," she told me with tears in her eyes. "So if they won't like who I am, I create somebody that I think they *will* like."

Vicki represents an extreme in vulnerability and neediness, to the point where it is almost addictive. Like many young people who spent their teenage years on drugs, she has missed growth opportunities and reached adulthood without quite knowing how she got there or what to do next.

Vicki has more work to do in therapy before she takes the action step of talking with her parents and looking to them for answers. When she does, it won't be easy. Her father is an emotional distancer and has been practicing that style for a long time. That's the way he dealt with the anxiety in his marriage before creating a triangle that included an extramarital affair. He will probably have a hard time providing answers, and Vicki may have to seek other people in her father's life—his brother, perhaps, to give her perspective.

Her mother will probably be more accessible, particularly when Vicki recognizes the similarities between her and her mother and feels able to discuss with her mother how she believes her past is influencing her behavior now.

While Vicki insists that her parents' divorce is largely responsible for her inability to relate well to men, I don't believe this is true. The divorce was upsetting, of course, and brought with it the difficult issues of violated trust, a stepmother whom Vicki sees as intrusive, and wariness about commitment. But it is her family style that is more responsible for her problems. It is the way her parents related to each other—*adaptation* by her mother to a marriage that made her unhappy, and *distancing* by her father who couldn't confront real problems—that is influencing Vicki's behavior today.

Vicki knows it will take time, but she is committed to breaking the cycle of her past and is working slowly to put the pieces in place.

CHAPTER THIRTY-FIVE

————/————

Donna:

"I'm Afraid of Being Betrayed"

Donna's parents had what you might call a "good divorce." While her parents were emotionally immature when they lived together, they understood the origin of their problems and managed to make better choices the second time around. Most important, they continued to coparent Donna in a healthy, cooperative way, and she was able to have a loving relationship, not only with her parents, but with her stepmother and stepfather. Donna says she feels enriched by her four parents and her large extended family. Nonetheless, she still has a brooding sense of being betrayed and struggles with fears of abandonment.

Donna was thirty-one when I met her. She had recently been graduated from medical school and was beginning her residency in dermatology. She came to me because she had spent the last ten years of her life wondering whether her marriage would last.

"I have no reason to believe that Anton would leave me," Donna told me. "He has never given me any reason to doubt that he loves me and our two children. But I keep having this nagging feeling that it won't last, that some day it will all blow up in my face."

Donna's parents were divorced when she was six and her brother was four. For the first three years after the breakup Donna's mother was depressed and couldn't function. Typically, Donna became her mother's emotional support and confidante. She was an overachieving little girl who grew up quickly, sympathizing with her mother and helping her through a difficult time. But Donna's closeness with her mother was *not* based on a negative view of her father as is often the case.

Once that initial period of unrest waned, Donna says she felt comfortable with her parents' divorce. She understood why they couldn't live together. Both of them were disorganized and immature. Her father was aggressive in business and a high achiever. Her mother was beautiful and a little elusive. Before she was married, she was pursued by men, and Donna believes that her father considered her a "prize" he had won. But their relationship never went beyond winning the prize. In their closest moments, Donna said, they sounded as though they were making small talk at a cocktail party.

After they married, they argued constantly and found the most immature ways to settle their disagreements. Donna said, for instance, that they bickered all the time about which one of them had lost the car keys. They settled the dispute by selling their car.

When they decided to divorce, however, they did it cooperatively and without the high conflict that had marked their marriage. They recognized that each of them was a good person—they just weren't good for each other.

Donna remembers no arguments about money or custody of the children or how the furniture should be split up. In fact, each of her parents continued to have contact with the other's extended family. "So I never felt I had lost a family at all," Donna said. "My dad's family came to my mother's wedding and my mother's family came to my dad's marriage ceremony and reception afterward.

"My parents' philosophy was that just because they were getting divorced, it didn't mean the family shouldn't go on. So we got together for family gatherings and no one bad-mouthed anyone else. It was probably as 'good' a divorce as you can get."

As frequently happens with girls who seem strong and well adjusted right after the divorce, Donna became rebellious when she turned sixteen. She dated older men her mom didn't approve of and began to think more about parties than she did about school.

At nineteen, she met Anton, twenty-six, the man she thought she wanted to marry. She says she was attracted to him because she found him trustworthy and because his parents have a stable marriage with no divorce in their background.

"I used to get really paranoid and jealous about my relationship with him," Donna remembers. "I had this constant fear it wouldn't work out even though it was working. I knew it was irrational and I couldn't figure out where it came from. It was obvious that Anton wasn't contributing to this. I was bringing it into our relationship."

During her courtship Donna would not live with Anton. It had nothing to do with morality or sexuality, she told me. "It is just that there is nothing you can't do outside of marriage today. But living together is one thing I can save."

Her fantasy, while she was dating Anton, was to have a traditional church wedding, have four children, live in a home with her loving husband, and never be divorced. A year later she and Anton married. They had the big wedding she wanted, attended by all of her mother's and father's original and new families. In the next six years, they had two children.

Meanwhile Donna, influenced by a stepmother who

urged her to "make something of herself and not be dependent on her husband," pursued a career in medicine. Her husband encouraged her and shared in the care of their children while she went to class and worked in the hospital. All the while, however, she continued to have nagging concerns about the stability of her marriage. "I can't explain it," she said. "I feel as though I haven't been hurt by my parents' divorce. In fact, I think I have gained in a lot of ways because I have the benefit of four different points of view—a father and a stepfather, a mother and a stepmother.

"And I have seen that divorce can be a positive thing and can solve problems. Both of my parents have made good second marriages and are much happier. Still . . ."

When Donna's mother and father joined her for a meeting with me, they reluctantly uncovered a possible cause of her uneasiness about her marriage. Just before her parents separated, Donna's father had had a brief affair with the wife of a longtime friend. While they made a conscious effort not to argue about it in front of Donna and her brother, they both agreed that Donna, even though she does not remember it, may have "picked up the vibrations."

Donna herself remembered feeling vaguely aware that her father had found a new "prize." And although she hadn't thought about it for a long time, she recalled the depression her mother experienced after the separation. In this light, her vague, unexplainable feelings about the fragility of her own marriage began to make sense. "Maybe, without being aware of it, I've always wondered—if my father could do this to my mother, could Anton do it to me?"

Donna followed up with more visits to her father, talking with him about both his marriages and why he thinks the second one worked for him while the first collapsed. She started to see through adult eyes how immature her father was when he married her mother and how much he changed over the years. And she became even more convinced that the divorce was necessary and resulted in improved living for both her mother and her father.

She compares herself with other adults from divorced families and is grateful that her parents were able to maintain the cooperation, communication, contact, and continuity that have helped her stay rooted.

"I've become even more conscientious about making my marriage work," says Donna. "I don't want to pass the legacy of divorce on to my kids. Even though it hasn't really interfered with my life, even though my parents divorced in probably the best possible way, even though my family connections are still strong, I went through a lot of my life with these unreasonable fears about being abandoned."

Donna is one of the fortunate daughters of divorce. Because her parents were able to cooperate around their roles as parents and make her feel comfortable with their new families, the lines of communication remained open. They were able to do what so many adults of divorced parents cannot—talk together about their past, learn what went wrong and why.

Nonetheless, as we discussed earlier, even "good" divorces have residual effects on children. Fear of betrayal is one of the most common. Donna's job now is to recognize that she is not her mother or her father and does not have to spend her life reacting to the way they treated each other. She says that drawing the connection between her father's affair and her anxiety about the stability of her marriage has helped calm her.

Now she is working to convince herself that "Anton is Anton, not my father."

Epilogue

Other things may change, but we start and end with the family.

—Anthony Brandt

Each of us comes from a family that began long before we became one of its members. What is passed on to us from that family—its unique values, rituals, wisdom, folklore, thoughts, feelings, and style of relating—helps shape us and determines what we will, in turn, pass on to our children and grandchildren. Fortunately we all have the ability to retain the richness of our family heritage while we "unlearn" automatic emotional responses that interfere with and damage our relationships with others.

Once you have studied this book and thought about your family patterns and the reactions you are still having to them, once you have answered the questions about your own behavioral maturity, you will be ready to take the first steps toward changing your behavior. Consider thoughtfully the following important—and revealing—ten questions.

1. If you review three generations of your family, what are your predominant family styles of relating? On what basis are you making those observations?
2. Describe how you have reacted to your family patterns over the years and how you can connect those reactions to your current intimate relationships.
3. What are the signs of dysfunction in your family?
4. Who in your family has tried to change them?
5. Would you describe those changes as temporary or permanent?
6. With which side of the family—your mother's or your father's—do you have more of an emotional commitment? Why?
7. How would you use your understanding of family styles to account for this?
8. Which issues would you encounter now if you were to increase contact with the other side of the family, the side to which you are less connected?
9. What would it take for you to become a significant member of your extended family?
10. What do you like most about your family? What do you like least?

When you are satisfied that you have explored these issues thoroughly, consider how you can use your new perspectives to make significant changes in your life. First, define in a general way how you tend to react when you are faced with stress. The next time you are in a tense situation, try to change that reaction. Take a deep breath, remember what you have learned about thinking and feeling; then *think* about how you want to react. Try a new kind of response: If you are a talker, try to listen; if you always avoid issues, try communicating; if you usually lose your temper, catch yourself and respond in a reasoned way.

Notice how the other person reacts to your new behavior and observe changes in the way you feel as a result. Then try to anticipate occasions that may provoke old reactions—your mother coming to visit, your wife showing up late at the restaurant, your partner forgetting your birthday—and make a conscious effort to substitute a new reaction.

Don't expect this to work overnight. It took years for your reaction patterns to build. Even though you now understand your family and yourself better, it does not mean that in stressful times you will be able automatically to apply all you know. You will make gains, then become frustrated because you revert to old patterns. But with practice you will be surprised at how new reactions will replace your former, more familiar ones.

Don't worry about becoming less spontaneous. You will find that you gain more flexibility and have more freedom of choice in the way you express yourself. Most important, you will have within your reach the ability to achieve the rich and rewarding personal relationships that give texture and meaning to life.

References

Introduction

1. Wallerstein, Judith S., Shauna B. Corbin, and Julia M. Lewis. "Children of Divorce: A 10-Year Study," *Impact of Divorce, Single Parenting and Stepparenting on Children*, ed. E. M. Hetherington and J. D. Arasteh. Hillsdale, New Jersey: Lawrence Erlbaum Associates, 1988. pp. 197–213.
2. Wallerstein, Judith S., and Sandra Blakeslee. *Second Chances.* New York: Ticknor & Fields, A Houghton Mifflin Co., 1989.
3. Hetherington, E. Mavis, Martha Cox, and Roger Cox. "Long Term Effects of Divorce and Remarriage on the Adjustment of Children," *Journal of the American Academy of Child Psychiatry,* Vol. 24, No. 5 (1985): pp. 518–530.

Chapter I: The Changing Family

1. National Center for Health Statistics, Advance Report of Final Divorce Statistics, 1987. Monthly Vital Statistics Report: Vol. 38, No. 12, Supplement II. Hyattsville, Maryland: Public Health Service, 1990.
2. Furstenberg, Frank F., Jr., "Child Care After Divorce and Remar-

riage," *Impact of Divorce, Single Parenting and Stepparenting on Children*, ed. E. M. Hetherington and J. D. Arasteh. Hillsdale, New Jersey: Lawrence Erlbaum Associates, 1988. pp. 245–261.

3. National Center for Health Statistics. Birth, Marriages, Divorces and Deaths for 1989. Monthly Vital Statistics Report: Vol. 38, No. 12, Hyattesville, Maryland: Public Health Service, 1990.

4. Stone, Lawrence, "A Short History of Divorce," *Family Therapy Networker* (November/December 1989), pp. 53–57.

5. Hetherington, E. Mavis, Jeffrey D. Arnett, and E. Ann Hollier. "Adjustment of Parents and Children to Remarriage," *Children of Divorce*. New York: Gardner Press, Inc., 1988. pp. 67–107.

6. Zaslow, Martha J., "Sex Differences in Children's Response to Parental Divorce." *American Journal of Orthopsychiatry*, Vol. 59, No. I (January 1989), pp. 118–139, and, Vol. 58, No. 3 (July 1988), pp. 355–378.

7. Castro, Teresa, and Larry Bumpass. "Recent Trends and Differentials in Marital Disruption." Available from Center for Demography and Ecology, University of Wisconsin–Madison (June 1987).

8. Lenore J. Weitzman did a 1985 study of California no-fault divorce law. A story about this study and others appeared in *The Philadelphia Inquirer*, August 27, 1989, Section K-I, "Painful Truths About Divorce" by Reid Kanaley.

9. ————*The Divorce Revolution: The Unexpected Social and Economic Consequences for Women and Children in America*. New York: Free Press, 1985.

10. Hoffman, Saul D., and Greg J. Duncan. "What Are the Economic Consequences of Divorce?" *Demography*. Vol. 25, No. 4 (November 1988), pp. 641–645.

11. Glick, Paul C. "The Role of Divorce in the Changing Family Structure: Trends and Variations," *Children of Divorce*. New York: Gardner Press, Inc., 1989. pp. 30–33.

12. Furstenberg, Frank F., Jr., "Child Care After Divorce and Remarriage," *Impact of Divorce, Single Parenting and Stepparenting on Children*, ed. E. M. Hetherington and J. D. Arasteh. Hillsdale, N.J.: Lawrence Erlbaum Associates, 1988. pp. 245–261.

13. Pittman, A. Frank, *Private Lies: Infidelity and the Betrayal of Intimacy*. New York: W.W. Norton, 1989.

14. Wallerstein, Judith S., Shauna B. Corbin, and Julia M. Lewis, "Children of Divorce: A 10-Year Study." *Impact of Divorce, Single Parenting and Stepparenting on Children*, ed. E. M. Hetherington and J. D. Arasteh. Hillsdale, N.J,: Lawrence Erlbaum Assoc. 1988. pp. 197–213.

15. Hetherington, E. Mavis, Martha Cox, and Roger Cox, "Long Term

Effects of Divorce and Remarriage on the Adjustment of Children," *Journal of the American Academy of Child Psychiatry*, Vol. 24, No. 5 (1985), pp. 518–530.

16. Some of Judith Wallerstein's comments come from an interview with her published in an article, "What Divorce Does To Kids," by Gloria Hochman in *The Philadelphia Inquirer Sunday Magazine*, December 9, 1979. pp. 28–40.

Chapter 2: Cast Out of Eden

1. Amato, Paul R., "Long-Term Consequences of Parental Divorce for Adult Well-Being." Report presented at 51st Annual Conference of the National Council on Family Relations, New Orleans, LA (November 3–8, 1989). Amato is a professor in the Department of Sociology at the University of Nebraska–Lincoln.

2. Kulka, R.H. and Helen Weingarten. "Long Term Effects of Parental Divorce." *Journal of Social Issues*, Vol. 35, No. 4 (1979), pp. 50–78.

3. Guidubaldi, John and Joseph D. Perry. "Divorce and Mental Health Sequelae for Children: A Two-Year Follow-Up of a Nationwide Sample." *Journal of the American Academy of Child Psychiatry*. Vol. 24, No. 5 (1985), pp. 531–37.

4. Robert Billingham of Indiana University reported findings from his study at a National Council of Family Relations meeting in New Orleans, November 1989.

5. Felner, Robert D., Lisa Terre, and Richard T. Rowlison. "A Life Transition Framework for Understanding Marital Dissolution and Family Reorganization." *Children of Divorce*. New York: Gardner Press, Inc., 1989. pp. 35–65.

6. Bumpass, Larry L., and James Sweet, *"Preliminary Evidence on Cohabitation from the National Survey of Families and Households."* August 1988, Center for Demography and Ecology, University of Wisconsin–Madison, Working paper #2 presented at 1988 meeting of Population Association of America. September 1988.

7. Bachrach, Christine A. "Characteristics of Cohabiting Women in the United States: Evidence from the National Survey of Family Growth, Cycle III." National Center for Health Statistics, Hyattsville, MD. Paper presented at annual meeting of the Population Association of America, Boston, March 27–30, 1985.

8. Glick, Paul C. and Graham B. Spanier, "Married and Unmarried Cohabitation in the U.S." *Journal of Marriage and the Family*, Vol. 42, No. 1 (February 1980), pp. 19–30.

9. Bennett, Neil G. Ann Blanc, and David Bloom. "Commitment and

the Modern Union: Assessing the Link Between Premarital Cohabitation and Subsequent Marital Stability." From a Speech Delivered at the Population Association of America, San Francisco, California, April 1986. Dept. of Sociology, Yale University.

10. Newcomb, Paul R. "Cohabitation in America: An Assessment and Consequences." *Journal of Marriage and the Family* (August 1979), pp. 597–603.

11. Tanfer, Koray, "Patterns of Premarital Cohabitation Among Never-Married Women in the United States." *Journal of Marriage and the Family*, Vol. 49 (August 1987). pp. 483–497.

12. Bonkowski, Sara E., "The Impact of Parental Divorce on Young Adult Children." Publication Pending. Bonkowski is associate professor at the School of Social Work, Aurora University in Illinois.

Chapter 3: The Difference Divorce Makes

1. Zaslow, Martha J., "Sex Differences in Children's Response to Parental Divorce," *American Journal of Orthopsychiatry*, Vol. 59, No. 1 (January 1989). pp. 118–139 and Vol. 58, No. 3 (July 1988), pp. 355–369.

2. Wallerstein, Judith S., and Joan B. Kelly. *Surviving the Breakup: How Children and Parents Cope With Divorce*. New York: Basic Books, 1980.

3. Wallerstein, Judith S. "Children of Divorce: Preliminary Report of a Ten-Year Follow-Up of Older Children and Adolescents." *Journal of the American Academy of Child Psychiatry*. Vol. 24, No. 5 (1985), pp. 545–553.

4. Some of Judith Wallerstein's comments come from interviews with her and were published in an article, "What Divorce Does to Kids," by Gloria Hochman in *The Philadelphia Inquirer Sunday Magazine*. December 9, 1979.

5. Cain, Barbara S. "Parental Divorce During the College Years." *Psychiatry*, Vol. 52, No. 135 (May 1989.), pp. 135–146.

6. Guidubaldi, John and Joseph D. Perry. "Divorce and Mental Health Sequelae for Children: A Two-Year Follow-Up of a Nationwide Sample." *Journal of American Academy of Child Psychiatry*, Vol. 24, No. 5 (1985), pp. 531–537.

Chapter 4: Relationships—Children and the Parents They Live With

1. Hetherington, E. Mavis, Martha Cox, and Roger Cox. "Long Term Effects of Divorce and Remarriage on the Adjustment of Chil-

dren." *Journal of the American Academy of Child Psychiatry*, Vol. 24, No. 5 (1985), pp. 518–530.

2. Wallerstein, Judith S., and Sandra Blakeslee. *Second Chances*. New York: Ticknor and Fields, 1989.

3. Southworth, S., and J. C. Schwarz. "Post Divorce Contact, Relationships with Father, and Heterosexual Trust in Female College Students." *American Journal of Orthopsychiatry*, Vol. 57, No. 3 (July 1987), p. 371.

4. Kalter, Neil, Barbara Riemer, Arthur Brickman, and Jade Woo Chen. "Implications of Parental Divorce for Female Development." *Journal of the American Academy of Child Psychiatry*, Vol. 24, No. 5 (1985), pp. 538–544.

5. Zaslow, Martha J., "Sex Differences in Children's Responses to Parental Divorce." *American Journal of Orthopsychiatry*, Vol. 59, No. 1 (January 1989). pp. 118–139 and Vol. 58, No. 3 (July 1988). pp. 355–369.

6. Hetherington, E. Mavis, "Effects of Father Absence on Personality Development in Adolescent Daughters." *Developmental Psychology*, Vol. 7, No. 3 (1972), pp. 313–326.

7. Cherlin, Andrew and Frank F. Furstenberg, Jr. "Divorce Doesn't Always Haunt the Kids." *The Washington Post*, March 19, 1989, Outposts Section C3.

8. Hetherington, E. Mavis, "Coping With Family Transitions: Winners, Losers and Survivors." *Child Development*, Vol. 60 (1989), pp. 1–14.

9. Hetherington, E. Mavis, and Frank F. Furstenberg, Jr. "Sounding the Alarm." *Readings*, Vol. 4, No. 2 (June 1989). pp. 4–8.

10. Furstenburg, Frank F., Jr., G. Spanier, and N. Rothschild. "Patterns of Parenting in the Transition from Divorce to Remarriage." *Women: A Developmental Perspective*, eds. P. W. Berman and E. R. Ramey. U.S. Public Health Service, National Institute of Health. Publication No. 82-2298, 1982. pp. 325–348.

11. Kelly, Joan B. "Sons of Divorce." *Vogue* (May 1988), p. 46.

12. Warshak, Richard A., and John W. Santrock. "Children of Divorce: Impact of Custody Disposition on Social Development." *Life-Span Developmental Psychology: Non Normative Life Events*. eds, E. J. Callahan, K. A. McCluskey. New York: Academic Press, Inc., 1983, pp. 241–263.

13. Warshak, Richard A., John W. Santrock, and Gary L. Eliott. "Social Development and Parent-Child Interaction in Father-Custody and Stepmother Families." *Nontraditional Families*, ed. M. E. Lamb. Hillsdale, New Jersey: Lawrence Erlbaum Assoc., 1982. 289–314.

14. Camara, K. A., and G. Resnick. "Interparental Conflict and Cooperation: Factors Moderating Children's Post-Divorce Adjustment." *Impact of Divorce, Single Parenting and Stepparenting on Children*, ed. E. M. Hetherington and J. D. Arasteh. Hillsdale, N.J.: Lawrence Erlbaum Associates, 1988. pp. 169–195.

15. Santrock, J. W., and R. A. Warshak. "Development, Relationships, and Legal/Clinical Considerations in Father-Custody Families." *In the Father's Role: Applied Perspectives*, ed. M. E. Lamb. New York: Wiley, 1986. pp. 135–163.

16. Zill, N., "Behavior, Achievement and Health Problems Among Children in Stepfamilies: Findings from a National Survey of Child Health." *Impact of Divorce, Single Parenting and Stepparenting on Children*, eds. E. M. Hetherington, J. D. Arasteh. Hillsdalc, New Jersey: Lawrence Erlbaum Associates, 1988. pp. 325–368.

17. Santrock, J. W., and R. A. Warshak. "Father Custody and Social Development in Boys and Girls." *Journal of Social Issues*, Vol. 35, No. 4 (1979), pp. 112–125.

Chapter 5: The Family After Divorce

1. J. R. Johnston, J. R., M. Kline, and J. M. Tschann. "Effects on Children of Joint Custody and Frequent Access." *American Journal of Orthopsychiatry*, Vol. 59, No. 4 (Oct. 1989), pp. 576–592.

2. Felner, Robert D., Lisa Terre, and Richard T. Rowlison, "A Life Transition Framework for Understanding Marital Dissolution and Family Reorganization." *Children of Divorce*. New York: Gardner Press, 1988. pp. 35–65.

3. Hetherington, E. Mavis, and Adeline S. Tryon. "His and Her Divorces." *Family Therapy Networker* (November/December 1989), pp. 58–61.

4. Bisnaire, Lise M. C., Philip Firestone, and David Rynard. "Factors Associated with Academic Achievement in Children Following Parental Separation." *American Journal of Orthopsychiatry*, Vol. 60, No. 1 (January 1990), pp. 67–76.

5. Furstenberg, Frank F., Jr., S. Phillip Morgan, and Paul D. Allison. "Paternal Participation and Children's Well-Being After Marital Dissolution." *American Sociological Review*, Vol. 52 (1987), pp. 695–701.

6. Furstenberg, Frank F., Jr., "Child Care After Divorce and Remarriage." *Impact of Divorce, Single Parenting and Stepparenting on Children*, ed. E. M. Hetherington and J. D. Arasteh. Hillsdale, New Jersey: Lawrence Erlbaum Associates, 1988, pp. 245–261.

7. Furstenberg, Frank F., Jr., and Kathleen Mullan Harris, "The Dis-
    appearing American Father? Divorce and the Waning Significance
    of Biological Parenthood." Paper presented at the Albany Confer-
    ence on Demographic Perspectives on the American Family: Pat-
    terns and Prospects. April 1990.

8. Goodman, Ellen, "Finding Fault with No-Fault Divorce," *The Phila-
    delphia Inquirer,* January 3, 1990, Section 7A.

9. Weitzman, Leonore J. *The Divorce Revolution: The Unexpected Social
    and Economic Consequences for Women and Children in America.* New
    York: Free Press, 1985.

10. Cherlin, Andrew, and Frank F. Furstenberg, Jr. "Divorce Doesn't
    Always Haunt the Kids." *The Washington Post,* March 19, 1989, Out-
    posts. Section C3.

11. "Who Gets Me for Christmas?" *Newsweek,* May 13, 1985. p. 74.

12. Hirshey, Gerri, "What Children Wish Their Parents Knew." *Family
    Circle,* August 9, 1988. p. 84.

13. Kunze, Jane Carolyn, "Role of Peer Relations in Children Coping
    With Divorce," Dissertation presented at George Washington Uni-
    versity Graduate School Arts and Sciences, February 18, 1990.

Chapter 6: The Legacy of Divorce

1. Hetherington, E. Mavis, "Coping with Family Transitions: Win-
    ners, Losers and Survivors." *Child Development,* Vol. 60 (1989): pp.
    1–14.

2. Hetherington, E. Mavis, and Adeline S. Tryon, "His and Her Di-
    vorces." *Family Therapy Networker* (November/December 1989), pp.
    58–61.

Chapter 7: The Web of Relationships

1. Furstenberg, Frank F. Jr. "Child Care After Divorce and Remar-
    riage." *Impact of Divorce, Single Parenting and Stepparenting on Children,*
    ed. E. M. Hetherington and J. D. Arasteh. Hillsdale, N. J.: Lawrence
    Erlbaum Associates, 1988, pp. 245–261.

2. Zaslow, Martha J., "Sex Differences in Children's Response to Pa-
    rental Divorce." *American Journal of Orthopsychiatry,* Vol. 58, No. 3
    (July 1988), pp. 355–378.

3. Bumpass, Larry, and James Sweet, "Children's Experience in Sin-
    gle Parent Families: Implications of Cohabitation and Marital Tran-
    sitions, *Family Planning Perspectives,* Vol. 21, No. 6. pp. 256–260.

4. Ahrons, Constance, "After the Breakup," *Family Therapy Networker* (November/December 1989). pp. 31–41.
5. Bray, James H. "Children's Development During Early Remarriage." *Impact of Divorce, Single Parenting and Stepparenting on Children*, ed. E. M. Hetherington and J. D. Arasteh. Hillsdale, New Jersey: Lawrence Erlbaum Associates, 1988. pp. 279–288.

Chapter 8: What Lies Ahead

1. London, Katheryn A., Joan R. Kahn, and William F. Pratt. "Are Daughters of Divorced Parents More Likely to Divorce as Adults?" Paper presented at Annual Meeting of the Population Association of America, New Orleans, April 21–23, 1988.
2. The multi-generational transmission of divorce doesn't seem to occur to the same degree for black people. If their parents divorced, their chances for ruptured marriages are only about fifteen percent higher than black men or women whose families did not divorce. Among black women, death of a father did not increase the risk of divorce at all.
3. McLanahan, Sara, and Larry Bumpass, *"Intergenerational Consequences of Family Disruption."* Report presented at the Annual Meeting, Population Association of America, San Francisco, April 1986.
4. Glenn, N. D., and K. D. Kramer. "The Marriage and Divorces of the Children of Divorce." *Journal of Marriage and the Family*, Vol. 49 (1987), pp. 811–825.
5. Klein, Edward "You Can't Love Without the Fear of Losing." *Parade* (March 5, 1989). p. 4.
6. Carey, Art. "Marriage in an Age of Divorce." *Bride's* magazine, (December 1985/January 1986), p. 100.
7. Lawson, Annette, and Colin Samson. "Age, Gender and Adultery." *The British Journal of Sociology*, Vol. 39, No. 3 (September 1988), pp. 409–440.
8. Weiner, Marcella, and Bernard Starr. *Stalemates: The Truth About Extra-Marital Affairs.* New Jersey: New Horizon, 1989.
9. Pittman, A. Frank. *Private Lies: Infidelity and the Betrayal of Intimacy.* New York: W.W. Norton, 1989.

Chapter 9: Lost in Time

1. McLanahan, Sara, and Larry Bumpass. "Intergenerational Consequences of Family Disruption." Paper presented at the Annual

Meeting of the Population Association of America, San Francisco, April 1986.

2. Klein, Edward. "You Can't Love Without Fear of Losing." *Parade* (March 5, 1989). p. 4.

Chapter 10: Looking Backward

1. Wallerstein, Judith S. "Children of Divorce: Preliminary Report of a Ten-Year Follow-Up of Older Children and Adolescents." *Journal of the American Academy of Child Psychiatry,* Vol. 24, No. 5: (1985), pp. 545–553.
2. Booth, Alan, D. B. Brenkerhoff, and L. K. White. "The Impact of Parental Divorce in Courtship." *Journal of Marriage and the Family* (February 1984), pp. 85–94.

Chapter 11: The Anxieties of Courtship

1. Gottman, J. M., and R. W. Levenson. "Assessing the Role of Emotions in Marriage." *Behavioral Assessment,* Vol. 8, (1986). pp. 31–48.
2. Booth, Alan, D. B. Brenkerhoff, and L. K. White. "The Impact of Parental Divorce in Courtship." *Journal of Marriage and the Family* (Feb. 1984), pp. 85–94.

Chapter 12: Pursuing Intimate Relationships

1. Bowen, Murray. *Family Therapy in Clinical Practice.* New York: Jason Aronson, Inc., 1978.

Chapter 13: Are You "Behaviorally" Mature?

1. My concepts of thinking and feeling, behavioral maturity, borrowing, and trading were influenced by my study of Bowen Family Systems Theory. For a more comprehensive look at that theory see: Kerr, Michael E., and Murray Bowen. *Family Evaluation: An Approach Based on Bowen Theory.* New York, W.W. Norton & Co., Inc., 1988. "Family Systems Theory and Therapy." *Handbook of Family Therapy,* Alan S. Gurman and David P. Kniskern, eds. New York: Brunner Mazel, 1981.
2. For more elaborate descriptions of concepts of family style and behavioral maturity, see: Bowen, Murray. *Family Therapy in Clinical Practice.* New York: Jason Aronson, Inc., 1978.

3. Papero, Daniel V. *Bowen Family Systems Theory.* Needham Heights, Mass.: Allyn and Bacon, Division of Simon & Schuster, Inc., 1990.

4. Rosenbaum, Lilian. *Biofeedback Frontiers: Self-Regulation of Stress Reactivity.* New York: AMS Press, 1988.

5. Beal, Edward, "Family Therapy Treatment of Adjustment Disorders." *Treatment of Psychiatric Disorders,* ed. T. B. Karasu (A Task Force Report of the American Psychiatric Association, Washington, D.C. APPI, 1989), pp. 2566–2577.

6. ———"Separation, Divorce and Single-Parent Families." *The Family Life Cycle: A Framework for Family Therapy,* eds. Elizabeth A. Carter and Monica McGoldrick. New York: Gardner Press, 1980. pp. 241–264.

7. ———"Theory and Practice in Working With Reconstituted Families." Presented at American Orthopsychiatric Association Annual Meeting, New York, April 1981, San Francisco, March 1982.

8. ———"Thoughts on the Divorce Process." Divorce: Physical, Emotional and Legal Processes, a Symposium presented at Georgetown University Medical School, January 1978, 1979, 1980, 1981, 1982.

9. ———"The Manifestations of the Mate Selection Process." Symposium presented at Georgetown University Medical School, 1981.

10. ———"Children of Divorce: A Family Systems Perspective." *Journal of Social Issues,* Vol. 35, No. 4 (1979), pp. 140–154.

11. ———"Child Focused Divorce." *Family Systems Theory: Clinical Application,* Ed. Peter Titelman, New Jersey: Jason Aronson, Inc., 1991.

Chapter 14: Find Your Family

1. Gottman, J. M., and R. W. Levenson. "Assessing the Role of Emotions in Marriage." *Behavioral Assessment,* Vol. 8, (1986). pp. 31–48.

2. The concept of triangles is central to the thinking of Murray Bowen. For more technical description see Michael E. Kerr's "Family Systems Theory and Therapy." *Handbook of Family Therapy,* eds. Alan S. Gurman and David P. Kniskern. New York: Brunner Mazel, 1981.

3. Kerr, Michael E., and Murray Bowen, *Family Evaluation: An Approach Based on Bowen Theory.* New York: W.W. Norton & Co., Inc., 1988.

Chapter 15: Divorce, Anxiety and Maturity

1. Camara, Kathleen, and Gary Resnick. "Interparental Conflict and Cooperation: Factors Moderating Children's Post-Divorce Adjust-

ment." *Impact of Divorce, Singleparenting and Stepparenting on Children,* eds. E. M. Hetherington and Josephine D. Arasteh. Hillsdale, New Jersey: Lawrence Erlbaum Associates, 1988. pp. 169–195.

Chapter 16: Becoming Free

1. Guerin, P. J., Jr., L. F. Fay, S. L. Burden, and J. G. Kautto. *The Evaluation and Treatment of Marital Conflict: A Four-Stage Approach.* New York: Basic Books, Inc., 1987.

Chapter 17: Where You Fit In

1. Minuchin, Salvador, Bernice L. Rosman, and Lester Baker. *Psychosomatic Families.* Cambridge, Mass.: Harvard University Press, 1978, pp. 23–50.

Chapter 23: Alice and Joyce, Edward and Carol

1. Booth, Alan, D. B. Brenkerhoff, and L. K. White. "The Impact of Parental Divorce in Courtship." *Journal of Marriage and the Family* Feb. 1984, pp. 85–94.

Epilogue

1. Questionnaire, Stress and Reactions, was designed for the Community Course at Georgetown Family Center, Washington, D.C.
2. Rosenbaum, Lilian. *Biofeedback Frontiers: Self Regulation of Stress Reactivity.* New York: AMS Press, 1988.

Bibliography

Ahrons, Constance. "After the Breakup." *Family Therapy Networker,* (November/December 1989), pp. 123–42.

———. "The Continuing Coparental Relationship between Divorced Spouses." *American Journal of Orthopsychiatry,* Volume 51 (1981), pp. 315–28.

——— and Roy Rodgers. *Divorced Families: A Multidisciplinary Developmental View.* New York: W. W. Norton and Company, Inc., 1987.

Amato, Paul R. "Long-Term Consequences of Parental Divorce for Adult Well Being." Presented at 51st annual conference of the National Council on Family Relations, New Orleans, November 1989.

Bachrach, Christine A. "Characteristics of Cohabiting Women in the United States: Evidence from the National Health Survey of Family Growth, Cycle III." Presented at annual meeting of the Population Association of America, Boston, March 1985.

Beal, Edward. "Child Focused Divorce." In *Family Systems Theory: Clinical Application,* edited by Peter Titleman. Northvale, N.J.: Jason Aronson Inc., 1991.

———. "Children of Divorce: A Family Systems Perspective." *Journal of Social Issues,* Volume 35, Number 4 (1979), pp. 140–54.

———. "Family Therapy Treatment of Adjustment Disorders." In *Treat-*

ment of Psychiatric Disorders, edited by T. B. Karasu (A Task Force Report of the American Psychiatric Association), Washington, D.C., 1989.

————. "Separation, Divorce and Single-Parent Families." In *The Family Life Cycle: A Framework for Family Therapy,* edited by Elizabeth A. Carter and Monica McGoldrick. New York: Gardner Press, 1980.

————. "Thoughts on the Divorce Process." Presented at the annual Divorce Symposium of Georgetown University Medical School, Washington, D.C., January 1978, 79, 80, 81, 82.

Bennet, Neil G. and Ann Blanc and David Bloom. "Commitment and the Modern Union: Assessing the Link between Premarital Cohabitation and Subsequent Marital Stability." Presented at annual meeting of the Population Association of America, San Francisco, April, 1986.

Bisnaire, Lise M. C. and Phillip Firestone and David Rynard. "Factors Associated with Academic Achievement in Children Following Parental Separation." *American Journal of Orthopsychiatry* Volume 60, Number 1 (January 1990), pp. 67–76.

Booth, Alan and D. B. Brenkerhoff and L. K. White. "The Impact of Parental Divorce in Courtship." *Journal of Marriage and the Family* (February 1984), pp. 85–94.

Bowen, Murray. *Family Therapy in Clinical Practice.* New York: Jason Aronson, Incorporated, 1987.

Bray, James H. "Children's Development During Early Remarriage." In *Impact of Divorce, Single Parenting and Stepparenting on Children,* edited by E. Mavis Hetherington and J. D. Arasteh. Hillsdale, N.J.: Lawrence Erlbaum Associates, 1988.

Bumpass, Larry and James Sweet. "Children's Experience in Single-Parent Families: Implications of Cohabitation and Marital Transitions." *Family Planning Perspectives,* Volume 21, Number 6 (1989), pp. 256–60.

————. "Preliminary Evidence on Cohabitation from the National Survey of Families and Households." Presented at annual meeting of the Population Association of America, Madison, Wisc., August, 1988.

Cain, Barbara S. "Parental Divorce During the College Years." *Psychiatry,* Volume 52, Number 135 (May 1989), pp. 135–46.

Camara, K. A. and G. Resnick. "Interparental Conflict and Cooperation: Factors Moderating Children's Post-Divorce Adjustment." In *Impact of Divorce, Single Parenting and Stepparenting on Children,* edited by E. Mavis Hetherington and J. D. Arasteh. Hillsdale, N.J.: Lawrence Erlbaum Associates, 1988.

Carter, Betty and Monica McGoldrick. *The Changing Family Life Cycle: A Framework for Family Therapy.* Needham Heights, Mass.: Allyn and Bacon, 1989.

Castro, Teresa and Larry Bumpass. "Recent Trends and Differentials in Marital Disruption." Center for Demography and Ecology, University of Wisconsin-Madison. June 1987. Photocopy.

Castro Martin, Teresa and Larry Bumpass. "Recent Trends in Marital Disruption." *Demography,* Volume 26, Number 1 (1989), pp. 37–51.

Everett, Craig. "Effects of Divorce on Children." *Journal of Divorce,* Volume 12, Numbers 2 and 3, 1989.

Felner, Robert D. and Lisa Terre and Richard T. Rowlison. "A Life Transition Framework for Understanding Marital Dissolution and Family Reorganization." In *Children of Divorce,* edited by Sharlene A. Wolchik and Paul Karoly. New York: Gardner Press Inc., 1988.

Friedman, Edwin H. *Generation to Generation: Family Process in Church and Synagogue.* New York: The Guilford Press, 1985.

Furstenberg, Frank F. Jr. "Child Care After Divorce and Remarriage." In *Impact of Divorce, Single Parenting and Stepparenting on Children,* edited by E. Mavis Hetherington and J. D. Arasteh. Hillsdale, N.J.: Lawrence Erlbaum Associates, 1988.

——— and S. Phillip Morgan and Paul D. Allison. "Paternal Participation and Children's Well-Being After Marital Dissolution." *American Sociological Review,* Volume 52 (1987), pp. 695–701.

——— and G. Spanier and N. Rothschild. "Patterns of Parenting in the Transition from Divorce to Remarriage." In *Women: A Developmental Perspective,* edited by P. W. Berman and E. R. Ramey. Bethesda, Md.: United States Public Health Service, National Institutes of Health, 1982.

Gardner, Richard. *The Boys and Girls Book about Divorce.* New York: Jason Aronson, Inc., 1970.

Gardner, Richard. *Psychotherapy with Children of Divorce.* New York: Jason Aronson, Inc., 1976.

Glenn, N. D. and K. D. Kramer. "The Marriage and Divorces of Children of Divorce." *Journal of Marriage and the Family,* Volume 49 (1987), pp. 811–25.

Glick, Paul C. "The Role of Divorce in the Changing Family Structure: Trends and Variations." In *Children of Divorce,* edited by Sharlene A. Wolchik and Paul Karoly. New York: Gardner Press, 1988.

Glick, Paul C. and Graham B. Spanier. "Married and Unmarried Cohabitation in the U.S." *Journal of Marriage and the Family,* Volume 42, Number 1 (1980), pp. 19–30.

Gottman, J. M. and R. W. Levenson. "Assessing the Role of Emotions in Marriage." *Behavioral Assessment,* Volume 8 (1986), pp. 31–48.

Guerin, P. J., Jr., et al. *The Evaluation and Treatment of Marital Conflict: A Four Stage Approach.* New York: Basic Books, Inc., 1987.

Guidubaldi, John and Joseph D. Perry. "Divorce and Mental Health Sequalae for Children: A Two-Year Follow-Up of a Nationwide Sample." *Journal of the American Academy of Child Psychiatry,* Volume 24, Number 5 (1985), pp. 531–37.

Hetherington, E. Mavis. "Coping With Family Transitions: Winners, Losers, Survivors." *Child Development,* Volume 60 (1989), pp. 1–14.

———. "Effects of Father Absence on Personality Development in Adolescent Daughters." *Developmental Psychology,* Volume 7, Number 3 (1972), pp. 355–69.

——— and Jeffrey Arnett and E. Ann Hollier. "Adjustment of Parents and Children to Remarriage." In *Children of Divorce,* edited by Sharlene A. Wolchik and Paul Karoly. New York: Gardner Press, 1988.

——— and Martha Cox and Roger Cox. "Long-Term Effects of Divorce and Remarriage on the Adjustment of Children." *Journal of the American Academy of Child Psychiatry,* Volume 24, Number 5 (1985), pp. 518–30.

——— and Frank F. Furstenberg Jr. "Sounding the Alarm." *Readings: A Journal of Reviews and Commentary in Mental Health,* Volume 4, Number 2 (June, 1989), pp. 4–8.

——— and Adeline S. Tyron. "His and Her Divorces." *Family Therapy Networker* (November/December 1989), pp. 58–61.

Hoffman, Saul D. and Greg J. Duncan. "What Are the Economic Consequences of Divorce?" *Demography,* Volume 25, Number 4. (November 1988), pp. 641–45.

Hu, Yuanreng and Noreen Goldman. "Mortality Differentials by Marital Status: An International Comparison." *Demography,* Volume 27, Number 2 (May 1990), pp. 233–50.

Isaacs, Marla Beth and Braulio Montalvo and David Abelsohn. *The Difficult Divorce: Therapy for Children and Families.* New York: Basic Books, Inc., 1986.

Johnston, Janet R. and Linda E. G. Campbell. *Impasses of Divorce: The Dynamics and Resolution of Family Conflicts.* New York: The Free Press, 1988.

Johnston, Janet R. and M. Kline and J. M. Tschann. "Effects on Children of Joint Custody and Frequent Access." *American Journal of Orthopsychiatry,* Volume 59, Number 4 (October 1989), pp. 576–92.

Kalter, Neil. "Research Perspectives on Children of Divorce." *American Journal of Orthopsychiatry,* Volume 59, Number 4 (October 1989), pp. 557–618.

Kalter, Neil, et al. "Implications of Parental Divorce for Female Development." *Journal of the American Academy of Child Psychiatry,* Volume 24, Number 5 (1985), pp. 518–30.

Kerr, Michael E. "Family Systems Theory and Therapy." In *Handbook of*

Family Therapy, edited by Alan S. Gurman and David P. Kniskern. New York: Bruner/Mazel, 1981.

———— and Murray Bowen. *Family Evaluation: An Approach Based on Bowen Theory.* New York: W. W. Norton and Company, Inc., 1988.

Kressel, Kenneth. *The Process of Divorce: How Professionals and Couples Negotiate Settlements.* New York: Basic Books, Inc., 1985.

Kulka, R. H. and Helen Weingarten. "Long-Term Effects of Parental Divorce." *Journal of Social Issues,* Volume 35, Number 4 (1979), pp. 50–78.

Kunze, Jane Carolyn. "Role of Peer Relations in Children Coping with Divorce." Dissertation, George Washington University Graduate School of Arts and Sciences, February 18, 1990.

Lawson, Annette and Colin Samson. "Age, Gender and Adultery." *The British Journal of Sociology,* Volume 39, Number 3 (September, 1988), pp. 409–40.

Levinger, George and Oliver C. Moles., eds. *Divorce and Separation: Context, Causes, and Consequences.* New York: Basic Books, Inc., 1979.

London, Kathryn A. and Joan R. Kahn and William F. Pratt. "Are Daughters of Divorced Parents More Likely to Divorce as Adults?." Presented at annual meeting of the Population Association of America, New Orleans, April 21–23, 1988.

McLanahan, Sara and Larry Bumpass. "Intergenerational Consequences of Family Disruption." Presented at the annual meeting of the Population Association of America, San Francisco, April 1986.

————. "Intergenerational Consequences of Family Disruption." *American Journal of Sociology,* Volume 94 (1988), pp. 130–52.

Medred, Diane. *The Case Against Divorce.* New York: Donald I. Fine, Inc., 1989.

Minuchin, Salvador and Bernice L. Rosman and Lester Baker. *Psychosomatic Families.* Cambridge, Mass.: Harvard University Press, 1978.

National Center for Health Statistics. *Advance Report of Final Divorce Statistics.* 1987. Monthly Vital Statistics Report, Volume 38, Number 12, Supplement 2. Hyattsville, Md.: Public Health Service, 1990.

————. *Births, Marriages, Divorces and Deaths for 1989.* Monthly Vital Statistics Report, Volume 38, Number 12. Hyattsville, Md.: Public Health Service, 1990.

Newcomb, Paul R. "Cohabitation in America: An Assessment and Consequences." *Journal of Marriage and the Family* (August 1979), pp. 597–603.

Papero, Daniel V. *Bowen Family Systems Theory.* Needham Heights, Mass.: Allyn and Bacon, 1990.

Pittman, A. Frank. *Private Lies, Infidelity, and the Betrayal.* New York: W. W. Norton and Company, 1989.

Rosenbaum, Lilian. *Biofeedback Frontiers. Self-Regulation of Stress Activity.* New York: AMS Press, 1988.

Santrock, J. W. and R. A. Warshak. "Development, Relationships, and Legal/Clinical Considerations in Father-Custody Families." In *The Father's Role: Applied Perspectives,* edited by M. E. Lamb. New York: Wiley, 1986.

———. "Father Custody and Social Development in Boys and Girls." *Journal of Social Issues,* Volume 35, Number 4 (1979), pp. 112–25.

Scarf, Maggie. *Intimate Partners: Patterns in Love and Marriage.* New York: Random House, 1987.

Southworth, S. and J. C. Schwarz. "Post Divorce Contact, Relationships with Father, and Heterosexual Trust in Female College Students." *American Journal of Orthopsychiatry,* Volume 24, Number 5 (July 1987), p. 371.

Stone, Lawrence. "A Short History of Divorce." *Family Therapy Networker* (November/December 1989), pp. 53–57.

Tanfer, Koray. "Patterns of Premarital Cohabitation Among Never-Married Women in the United States." *Journal of Marriage and the Family,* Volume 49 (August 1987), pp. 483–97.

Titelman, Peter., ed. *The Therapist's Own Family: Toward the Differentiation of Self.* Northvale, N.J.: Jason Aronson, Inc., 1987.

Visher, Emily B. and John S. Visher. *Step-Families: A Guide to Working with Stepparents and Stepchildren.* New York: Brunner/Mazel, 1979.

Wallerstein, Judith S. "Children of Divorce: Preliminary Report of a Ten-Year Follow-Up of Older Children and Adolescents." *Journal of the American Academy of Child Psychiatry,* Volume 24, Number 5 (1985), pp. 545–53.

——— and Sandra Blakeslee. *Second Chances.* New York: Ticknor & Fields, 1989.

——— and Shauna B. Corbin and Julia M. Lewis. "Children of Divorce: A 10-Year Study." In *Impact of Divorce, Single-Parenting and Stepparenting on Children,* edited by E. Mavis Hetherington and J. D. Arasteh. Hillsdale, N.J.: Lawrence Erlbaum Associates, 1988.

——— and Joan B. Kelly. *Surviving the Breakup: How Children Cope with Divorce.* New York: Basic Books, 1980.

Warshak, Richard A. and John W. Santrock and Gary L. Eliott. "Social Development and Parent-Child Interaction in Father-Custody and Stepmother Families." In *Nontraditional Families,* edited by M. E. Lamb. Hillsdale, N.J.: Lawrence Erlbaum Associates, 1982.

Warshak, Richard A. and John W. Santrock. "Children of Divorce: Impact of Custody Disposition on Social Development." In *Life-Span Developmental Psychology: Non Normative Life Events,* edited by E. J. Callahan and K. A. McCluskey. New York: Academic Press, Inc., 1983.

Weiner, Marcella and Bernard Starr. *Stalemates: The Truth About Extra-Marital Affairs.* Far Hills, N.J.: New Horizon, 1989.

Weiss, Robert S. *Marital Separation.* New York: Basic Books, Inc., 1975.

Weitzman, Lenore J. *The Divorce Revolution: The Unexpected Consequences for Women and Children in America.* New York: Free Press, 1985.

Zaslow, Martha J. "Sex Differences in Children's Response to Parental Divorce." *American Journal of Orthopsychiatry,* Volume 59, No. 1 (January 1989), pp. 118–39 and Vol. 58, No. 3 (July 1988), pp. 355–69.

Zill, N. "Behavior, Achievement, and Health Problems among Children in Stepfamilies: Findings from a National Survey of Child Health." In *Impact of Divorce, Single Parenting and Stepparenting on Children,* edited by E. Mavis Hetherington and J. D. Arasteh. Hillsdale, N.J.: Lawrence Erlbaum, Associates, 1988.

Index